WEMBLEY

WEMBLEY

THE GREATEST STAGE

**The Official History
Of 75 Years
At Wembley Stadium**

by Tom Watt

& Kevin Palmer

SIMON & SCHUSTER
A VIACOM COMPANY

First published in Great Britain by Simon & Schuster UK Ltd, 1998
A Viacom Company

1 3 5 7 9 10 8 6 4 2

Simon & Schuster UK Ltd
Africa House
64-78 Kingsway
London WC2B 6AH

Simon & Schuster Australia
Sydney

A CIP catalogue record for this book is available from the British Library.

ISBN 0-684-84051-0

Designed by Design 23
Reprographics by Jade Reprographics Ltd, Braintree, Essex.
Printed and bound in Great Britain by Butler & Tanner Ltd, Frome, Somerset.

CONTENTS

Preface

Wembley is not the biggest, the oldest or the most luxurious stadium in the world, but it is certainly the most famous. On the 75th anniversary of its opening year and months before work begins to turn it into England's new national stadium soon after the Millennium, *The Greatest Stage* tells Wembley's remarkable story so far.

The reason the stadium is celebrated, despite any shortcomings, by sports people and spectators alike lies in a unique tradition; Wembley has been the setting, year on vintage year, for now legendary games, events and achievements since its first FA Cup Final in 1923. *The Greatest Stage* is not the history of a building, or of a business, nor can it be an exhaustive catalogue of names, games and statistics. Instead, the book tries to describe the development of the sense of tradition which has made Wembley instantly recognisable and admired around the world.

If England is historically the home of football, Wembley is, without question, the home of the English game: of the world's oldest knock-out competition, the FA Cup and of England's national team. The chronologically arranged chapters of *The Greatest Stage* reflect that heritage - what has happened at Wembley reflects what has happened to the national game. It details, too, how other sports and other entertainments have been drawn to and, in turn, have left their mark on Wembley's history.

The chapters take a long view. After each one is a 'Wembley Scrapbook' covering the same period, which uses interviews, first person accounts and illustrative material to offer snapshots of particular landmarks in the Wembley story. The intention is that these immediate, first-hand impressions can be set against the conventional narrative history. The Wembley tradition, after all, is composed of those experiences: every event at the stadium is enriched by the spirit of all those which have preceded it.

A book like *The Greatest Stage* would be impossible without the help, advice and goodwill of many people. Guidance from the staff at Wembley has been freely given particularly by Tony Nikolic, Martin Corrie, Peter O'Malley and Charlie Shun. The Football Association too, especially the librarian David Barber, deserves many thanks. Much of the illustrative material in *The Greatest Stage* has been drawn from the archives of Soccer Nostalgia Ltd and Mirror Group Newspapers: the generosity of Graham Smith and his colleagues, the goodwill of *Mirror* editor Piers Morgan and the hard work of Tony Ward and the staff at the *Mirror's* picture library have been crucial in helping to bring this telling of the Wembley story to life. The book's early chapters draw heavily on the archives of Sir Robert McAlpine Ltd, the company that built the stadium. Their co-operation has been invaluable. Thanks also to Joe Palmer, Pat Quigley, Tony Henshaw, John Martin and Ben Jones at Action Images. Thanks are due, too, for important contributions from Ken Aston, Norman Jones, Nick Hornby, Andy Porter, Wally Morris, Richard Shepherd, Steve Stride, Tony Stephens, David Sadler, Paul Fletcher, Chris Palmer, Laura Thompson, John Gibson, Patrick Barclay, Tony Banks, Keith Loring, Andy Wilson, Cliff Butler, Tina Evans, Jason Tomas, Howard Holmes, Derek Tapscott, Patsy Martin and Dave Davies. On the bricks and mortar front, Judi Spector's typing has been admirably accurate and prompt, Martin Fletcher, Jacquie Clare and Katharine Young at Simon & Schuster have been admirably constructive and patient, copy-editor Jeremy Alexander admirably painstaking and precise.

Above all, of course, *The Greatest Stage* owes much to the time and effort of the dozens of figures from Wembley's history whose experiences have done so much to create the Wembley story and whose words, here, illuminate the telling of it. Thanks, in equal measure, to those interviewed specifically for *The Greatest Stage* and those who have given kind permission to use material first published or broadcast elsewhere. *The Greatest Stage* is dedicated to them and to all who have played or watched at Wembley: the story belongs to them. Our hope is that the book will do justice to their own memories of the most famous stadium in the world.

TOM WATT, KEVIN PALMER; JULY 1998

CUP FINAL CHAOS THAT WAS NEARLY A DISASTER

Stadium Gates Stormed by 100,000 People— Pitch Overrun and Play Interrupted.

DOCTORS TREAT CLOSE ON 1,000 CASUALTIES

Broken Limbs and Serious Injuries in Great Rush and Struggle With the Police.

THE KING'S PART IN SAVING THE SITUATION

How near was chaos to disaster at Wembley yesterday, at the first Cup final to be played in the arena of the new Stadium, can be judged from the toll of casualties revealed last night.

Nearly 1,000 people were treated for injuries, there ....
broken bones. There were 200,000 ....
Barricades were storm.............
unmanage.............

HOW STADIUM GATES WERE RUSHED.

Official Figure of 100,000 Who "Got Through."

200,000 CROWD.

An official statement issued by the Stadium authorities last night said:—

At 1.30 p.m. a complete inspection was made of the packing of the crowd, and at 1.45 p.m., when the returns showed that the standing accommodation was nearly full, instructions were given for all gates to be closed
Information was taken.....
London termed.....

GERMANY TO REVIVE RESISTANCE IN RUHR.

Coming Note to Allies Merely a Bait?

TURK PEACE NEEDS.

Sir Horace Rumbold's Hopes for the Conference.

PARIS, Saturday.

It is reported from Dusseldorf that a semi-official German Note published at Essen announces that the Reich has decided to continue its passive resistance to the Ruhr occupation.

The Note declares that no change can be looked for in the German tactics, which have proved their value, until a complete settlement of the questions in dispute has been come to between the parties.

Such settlement must include the immediate evacuation of the Ruhr.

The Temps, in an inspired leader, says France will draw up no new plan for reparations in anticipation of direct proposals from Germany. The French Government does not admit any state of payment should be drawn up under pretext of adjusting, reducing, or recovering easily the German debt.

Neither will France lend herself to any preliminary discussion on the subject of her security.

"BAIT FOR BRITAIN."

As long as Germany continues her passive resistance, Germany can have neither a sound Budget, a stable exchange, nor credit. She can only ruin herself by exporting gold remains to her.—Exchange.

Writing in the Echo de Paris Pertinax says the Germans are turning their eyes towards London rather than towards Paris.

They are anxious, he declares, to prove that they are acting in conformity with British views and hope, in return, that Lord Curzon will assume the rôle of an impartial judge as between France and Germany.—Reuter.

A message says that to-morrow afternoon the Cabinet and the Premiers of all the Dominions meet in a final conference in which to prepare the German Note to the Allies is Central News.

LAUSANNE PROGRESS.

Goodwill Shown by the Turkish Delegates.

PARIS, Saturday.

The Lausanne correspondent of the Petit Parisien has had a conversation with Sir Horace Rumbold, the British plenipotentiary, who said: "I am convinced with the Turks have a sincere desire for peace, and their reticence is only Oriental habit."—Central News.

According to Reuter, Sir Horace Rumbold is reported as saying that the Turks had every reason to desire peace.

LAUSANNE, Saturday.

Committee No. 3 sat for two hours to-day and settled practically all of the economic clauses of the Treaty, the Turks showing a spirit of goodwill.

Discussion of the Chester concession will be excluded from the Lausanne Conference, and negotiations will take place instead between the interested parties and the Turkish Government.—Reuter.

A deadlock, says the Exchange, was reached on Article 107, which deals with patents granted by Constantinople since the Armistice to the British and Americans.

The Turks say they will not recognise any act of the Constantinople Government.

OUR MESPOT BURDEN.

Sir Percy Cox : Perhaps British Will Leave in Four Years.

PLAYERS MOBBED.

The players pushed themselves through, and appealed to all around them for a chance to play. By and by the players themselves were mobbed, and could neither get in nor out. By slowly maintained pushing and backing by the police horses the pitch, finally, was cleared, and at 3.45, the seemingly impossible happened, and Watson kicked off for West Ham.

But the trouble was not over. Play had been in progress only thirteen minutes when the crowd .....a on to the pitch again just in front .....
Gray .....
penal .....
tende .....
On .....
slow .....
littl .....
rea .....

.......ams ex-.......
into congestion, the crowds waiting to get into the stations, and the large number of private vehicles making road traffic extremely difficult.

It was not until 7.45 p.m. that the "all clear" was given for omnibus traffic, which the L.G.O.C. Controller described as "absolutely abnormal," and, as far as the East End was concerned, "absolutely terrific."

WEST HAM'S WELCOME.

Enthusiastic Reception by Huge Crowds on Their Return Home.

The West Ham team had dinner after the match at Brent House, Golders Green.

On their arrival last night at Canning Town they were given an enthusiastic reception by large crowds. The Mayor and Councillors of .....
Ham met them, and there was a procession .....of the main roads, illuminated .....being used. .....in the West .....went .....

MANY WOMEN CRUSHED.

Ambulance Men Who Could Not Find Path to Attend Victims.

Marvellous indeed is the fact that there was no fatality.

Nearly a thousand people were treated by the first aid detachment during and after the match.

Most of them were suffering from minor injuries, but there were quite a number of broken legs and collar-bones and serious eye injuries, while there were hundreds of fainting cases.

Sixty persons in all were sent to various hospitals.

Most of the injuries were the result of the stampeding of the crowd.

A number of women were badly crushed against the railings.

The ambulance men experienced much difficulty in attending to the cases, as the gangways became impassable for stretchers.

One man had to sit for two hours with a broken shoulder blade because the Red Cross men could not get through the crush.

The King, from his position on the stand, could see the various victims of the crush as they were being carried to the clearing station underneath the arches above the royal box, and it was noticed that he displayed very great concern.

It is certainly not too much to say that the tactful behaviour of the police averted what might have been extremely ugly consequences.

The crowd showed a very dangerous temper when it was suggested that the match might be impossible.

Our Citadel Has Been Stormed

1923

Saturday, April 28 1923: a lovely day for football, fine, warm, a gentle westerly breeze. A day, too, to witness history being made: the Football Association Challenge Cup Final had, at last, found a permanent home. The game's most glamorous annual fixture would kick off at 3 p.m. at a marvellous new sports ground, the Empire Stadium on Wembley Hill, Bolton Wanderers taking on West Ham United in the presence of His Majesty the King.

It promised to be an auspicious occasion, with every prospect of 90,000 places on the terraces being taken up by supporters paying their one shilling admission at the turnstile on the day. England's largest and newest arena, 'constructed', according to its contract with the Football Association, 'to provide accommodation for not less than 125,000 spectators', was ready to welcome all-comers.

In the event, upwards of 300,000 people, a mixture of the curious and the committed, turned up. Two-thirds of them, indeed, during an anarchic hour and a half in the early afternoon, managed to find their way into the arena itself. Sunday's headlines were inspired not by the stadium, Bolton's 2–0 win or even George V; instead, what *The Times* described, aghast, as 'a mammoth congregation' was to make Wembley world-famous overnight.

With hindsight, it is not surprising this Cup Final should have led to such scenes of enthusiastic mayhem. The stadium, after all, had been the subject of intense public interest for the past three years, since it had been proposed by the then Prince of Wales as the centrepiece of a forthcoming British Empire

Exhibition. A sense of anticipation was all the keener for the fact that building work had been completed only on the Wednesday before Wembley's scheduled opening day.

The King himself, recently married, was responsible for drawing further patriotic thousands out to a little-known suburb in North-West London. George V inspired uncomplicated and affectionate admiration, effortlessly keeping his head above troubled political and economic waters. If the Cup Final made for a day to forget fuel shortages, unemployment, strikes and the crisis in Ireland which beset post-war Britain, the chance to glimpse and cheer the King, it seems, would make it all the more passionate a day to remember.

Huge and unruly Cup Final crowds were nothing new. Ten years previously over 120,000 had besieged the Crystal Palace arena to watch the great teams of the day, Aston Villa beating Sunderland by the only goal. Dozens clambered on to roofs and into trees to secure a vantage point from which they passed on news to disappointed thousands locked outside.

Come 1923, however, and the fourth Final following the resumption of football after the Great War, the authorities – the FA and the Empire Exhibition company (the latter responsible for arrangements on the day) – had grown complacent after smaller, more orderly crowds had attended the previous three at Stamford Bridge. The first Wembley Final, therefore, found the stadium unprepared for the human tide by which it was about to be engulfed.

The match itself looked an attractive confrontation. Bolton Wanderers were aristocrats in footballing terms, an established First Division side, beaten pre-war finalists, fashioned in the charismatic image of their tall, stylish inside-forward David Jack who, by the end of the decade, would be the celebrated subject of the game's first £10,000 transfer. West Ham, meanwhile, then as now an unpretentious club reflecting more than most of its metropolitan rivals the aspirations of a local community, were looking to become the first Second Division side to win the Cup, although a successsful

1922–23 season had just secured their promotion to the First.

Little wonder that for a first appearance by its heroes in a Cup Final most of the East End should decamp to North-West London. Supporters streamed into the capital from Lancashire, too, travelling the day before or overnight by charabanc and mail packet. The prospect of a day out in London made suffering the privations of pre-motorway and InterCity travel seem all the more worthwhile. Half a dozen well-heeled Wanderers fans made the trip in style, chartering a Daimler Hire plane from Manchester Aerodrome to fly down and back the same day.

There is no doubt, too, that thousands of Londoners, uncommitted to either team, woke up on the Saturday morning, saw the sunshine and resolved to spend the afternoon amid the partisans. Wherever they came from, the stadium was easily reached. From stations dotted along the Marylebone Road, Wembley was quarter of an hour away by rail.

The Empire Stadium was advertised as opening its turnstiles, 104 of them, for the first time half an hour before noon. By then thousands were streaming south from Wembley Park station, intent on a decent vantage point somewhere on the terraces. They made their way towards the Twin Towers, stark and unfinished concrete on the skyline, across a building site which a year later would open as the Empire Exhibition.

At 11.30, as promised, the first supporters gained admission. Filtering through the cloister of corridors beneath Wembley, they climbed staircases up into the arena, to be confronted by a sweep of terracing, some half a mile around its oval circumference, the clean line where the outside wall met the sky at the bowl's highest vantage point broken only by sections of roof over the seated areas, room for 25,000 spectators in two blocks opposite each other at the halfway line.

The terracing itself was broken into two tiers of timber steps filled in, on the lower tier, with packed cinders and, on the upper, with concrete. At the foot of the vast standing sections ran five concentric rings of bench seats, closest, in theory, to the action and, at five shillings (25p), less than half the price of the cheapest seats in the stands. Beyond the 'ring' stretched the fresh green of Wembley's first pitch, which had been cut from the golf course which lay elsewhere in the Exhibition grounds.

During the next hour and a half the steps of the terraces gradually diappeared from view as supporters found their way into position, gathering first around safety barriers and adjacent to stairwells where surer footing could be found, relatively stable amid the eddying flow of later arrivals swirling haphazardly around them.

By 1 p.m. those who had been in position for an hour or so knew they were in the middle of a rare old crush. Those still trying to make their way in found the way blocked by walls of people who could themselves squeeze no further than the top step of the staircases leading out on to the terraces. Before long the staircases themselves were full, two hundred or so people packed into each, fretting at the prospect of an afternoon to be spent watching the patch of sky beyond the caps and bowlers above and ahead of them.

From the relative comfort (at this stage) of the stand Sir John Squire was making notes of the remarkable scene unfolding before him: '1.10 . . . What a sight. This is two hours before the start, and except for a few reserved seats there doesn't seem to be even standing room for a person more. A vast, elliptical basin. A hill of people all around and a clean rim far up, cutting the sky . . .'

Belatedly, at 1.30, stadium officials toured the arena to inspect the 'packing' of the crowd. Not long afterwards those totting up returns at the west end of the ground, in a room now shoulder deep in cash, realised that the standing accommodation was full to bursting. The order went out to shut the gates and all London rail stations were telephoned with the news that the turnstiles had been closed.

Of course, thousands of supporters were already on their way to join those waiting outside, who now began to cluster around the stadium entrances, almost certainly unaware that the turnstiles were no longer open.

As the crush without became as intense as the crush within, reinforcements were called in from neighbouring police stations despite the fact that, at this late stage, they would be unlikely to make anything but slow headway through the multitude.

At 2.15, the irresistible force got the better of the immovable object. As barriers were broken down at entrances from one end of the stadium to the other, something like 100,000 more people forced their way in. It is an immutable law of the crowd: however uncertain what lies ahead, turning back is physically out of the question.

Over railings, under turnstiles, through barbed wire fencing they streamed. Once past the stadium's outer defences, the crowd coursed through Wembley's arteries, the network of corridors, gangways and staircases beneath the stands, searching feverishly for a way out into the daylight of the arena. Inner entrances and gangways to the reserved seats were hurriedly secured. Those that held fast prevented ticket holders reaching their seats. Those that did not allowed a lucky few to occupy those seats on their owners' behalf. Sir John Squire was dumbstruck as all semblance of order fell away: 'There isn't room for another soul, and yet they are still pouring in through the entrances – the crowd has burst in. They are all over the ground now.'

Amid the chaos, of course, there could be no standing on ceremony. The Bolton team had reached the ground long since. The charabanc bringing directors and staff from their weekend headquarters in Russell Square, however, had ground to a halt in the jam. One of that party was to remember: 'We left the motorcoach, made our way across some fields, crossed a railway line and, at the outer barriers of the stadium, came upon a man with a spade who was digging a hole under the fence. Through the hole he went; we followed. As we climbed another fence we met a policeman, who grinned and said, "You're wasting your time." '

Meanwhile, inside the ground, the pressure on the terraces, made worse by the continuing attempts of the crowd below the stands to find a way out into the spring sunshine, meant that eventually the only safe place to be was on the field of play. Once the first few had clambered over the benches at the foot of the terraces and on to the running track, thousands more followed. Within minutes the pitch was lost beneath a small ocean of flat caps, people milling across the arena able to move and breathe again at last. The faces in the grainy photos and flickering newsreels of the day seem cheerful, dazed, relieved – and with good reason: although nearly 1,000 people were treated for minor injuries during the course of the day, between 2.30 and 2.45 on that Saturday afternoon over a quarter of a million people, gathered to witness the Cup Final, came within perhaps a hair's-breadth of disaster.

The arrival of the King was crucial in easing the pressure on Wembley's beleaguered defences. Thousands broke off trying to push their way in and turned to cheer the progress of George V's carriage through their midst. Once inside, the monarch looked out upon the pandemonium described by Sir John Squire: 'Our citadel has been stormed and there are thousands of them, all covered with favours. They force their way through us, press in on the track and spread over the field: nothing but people.'

By this time mounted police, called out from West Hampstead, had nosed their way on to the field, among them Constable George Scorey on his white horse Billy, the pair set to become the heroes of the hour. Their efforts to edge the crowd back towards the stands were helped by the sight of King George taking his place in the Royal Box as, patriots all, supporters around the arena fell silent before a spontaneous rendition of the National Anthem.

Outside, it had become clear that no one else stood a chance of being inside even should there be a football match to watch. The railway companies, the Metropolitan and the London and North Eastern, began to run trains back towards the West End, while fences put up to keep supporters off the main Exhibition site were hurriedly taken down to speed the flow of disappointed fans away from the stadium.

Impossible as it must have seemed, the show had to go on. By the scheduled kick-off time the bands of the Irish and Grenadier Guards, as well as the Bolton and West Ham teams, were out on the field of play along with several thousand uninvited guests. But the White Horse, his colleagues and the players themselves prodded patiently, clearing spectators back inch by inch towards what remained of the touch-line.

Mr Asson, the West Bromwich referee, called together the captains, Joe Smith of Bolton and George Kay of West Ham. Even as they tossed the coin for choice of ends a pair of mounted policemen galloped past them to push back a group of spectators spilling over the far goal-line. Mr Asson muttered, 'Let's start the game and hope that we can finish it', put his whistle to his lips and, at fourteen minutes to four, within walls of spectators pressed ten and twenty deep along all four touch-lines, the first Wembley Cup Final was underway.

The opening minutes were understandably frantic: after the interminable time spent making the game possible, there remained every chance that it might not be concluded. Each hurried pass, each desperate clearance might prove to be the afternoon's last. Bolton, quicker to settle, took the lead in the fourth minute. Half-back Seddon played a long pass down West Ham's left. Although Young beat Butler to it, the West Ham full-back could only clear the ball into the path of David Jack, who stepped forward a pace or two before hitting a cross-shot past Hufton: Wembley's first goal.

Shortly afterwards the game had to be held up for a further ten minutes as those behind pushed the crowd along the touch-line on to the pitch once more. When play restarted, West Ham's forwards, of whom much had been expected, wrested control and during the only period they dominated, ought to have equalised. Pym misjudged a Ruffell corner but Watson, the West Ham centre-forward, a few yards out in front of an open goal, snatched at the chance and lifted the ball over the bar. Moments later the Bolton keeper redeemed himself, sticking out a foot to deflect Richards' cross-cum-shot to safety after the winger had cut in past Jennings and Finney.

By half-time Bolton were back in charge. John Smith was unlucky to have had a goal disallowed, impossibly for offside after Butler had cut the ball back to him from the byline. With the game still there to be won, the referee decided not to take teams off at the break: if he had, wrote the man from *The Times*, 'the match would not have been finished on Saturday'.

Instead the teams changed ends after a short rest and, within ten minutes of the restart, Bolton made the game safe with a second goal. Picking up the ball in a deep position John Smith released Vizard down the left. The Bolton winger eluded Henderson – did a spectator's leg keep the ball in play? – before pulling his cross back into the area. Smith had made up the ground to arrive with a left-footed half volley. The ball flew up under the bar, where the net had been pulled taut by the feet of the crowd behind the goal, and rebounded into play. Mr Asson, however, did not hesitate to point play back to the centre and the Cup was as good as won.

Shortly afterwards, the story goes, George Kay suggested abandoning the game, to which his Bolton counterpart, Joe Smith, responded by assuring the referee that his team would continue playing until nightfall if it meant seeing the game through to its conclusion. The crowd certainly sensed the match was over as a contest and, having waited so long for proceedings to get underway, thousands were streaming away with almost half an hour left to play.

Come the final whistle, however, enough remained for the pitch again to disappear under a tide of happy Wanderers fans. Finney, the young Bolton full-back, got his hands on the ball before it could be lost in the swirling crowd. It took some time for the police to clear a path through to the Royal Box for the winning team. Up stepped Joe Smith to collect the Cup from George V before introducing Bolton's players. The King then drove away, according to *The Times*, 'amidst a scene of heartfelt enthusiasm'.

By the time Smith and his team-mates had found sanctuary in the dressing-room the Bolton captain seemed, to one observer, 'as happy as a schoolboy'. 'Tell them,' Smith declared, 'our great ambition to bring the Cup for the first time to Bolton is realised. This is the proudest day of our lives.'

He might have added that, if not the proudest, the day had certainly been the most extraordinary in the lives of many of the 200,000 who had got inside to be a part of an occasion they had sensed might prove momentous. The first and, in its way, the most remarkable drama of the stadium's history had been played out on Wembley's stage, stars and groundlings literally shoulder to shoulder for the duration.

By the time the winning team got back to Lancashire with the Cup, news of events in North-West London had made headlines everywhere: the feverish excitement and cheerful disorder, tiny heroics and unlikely dignity, a cracking game of football – what a very English way to spend a Saturday afternoon. The opening day had assured Wembley was already on its way to becoming the most famous stadium in the world.

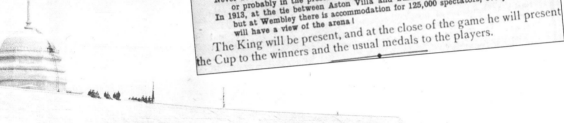

The King to See Struggle Between West Ham and Bolton Wanderers.

VAST STADIUM TO BE USED FOR FIRST TIME.

Accommodation for 125,000 Spectators — Big Invasion of Enthusiasts from Northern Towns.

This is "Cup-tie Day," and at the vast new Stadium at Wembley West Ham United and Bolton Wanderers will fight for the Football Association's famous Cup.

Never before will a football match have been played in such wonderful surroundings or probably in the presence of so vast a throng. In 1913, at the tie between Aston Villa and Sunderland, 120,000 watched the game; but at Wembley there is accommodation for 125,000 spectators, every one of whom will have a view of the arena!

The King will be present, and at the close of the game he will present the Cup to the winners and the usual medals to the players.

1923: TOM JALES

I was ten years old in 1923. I was born in a pub down Ironmonger Row. There was a chap my mum used to get to look after me. She'd pay him to keep me out of the pub! He was four or five years older than me, Bobby Hines his name was. He lived near us in Central Street. He asked my mum if he could take me to Wembley for the Cup Final. There was no tickets for that first Final, so we went off at about ten in the morning.

There'd been a big build-up but they weren't expecting that crowd. There were already thousands of people when we got there. We went on the tube from the Angel to Wembley Park. It wasn't like now: you had to make your way over waste ground to get to the stadium, stepping on bricks and stones where they were building the exhibition I suppose.

When they saw how many were there they opened the gates, sometime after eleven. We got in and found a place down near the front, I think in around what's now 'A' block. But of course, when it got near to kick-off, they were still coming in and people started going over the barriers and on to the pitch. Bobby said to me: *Come on, we won't see anything if we stop here.* So over we went. There was no one stopped us. We ended up on the touch-line and during the game people were actually stepping on to the pitch. I suppose the game shouldn't have been played, really.

There were lots of kids like me there, too. I was lucky I had Bobby to look after me, what with people swaying backwards and forwards to see what was going on, spilling on to the pitch. It was all a bit overwhelming leading up to kick-off. I was a bit scared by it all, to be honest. It was even worse trying to get out. People started leaving twenty, thirty minutes from the end because they were worried about the crush and, coming home, Wembley Park was murder, people trying to get on the tube. The whole thing was an experience, I should say.

INTERVIEW, 1997

SUNDAY PICTORIAL, April 29, 1923

FINAL WEEKS OF £7,000 FILM CONTEST—See Page 5

SUNDAY · PICTORIAL

SALE MORE THAN DOUBLE THAT OF ANY OTHER SUNDAY PICTURE PAPER

No. 424. | Registered at the G.P.O. as a Newspaper | SUNDAY, APRIL 29, 1923 | [24 PAGES] | Twopence.

WEMBLEY STADIUM STORMED BY EXCITED CUP FINAL CROWDS

A striking aerial photograph of the scene at Wembley Stadium yesterday after the gates had been closed. All accommodation is packed, spectators flood the playing pitch, while thousands clustered outside are clamouring for admittance.

One of four daring souls who climbed a drain-pipe to secure an entrance at the back of the lofty covered stand.

...lice arriving by motor-van at the ground in response to a call for reinforcements.

...derers yesterday, when ...Stadium, Wembley. The ...ordinary scenes. Tha... ...h the spectators within

The crowd ... had broken through to the running track ... itself. The crowd outside rushed the grou... confusion even greater. With the arrival ... pitch just clear. Pictures of play on page 24

RING SEAT

British Empire Exhibition.

THE EMPIRE STADIUM, WEMBLEY.

The Football Association Cup Competition.

FINAL TIE.

SATURDAY, APRIL 28th, 1923,
Kick-off 3 p.m.

Entrance 5 Seat 6406

C. Henry McMahon

Chairman, Management Committee

Price 5/-.
Including Tax. [SEE BACK]

This portion to be retained.

1923: PC GEORGE SCOREY

Before that day in April, 1923, in the Mounted Branch of the Force I'd helped to control a lot of great crowds but I'd never seen anything like the sight of Wembley Stadium that afternoon. A number of us were on reserve and had been suddenly called up to deal with the situation but, as my horse picked his way on to the playing field, I saw nothing but a sea of heads. I thought *We can't clear it, it's impossible!* Then I said to myself *I won't be beat* and I happened to see an opening near one of the goals. The horse was very good, easing them back with his nose and his tail until we got the crowd back along one of the goal-lines. We continued up the touch-lines until some of them got a bit stubborn. *Don't you want to see the game?* I said. They said *Yes* and I said, *So do I. Now those in front join hands.* Then I gave the word to heave and they went back, step by step, until they reached the line. Then I told them to sit down and we went on till, with the help of the other mounted men, the pitch itself was eventually cleared.

I'm certain that any success I had was due mainly to my horse. Perhaps because he was white he commanded more attention but, more than that, he seemed to understand what was wanted of him. The other helpful factor was the good temper of the crowd.

BBC RADIO INTERVIEW, 1944

RICHARD H. PYM
BOLTON WANDERERS

1923: DICK PYM

We used to be able to see Wembley being built every time we played in London. On the train going back to Bolton we'd look out of the window, see the stadium in the distance and wave our hands, to say *See you later!* And it turned out that way. It was a special occasion with Wembley being opened.

We were tucked away in the dressing-room and all we were concerned about was getting a bit of massage – a drop of olive oil on our legs – and didn't know what was going on upstairs. We used to give ourselves about half an hour to change but, when we were all ready, somebody came in and said to the trainer: *You'll have to wait a bit*. We were there three-quarters of an hour. Poor old George Eccles, our trainer, said: *Now, don't get excited, Dick*. I said: *You don't want to worry about me, I'm all right*. I sat on the table reading the programme. When we got out on the pitch all we could see of the ground was the top of the crossbars and a foot of the uprights. Just one mass of people.

We came out through the crowd who made a way for us. The police got to work and we joined hands and tried to get the crowd back, talked to them: *Let's have a game. Let's have a game*. Most of the crowd looked dazed, as if they were intoxicated: they weren't but they'd taken that much of a buffeting. Then, of course, the White Horse came on the scene. I suppose he was more prominent than we were but I've always thought the two teams had as much to do with getting the crowds back as the man on the White Horse.

BBC TV INTERVIEW, 1993

Yours sincerely R.H. Pym
D. Pym.
BOLTON WNDRS

CE Willis Photo

1923: TED VIZARD

I think I can safely say that the 1923 Final was one of my own greatest thrills, and I can remember almost every detail of it. For instance, the rumour that went round that, even if the game were played, it would never be recognised as official; the corridors and tunnel from the dressing-rooms to the arena looking like ARP casualty stations; the anxiety as to where our wives and relatives were in all that vast crowd; and, after finally shoving our way on to the pitch, the unforgettable sight of a solid wall of spectators round the touch-lines – it felt as though we were going to play football in a human box.

Then the game started and within a few minutes we were one up. That early goal was just what we wanted to put us on our game after that long, anxious wait in the dressing-room. I shall never forget David Jack's shot flashing past Ted Hufton, nor the pass that JR Smith gave me later in the game and my close dribble down to the corner flag. Then, cutting in along the goal-line I saw JR Smith run into position and, as he fastened on to my centre, I watched him screw the ball into the net before the West Ham defenders realised what had happened. I had paved the way for the goal that just about settled the issue in this unforgettable match.

BBC RADIO INTERVIEW, 1944

E.T. VIZARD.

PHOTO C.E. WILLIS

EDWARD T. VIZARD
BOLTON WANDERERS

BRITISH
EMPIRE
EXHIBITION
1924

OFFICIAL
GUIDE

Price One

FLEETWAY PRESS L

OFFICIAL GUIDE
BRITISH EMPIRE
EXHIBITION 1925

George Sheringham

PRINTED & PUBLISHED BY
Fleetway Press Ltd.

PRICE ONE SHILLING
COPYRIGHT

The Home Of British Sport

1923-29

'In the vicinity of the metropolis there are few places so free from interruption as the grounds at Wembley; and, indeed, in the course of my experience, I have seen no spot within so short a distance of London more perfectly secluded from those interferences which are the common effects of divided property and a popular neighbourhood.'

Seclusion? Freedom from interruption? Obviously, Humphry Repton could not have imagined the scene two centuries on: cars and coaches snaking towards the stadium from every direction; thousands, decked in club colours, striding down Wembley Way past food stalls and souvenir stands; thousands more eddying around the concourses, meeting mates, gulping last pints, arguing the toss; helicopters chuntering overhead; journalists scribbling, broadcasters gabbling, below; the whole world seemingly at Wembley or at least watching, listening, waiting elsewhere for the latest news.

Repton, one of the eighteenth century's most celebrated landscape architects, was engaged in 1792 by Richard Page to remodel Wembley Manor House and turn the surrounding farmland into a 'pleasant, well-wooded park'. Fifty years later the site had new owners, the Gray family, the House had become Wembley Park Mansion and Repton's landscape had matured in private splendour, 'amongst the copses and osier beds . . . a mass of wild flowers, with dragonflies darting over the water and then vanishing into the deep shades of the plantations'.

London, however, seven miles distant in Repton's day, was on Wembley's doorstep by the end of the nineteenth century. Like so much of Britain, the borough was changed for ever by the arrival of the railway. In 1880 the Metropolitan Railway Company, looking to extend their line which already ran from Baker Street to Willesden Green, bought forty-seven acres of John Gray's Wembley estate. Ten years later Wembley Park was a station on the way to Harrow (during building work fossilised remains of an elephant and hippopotamus were discovered, an exotic past hinting at an equally exotic future) and the entire 280-acre Wembley estate had been bought by the Metropolitan's chairman, Sir Edward Watkin, for £32,929.18s.7d. Sir Edward had grand designs for Wembley Park. At the centre of his plans for a great pleasure ground on the site was a proposal to build a tower to rival Gustave Eiffel's, which overlooked the Seine in Paris. Whatever the French can do, reasoned this quintessential Victorian industrialist, the British should be able to do better or, at least, bigger and higher.

A first prize of 500 guineas was offered in a public competition to design a 'Great Tower in London'. The winning entry included 'restaurants, theatres, dancing rooms, Turkish baths and rooms for exhibiting all kinds of scientific and amusing novelties' to be fitted in on a platform halfway up the 1,150-foot high steel structure. Sir Benjamin Baker, designer of the Forth Bridge and the Aswan Dam, was engaged as chief engineer. Work began in 1892 but the tower barely got off the ground. Three years later, with the first 155-foot high section in place, its foundations started to subside and construction ground to a halt.

Beneath and around the legs of what became known as Watkin's Folly, however, sport had come to Wembley. The park, which opened in 1894, included football and cricket pitches (on one of which an Australian touring side bowled out the local cricket club for 65 and 37) and a Trotting Ring with its own wooden grandstand. Indeed, but for objections raised by local residents, Wembley might have been home to a racecourse long before the stadium was even thought of. With a boating lake and a variety theatre, too, the park was, briefly at least, something worth the fuss, as advertised in the *Daily Mail*: 'Every day throughout the week. Cyclists' Camp, Balloon Ascents and Parachute Descents, Boating, Variety Entertainments. Band under the direction of Mons. Carl Vorzanger. Illuminated Tower. Admission One Shilling.'

But the money, and perhaps the overweening ambition, eventually ran out. The tower, now unsafe, was closed in 1902. In 1907 the process of dismantling was complete; an explosive called Roburite was used to destroy its foundations. The site's proximity to Central London, though, ensured that Wembley remained an attractive proposition. The Tower company hastily reconstituted itself as a real estate concern, with plans to redevelop Wembley as an exclusive garden suburb: 'High-class residences, shops, bank etc. with tennis lawns and motor houses,' promised the prospectus. An 18-hole golf course, then as now the hallmark of a posh suburb, was set out in 1912.

The best laid plans of the local council and attendant house builders were rudely interrupted by the 1914–18 war. Although some homes and a network of new roads, as well as a new rail line and station serving Wembley Hill, were already in place, the Armistice and an end to hostilities proved to mark a radical new beginning for Wembley.

The idea for an Empire Exhibition to celebrate Britain's ties with its colonies had been mooted before the Great War. Peacetime found the nation demoralised, thousands of servicemen returning to unemployment, and the economy in the midst of a slump in world trade. Little wonder that Lloyd George, the prime minister, was quick to promise government support for a project which promised jobs, distraction and the opportunity to market British industry to the world.

Wembley Park was chosen as the Empire Exhibition site, despite being criticised by *The Times* for being 'some way out of London'. Wembley and the idea for the Exhibition met with approval from the Dominion Prime

Ministers and, with the support of King George V, the Prince of Wales and Lloyd George's government, a private corporation, The British Empire Exhibition (1924) Inc., set about raising funds.

In difficult times subscription to the project was at first less than encouraging. Given that the stadium, the Exhibition's centrepiece, is now all that remains, it was fitting that the prospects for sport, and football in particular, were to prove crucial in ensuring the commercial viability of the entire project.

At an appeal for funds held at the Mansion House, the Prince of Wales promised employment for thousands of ex-servicemen before going on to describe his vision for the new Empire Stadium as a 'great national sports ground'. Money started pouring in, including over £100,000 from the City of Glasgow – the down payment, perhaps, on what was to become a home away from home for generations of Scottish fans.

Just as important, in terms of firing public enthusiasm for the Exhibition, was the signing of a twenty-one-year contract with the Football Association. Discreet visits to the site had been made by the Ground Committee in preceding months as the FA sought a permanent home for the FA Cup Final. The decision that was to make Wembley the home of English football was recorded in the FA Council's minutes of 30 May 1921:

14. Ground for the Final Tie. The Finance Committee recommended that the Council enter into an agreement with the British Empire Exhibition for the playing of the Final Tie, and such other matches as may be agreed, upon a ground to be constructed at Wembley Park by the British Empire Exhibition. The Council approved the recommendation and authorised the Finance Committee to proceed with the completion of the arrangements.

Those 'arrangements' included the FA putting £10,000 into an Exhibition pot which now contained upwards of one million pounds. Sir Robert McAlpine & Sons were engaged as contractors for the entire Exhibition site in January 1922. Work on the stadium started at once. The first turf was cut by the Duke of York on the 10th, with construction of the stadium getting underway three months later. The Exhibition was not due to open until 1924 but the Empire Stadium had to be completed in some 300 working days to be ready for its first Cup Final in 1923.

The top was sliced off Wembley Hill, the site of Watkin's Folly, removing some 150,000 tons of clay. Designed by Sir John Simpson and Maxwell Ayrton and engineered by Owen Williams, the new stadium was a monument to the possibilities of ferro-concrete: a framework of wooden boards and steel reinforcement rods; 25,000 tons of concrete funnelled into place from the world's largest Insley Tower to create foundations and the outside walls; 900 tons of steel girders on which to support the stands and terraces; 37 concrete arches of 50-foot span reminiscent of McAlpine's trademark railway viaducts; a sweep of entrance terrace flanked by a pair of domed concrete towers 126 feet high; some half a million rivets to hold the whole thing in place; and a bill for £300,000.

The stadium was finished in the nick of time, three days before Bolton were to play West Ham. During that same week the stands and terraces were tested by the dead-weight of sandbags and by the synchronised sitting, standing and marking time of a battalion of 1,200 men. The story goes that rather than remove or dismantle one of the narrow-gauge trains used to transport material into and out of the site, the thing was simply buried in the arena.

The Final, famously, did not run according to plan. As the FA report explained, in terms less melodramatic than the contemporary news accounts, 'the ground and playing pitch was raided and the playing of the match delayed for nearly an hour'. The mistake, perhaps, had been in assuming the stadium, designed to hold 127,000, could accommodate all those wanting to see Wembley's first Cup Final; or in the decision, based on that assumption, to make terrace tickets available at the turnstiles on the day; or in the haphazard allocation of administrative responsibilities between the FA and the Exhibition company. The Labour MP Jack Jones, wanting his say, blamed inadequate policing: 'They can turn out nine hundred strong for a Royal wedding, but when it comes to the people's amusement there is, of course, a difference.'

Wherever the buck was to stop, the inquest was underway by the time the Cup had found its way through the throng to the winners' dressing-room. A disgruntled 'Olympian' wrote in the *Bolton Evening News*: 'Never in the history of the game has there been such a tragedy, and for the credit of those who are responsible for the good government of soccer, the most popular of all pastimes, it is to be hoped it will never be repeated ... Such a debacle will do unquestionable harm to the game.'

What seemed to upset Olympian most was that some ticket-holders had been unable to reach their seats. Pre-empting the brickbats from those who had been so expensively disappointed, within a fortnight the FA published an apologetic notice: 'The Football Association deeply regrets the incidents and inconvenience caused to the public and will, upon production of any tickets with counterfoil attached, return the cost to holders who travelled to the stadium and were prevented from taking their seats.' £4,100 had to be refunded.

Deciding what had to be done to avoid 'a recurrence of the incidents of the 28 April 1923' took longer. Responsibility (and a flurry of more or less constructive suggestions) passed back and forth between the FA and the Exhibition company. Several changes were agreed: extra entrances on to the terracing and its division into numbered pens, increased security in and around the arena, removal of the rings of pitch-side bench seats, installation of the new Ellison bent arm turnstile. Most significant, however, was the announcement that, despite concerns that forged tickets might appear as a result, the 1924 Cup Final and all football matches at Wembley thereafter would be all-ticket affairs.

George V, a significant presence at the 1923 Cup Final, had been reported as saying, on his first sight of Wembley's besieged pitch that afternoon: 'I fear the match may not be played.' The King was back at the stadium a year later. This time his words went round the world. 'I declare this Exhibition open' composed the first live radio broadcast by a British sovereign to his subjects.

On 23 April 1924, George drove from Windsor to Alperton and then by state carriage to Wembley to inaugurate the British Empire Exhibition, a combined trade fair and prototype theme park whose palaces, pavilions and halls fanned out from the stadium to cover several square miles, each housing displays from an outpost of the Dominions. Enormous ferro-concrete caverns showed off the best of British in industry, engineering and the arts, while four rail systems carried visitors around the site before dropping them at the entrance to an amusement park described as 'the last word in sensations, for the entire world is being searched for novelties and attractions'.

The stadium itself was the venue for a series of spectacular Exhibition events. On opening day an imperial choir filled half the arena. Millions passed through the turnstiles in the coming months to witness a Pageant of Empire which saw one end of the bowl draped in sheets to represent the white cliffs of Dover, a torchlit Military Tattoo, a Boy Scouts' Jamboree, CB Cochran's International Rodeo (much to the disquiet of the RSPCA), a 'London Defended' show during which planes hung with fairy lights flew over the stadium, dropping incendiary bombs to be extinguished by squads of firemen waiting below, and a succession of circuses and firework displays.

One-off sports events were tried too, during 1924, though with less success. A match between the Army and the RAF was the only time rugby union was played at the stadium before World War II. A light-heavyweight bout between Jack Bloomfield and the American Tom Gibbons was so sparsely attended that the latter demanded his fee in cash before stepping into the ring. Two Cup Finals, though, attracted near-capacity crowds on April Saturdays in 1924 and 1925 during the life of the Exhibition. Fans made their way through the Exhibition grounds to watch Newcastle beat Aston Villa 2–0 and Sheffield United beat Cardiff City by a single goal.

During the first twenty years of Wembley's history only one other fixture shared the limelight with the FA Cup Final. England versus Scotland in 1872 had been the first ever international match. By the 1920s, therefore, the fixture had a tradition as venerable as that of the two countries' national cup competitions. The new Empire Stadium became its English venue every other year.

The first Wembley meeting took place eleven days before the Empire Exhibition opened in 1924. Charles Buchan was the England star in a 1–1 draw: 'Two and even three Scottish defenders followed him, no matter how he moved,' according to the *Daily Mail*. It was the start of a fortnight to remember for the Villa inside forward Billy Walker: 'I was at Wembley two weeks running in April 1924, first in an international and the following Saturday in the Cup Final! In the international against Scotland I scored England's only goal. Next Saturday, in the Cup Final, I crashed into the goalpost and knocked myself out!'

That first Wembley international drew a disappointing crowd, the stadium less than half full. In 1926, the fixture was played in Manchester but, by the time it returned to London in March 1928, Scots fans had worked out the way to Wembley. Indeed, when the Scotland team arrived at their head-quarters, the Regent Palace Hotel in Piccadilly, they found the premises crammed with a tartan army apparently intent on drinking the West End dry. The players took little persuading to join the party and the evening disappeared in high spirits to tunes from the inevitable piper.

The captain, Jimmy McMullan, had his work cut out getting his players upstairs. Wisely he kept his own tactical counsel and issued a simple last instruction: 'All I've to say is go to your bed, put your head on your pillow and pray for rain.' If not the ideal preparation, the Scots got their rain, which was sheeting down when they woke the following morning. The smallest forward line in international history, Scottish fans were convinced, needed only a slick playing surface on which to turn over bigger, more ungainly, opponents.

When the Scottish team arrived at Wembley one observer was moved to remark that they appeared 'undernourished'. Memorably, however, the forwards – Jackson, Dunn, Gallacher, James and Morton – filled their boots at the expense of a cumbersome England defence. The 5–1 scoreline did scant justice to an hour and a half of dazzling passing and sleight of foot to set up a hat-trick for Jackson and two goals for James.

It had taken 200,000 spectators and a white horse to make Cup Final history at Wembley. It took just eleven Scotsmen to make the same impact on it as an international venue, humiliating the home side to a degree that would not be matched for twenty-five years. For the Scots, christened the Wembley Wizards, not only the margin but the manner of the victory established a precedent all Scottish teams have sought to emulate since. As the *Daily Mail* reported, 'Scotland's whole team played with a dominant mastery that was made to appear sheer effrontery.'

Though Wales did not play at Wembley until 1940, Cardiff City's appearances in two twenties Cup Finals were celebrated, by the Welsh at least, as fully-fledged international occasions. Led by the hangdog, chain-smoking Fred Keenor, Cardiff steamed up to Paddington with the support of not just their city but their country behind them.

In 1925 a mistake by the City half-back Wake ('not Awake', according to the *South Wales Football Express*) gifted Sheffield United's Fred Tunstall the winning goal. Two seasons later, however, Cardiff's victory over Arsenal was described by the *South Wales Football Echo* as 'a 1–0 victory for Wales'. The 1927 Final, though by all accounts a dour contest, was memorable on several counts, not least that the FA Cup left England for the first and only time. Ironically the match turned on a mistake by Arsenal's Welsh goalkeeper, Dan Lewis, who fumbled Hugh Ferguson's speculative shot and scooped the ball into his own net for the only goal.

The depression had hit South Wales particularly hard. The General Strike of 1926 had been the cue for nearly a year of bitter industrial dispute in and around the Welsh pits. Little wonder that, as the Cardiff players celebrated Ferguson's winner, thousands of Welsh fans in the crowd turned to cheer David Lloyd George, sitting in the Royal Box with a daffodil worn proudly on his lapel, who was heard to remark: 'One would think I had kicked the goal.'

The former prime minister, it is safe to assume, had found his Cup Final ticket easy enough to come by. Such was the demand, however, that the number of forged tickets in circulation before the game led some to call for pay-at-the-gate admission to be reintroduced at Wembley. Some fans even fell foul of bogus officials outside Wembley who 'collected' and then resold their tickets.

The 91,000 or more who got inside took part in the inauguration of what was to become an enduring Wembley tradition. At 1.45 and again at 2.45, the Man in White, Mr TP Ratcliff, climbed his podium to conduct community singing to the accompaniment of the band of the Grenadier Guards. The secretary of the FA, Sir Frederick Wall, chose the songs and included his favourite hymn, *Abide With Me*, which has been sung at every Cup Final since. Paul Gardner describes in *The Simplest Game* how 'the last note slides into a sustained cheer as banners wave and rattles rattle, a cheer that turns suddenly to an amorphous deafening roar of relief and expectation ... as the two teams walk sedately ... on to the field'.

One reason for the introduction of community singing was that the Final was for the first time being broadcast live on radio. The *Radio Times* promised that 'listeners all over the country will be able to hear in their own homes the story, told from the ground during the actual progress of the game'. To help fans follow George Allison's commentary, the BBC printed a picture of the Wembley playing area divided into numbered squares, the position of the ball in play would then be announced quietly from time to time by Allison's assistant, Derek McCulloch. Allison was an Arsenal director at the time, but impartiality, the BBC judged, was less important than his and his number two's cool heads. 'The thrills of a big occasion have no terrors for them ...'

Between Cardiff's visits Bolton returned to defeat Manchester City, thanks to a David Jack goal and a sterling show from keeper Dick Pym, in what seemed for a time as if it might be Wembley's last Cup Final. The Empire Exhibition's first season, in 1924, had been an outstanding success, attracting seventeen-and-a-half million visitors through the summer. The novelty, though, had worn off by the following year and terrible weather dampened enthusiasm further. With the Exhibition sustaining heavy losses (guarantors had to stump up 17s 6d in the pound), the Government decided against sending good money after bad: the Empire Exhibition closed for good on 31 October 1925, the operating company going into liquidation a few weeks later.

What was to be done with a site which had cost £12 million to develop and now stood desolate, in the words of one observer 'a vast white elephant, a rotting sepulchre of hopes and the grave of fortunes'? Put up for auction as a single lot, it was withdrawn without reaching its reserve of £350,000. Eventually Mr Jimmy White, describing himself as a speculator and entrepreneur (his obituary, less generously, read 'sporting racketeer and racehorse punter'), paid a £30,000 deposit, promising to pay a further £270,000 as he broke up and sold the Exhibition buildings. The demolition work was sub-contracted to Arthur Elvin, with whose fortunes Wembley's would be entwined for the next thirty years.

The Empire Exhibition had promised jobs for thousands of ex-servicemen, including some seventy per cent of the workforce which worked on its construction. Elvin, the son of a Norwich policeman, had been taken prisoner of war after a forced landing in his Air Force biplane. In his early twenties and penniless, he tipped up at the Exhibition and was found a job, at £4 10s a week, as an assistant in a tobacco kiosk. Over the next two summers he acquired a wife and the tenancy of eight kiosks of his own, with a profitable sideline in Exhibition confectionery and souvenirs.

Given the demolition contract by White, Elvin soon realised that money could be made selling off some of the Exhibition buildings whole. The West Africa, East Africa and Ceylon buildings, all disposed of locally, became furniture, jam and coach-building factories; the New Zealand building became a London dance hall, the Palestine building a Glasgow laundry and the Sierra Leone building a restaurant in Tranmore, County Waterford, while a job lot of cafés were rebuilt as a grandstand at Bournemouth and Boscombe F.C. As one of Elvin's workmen, Edmond McElligot, remembered: 'As we took it down, lorries came in a continual stream to take it away.'

Once the Exhibition had closed, the stadium itself was no longer a commercial proposition and, with only a Cup Final every year and an international every other on the books, its demolition, too, was privately and publicly discussed. By early 1927, however, Elvin was in a position to make White an offer for it of £122,500: £12,500 down on a ten-year mortgage. White agreed, but that summer, facing bankruptcy himself, committed suicide. White left Elvin owing the balance on the stadium to the Official Receiver who gave him two weeks, rather than ten years, to pay up or lose his deposit.

It proved an exciting and profitable fortnight for the young entrepreneur. Elvin assembled a syndicate which came up with £150,000, enough to buy the stadium and afford the man in the middle a tidy profit besides. At 6.30 p.m. on 17 August, Elvin concluded business with the Receiver and, the following day, got his feet under the desk as managing director of Wembley Stadium and Greyhound Racecourse Company.

The Cup Final was secure for the time being and, as a spectacle, the Wembley fixture in 1928 did not disappoint. Huddersfield, the team of the decade, went into the match firm favourites to beat Blackburn Rovers. They had been chasing the League title all season and in the winger Alex Jackson they had a match winner who had already laid low the best England had to offer at Wembley, with a hat-trick for Scotland a few weeks previously.

The game, though, turned out to be a first episode in the stadium's continuing love affair with the underdog. As the *Sunday Times* reported, the game's decisive moment had occurred before many of the 92,000 spectators had settled into their places: 'Huddersfield won the toss and, although they crossed the half-way line, barely thirty seconds had ticked off when the Rovers were a goal up. In the excitement of the moment it was difficult to say precisely what happened, but when the ball came across from the right – Healless swung it into the goal – Puddefoot bundled goalkeeper Mercer into the net, while Roscamp touched the ball through ... So unexpected, indeed, was the goal that, strange as it may seem, people had no time to cheer.' The Blackburn half-back, Campbell, 'stuck to Jackson as if it were his only mission in life' and, although the Huddersfield winger touched in his side's consolation goal, the 3–1 scoreline ensured 'it was a grand finale for Lancashire and Huddersfield could not complain'.

1921: EDWARD, PRINCE OF WALES
It is, I am sure, unnecessary for me to emphasise the importance of the British Empire
Exhibition, not only its permanent character as the home of the British Trade
Exhibitions and British Sport but also in its particular purpose as a means of developing
the resources and trade of the Empire. I am convinced that it is only by a general revival
of trade that we may hope to reduce the amount of unemployment in this country and
bring happiness and prosperity to the homes of thousands of our fellow countrymen who
have been passing through a long-drawn period of depression and distress.
SPEECH, LONDON, 1921

1923: SIR McALPINE

When Titus of Ancient Rome built the vast Amphitheatre, known on account of its colossal size as the Colosseum, taking sixteen years to do the job, it probably did not enter his imperial mind that one day a Stadium almost three times as large, and infinitely more enduring, would be constructed in less than a tithe of the time by a nation whose people he and his forbears thought it scarcely worthwhile to conquer. Yet the task has been done, and in its accomplishment all records for speed of erection, size, beauty, accommodation and – in the opinion of experts – permanency have been beaten. The Stadium at the British Empire Exhibition – the shop window for the British Dominions whose blinds will be pulled in 1924 at Wembley – is a triumph of modern engineering and a permanent monument to the athletic proclivities of the greatest sports-loving nation on earth.

THE STORY OF THE BUILDING OF THE GREATEST STADIUM IN THE WORLD, ROBERT McALPINE & SONS, 1923

Sir ROBERT McALPINE, Bart.
The Senior Partner.

1925: LES SANDERSON

Our family party included my father, an uncle and aunt, and a cousin. We travelled on an excursion train which left Midland Station around midnight on the Friday and returned on a similarly late train from London the following night – in between enjoying a marvellous twenty-four hours during which I thought I was in heaven.

The meals that weekend were part of the trip and after breakfast on Saturday morning my cousin, who was connected with the *Daily Mail*, took us on a tour of the sights. Then, after lunch, he joined us on the train to Wembley, which was then a new stadium staging only its third Cup Final.

We had three-bob (15p) seats in one of the corner areas of the ground, at the end where the players came out; and we were ideally placed for a perfect view of Tunstall's goal on the half-hour. Gillespie had starved Tunnie of the ball until then, but now the skipper suddenly fed him and the best outside-left I ever saw sped down the wing and shot the ball under the body of Farquharson, the Cardiff goalkeeper.

INTERVIEW, 1998

FINAL TIE

Of the Football Association English Cup Competition

APRIL 25th, 1925

METROPOLITAN RAILWAY

FOOTBALL CUP FI[NAL]
at the
STADIUM, WEMBLEY

Cheap Third Class Retur[n]

WILL BE ISSUED TO

WEMBLEY

STADIUM

British Empire Exhibition
Wembley

Official Programme - 6d.

PROGRAMME & SOUVENIR
of the
FOOTBALL ASSOCIATION'S
ENGLISH CUP COMPETITION
FINAL TIE
1924
IN THE STADIUM AT
THE BRITISH EMPIRE
EXHIBITION, WEMBLEY.

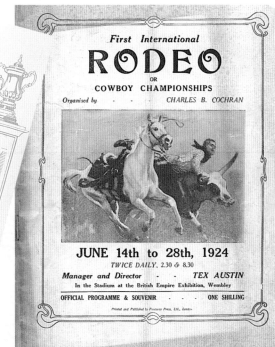

First International
RODEO
OR
COWBOY CHAMPIONSHIPS
Organised by - - - CHARLES B. COCHRAN

JUNE 14th to 28th, 1924
TWICE DAILY, 2.30 & 8.30
Manager and Director - - - TEX AUSTIN
In the Stadium at the British Empire Exhibition, Wembley
OFFICIAL PROGRAMME & SOUVENIR - - - ONE SHILLING
Printed and Published by Fleetway Press, Ltd., London.

FINAL TIE
Of The Football Association Challenge Cup Competition.
APRIL 23rd 1927
STADIUM
WEMBLEY
Official Souvenir Programme 6d

EXPERT CRITICISM By FRANK THOROGOOD
AND THE FINEST PICTURES OF TO-DAY'S CUP-TIE
in Monday's London
Daily News

PRINTED & PUBLISHED BY FRED BLOWER 132 HIGH STREET, WATFORD

FINAL TIE
Of The Football Association Challenge Cup Competition.
APRIL 24th 1926
STADIUM
WEMBLEY
Official Programme 6d

THE BEST PICTURES
and the most Expert Criticism will appear in
THE
SUNDAY NEWS
(Formerly known as Lloyds Sunday News)
TO-MORROW
Order it as you go home

PRINTED & PUBLISHED BY *Fleetway Press Ltd* 3 to 9 LANE ST. LONDON W.C.1

1927: ARTHUR ELVIN

After getting out of a German prison camp, following the Armistice in 1918, I got a job in charge of labourers dismantling ammunition dumps in France. That's how I learnt the technique and trade of demolition. And it was while I was working in a tobacco kiosk at the Exhibition that I got the idea of soliciting orders from the various firms interested for the demolition of their pavilions and displays.

With the profits I decided to bid for most of the buildings that had been bought in a block by the late Jimmy White. I badgered him for weeks before I got what I wanted, but I got it, and then I dismantled and resold them all well within the nine months' clearance time. This deal yielded quite a lot of money. Mind you, it wasn't all quite so simple as it sounds. Still, *Now*, I thought to myself, *I'll have the stadium.*

BBC RADIO INTERVIEW, 1944

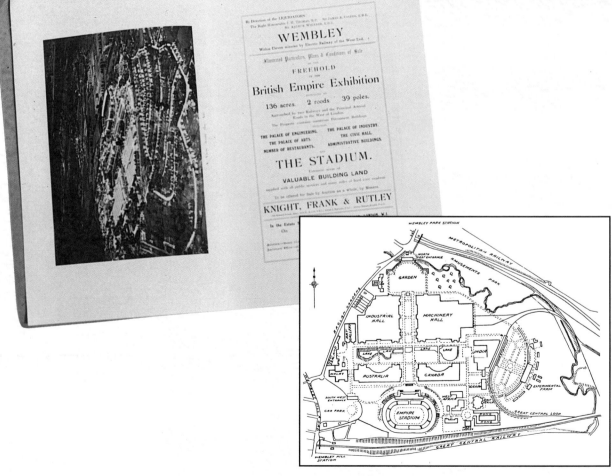

WILL THE ENGLISH CUP LEAVE ENGLAND AT LAST?

1927: ERNIE CURTIS

I was glad when the time came and we went out on the pitch. I remember the weather was quite good. It was a fine day. A lot of people said beforehand that it was a bad pitch to play on because they were getting pulled muscles and God knows what. But I found it was like a bowling green to play on: nothing to worry about as far as the pitch was concerned. In fact I thoroughly enjoyed it, seeing as we won. A lot asked me: *What did the King say to you?* To be honest, I couldn't tell you because he mumbled, so I always tell people that the King said: *Hello, Ern,* and I said: *Hello George. I'll see you after the match.*

It was funny really, it was actually the first time I'd played on the wing in my life. It was a strange position but I was just glad to be there. The game itself, I thought, was evenly matched. It was one of those days when you thought whoever scored first would win. Once you get on that field you don't notice the crowd. You forget they're there. The only time you remember them is when they give you a roasting. I missed a chance about ten minutes before the end. I think they'd have shot me if we hadn't won.

It was up and down most of the time. When the full-time whistle went, that was a big relief to me. I couldn't get up to that Royal Box quick enough! You can see from some of the photographs we had taken I have hold of that Cup Winners' medal like it was a lump of gold: which it was. It was certainly a big day for me. Oh, the dressing-room was alive, champagne flowing all over the place.

That night we stopped at the Palace Hotel in Bloomsbury. They laid out the floor with a green baize and laid out the tables in formation: goalkeeper, two full-backs, three half-backs, five forwards. The ladies who were with us, wives and girlfriends, they cleared the tables afterwards and let them play football on it. It was a really good night. Of course, when we got back to Cardiff, there were over 200,000 people waiting to see us.

BBC WALES INTERVIEW, 1979

Lewis, the Arsenal goalkeeper, dropping the ball after Ferguson's shot. He tried to smother it.

FIRST IN THE FIELD.

F. KEENOR (Cardiff). C. M. BUCHAN (Arsenal).

Two Captains
and
Twenty
PLAYER'S

20   11½D.

"It's the Tobacco that Counts"

1927: GEORGE ALLISON

I told myself that I was describing the game for one person only, a person to whom you could talk naturally. The one person I assumed I was talking to was a sweet old lady up in Redcar, my mother. The rest of the ten million were eavesdroppers. My mother could never get to see a football match, although she was keenly interested in the game. I talked directly to her. She sat in her room with headphones on. More than once I just stopped myself from addressing her by name. When one of those sports around the box told me that a scramble I could not quite see had resulted in a corner, I told my mother that some good-natured spectator had let me know what was going on.

ALLISON CALLING, STAPLES PRESS, 1948

LATEST WIRELESS INVENTION!
NON-VALVE MICROPHONE BAR (PATENT) AMPLIFIER
WILL WORK A LOUD-SPEAKER FROM YOUR CRYSTAL SET

NOT THIS
NOR THIS
NOR THIS

VALVE
ACCUMULATOR
HT BATTERY

BUT THIS

MAKES WEAK CRYSTAL OR VALVE RECEPTION LOUD and CLEAR IN HEADPHONES
ENABLES EVEN VERY DEAF PERSONS TO HEAR FROM CRYSTAL SETS

Complete Amplifier

Order from your Dealer or from Sole Manufacturers and Patentees

NO VALVES OR ACCUMULATORS DISTORTION FRAGILE PARTS

Price **38/-** Post Free

FULLY ILLUSTRATED LISTS FREE
NEW WILSON ELECTRICAL MFG., CO., LTD.
18 Fitzroy Street, Euston Road, London, W.1. Phone: Museum 6979.

GOAL!!

MILLIONS TO "HEAR" FOOTBALL CUP FINAL TO-DAY

1928: BILL HOPKINSON

In 1928 Huddersfield were runners-up in the League and we lost the Cup Final to Blackburn Rovers. They scored in the first minute when a chap called Roscamp bounced our goalie over the line. I went to Stamford Bridge when we were in the Cup Finals in 1920 and 1922. 1928 was the first time I'd been to Wembley. Went down with Dean and Dawsons travel agents. You paid nineteen shillings. They took you down on a coach. You had a tour of London and they took you to Lyons Corner House for a meal. Then there was a night's lodging and next day they took us out to Wembley. Then they brought us back for the Sunday. Lyons Corner Houses were noted for their meals then; and the hotel was in Russell Square. They gave us our tickets for the match on the coach. Huddersfield were doing very well at that time. Fifteen or twenty thousand people would travel down – by road, by coach, by train. Remember, then, it took you about eight hours to get down if you had your own car, down the old A1.
INTERVIEW, 1998

FINAL TIE
of the
FOOTBALL ASSOCIATION CHALLENGE
CUP COMPETITION

April 21st 1928

WEMBLEY STADIUM

EXPERT CRITICISM
BY FRANK THOROGOOD
and the finest pictures of to-day's Cup-Tie
in Monday's
Daily News & Westminster

PRODUCED & PUBLISHED BY FRED. E. BLOWER & CO, 132 HIGH ST, WATFORD

1928: RALPH L. FINN

It was 1928 and it was raining. Someone came for us in a van, piled a whole bunch of us into the back and raced us to Wembley. Perhaps the very fact that we got there at all was a good omen, for the way that vanman drove was enough to frighten one off vans, roads and football matches for ever.

It was a footballer's day, such a day as ball-players dream of and harum-scarum kickers of the ball dread; for you could beat your man by a deft swerve of the shoulder, could get him groping by a slight feint and, if you were a defender, you could lie down on your posterior and go sliding half the length of the field to make your tackle. Conditions favoured neither defenders nor attackers; they favoured footballers.

MY GREATEST GAME, SATURN PRESS, 1951

Gallaher's Cigarettes.

ALEC JAMES
PRESTON NORTH END

ENGLAND

Goal
A. E. HUFTON
(West Ham United)

Right Back
F. R. GOODALL
(Huddersfield Town)

Left Back
H. JONES
(Blackburn Rovers)

Right Half-Back
W. EDWARDS
(Leeds United)

Centre Half-Back
T. WILSON
(Huddersfield Town)

Left Half-Back
S. M. BISHOP
(Leicester City)

Outside Right
J. H. A. HULME
(Arsenal)

Inside Right
R. KELLY
(Huddersfield Tn.)

Centre Forward
W. R. DEAN
(Everton)

Inside Left
J. BRADFORD
(Birmingham)

Outside Left
W. H. SMITH
(Huddersfield Tn.)

Outside Left
A. MORTON
(Rangers)

Inside Left
A. JAMES
(Preston N.E.)

Centre Forward
H. GALLACHER
(Newcastle Utd.)

Inside Right
J. DUNN
(Hibernian)

Outside Right
A. JACKSON
(Huddersfield Tn.)

Left Half-Back
J. McMULLAN
(Manchester City) Captain

Centre Half-Back
T. BRADSHAW
(Bury)

Right Half-Back
J. GIBSON
(Aston Villa)

Left Back
T. LAW
(Chelsea)

Goal
J. D. HARKNESS
(Queen's Park)

Right Back
J. NELSON
(Cardiff City)

SCOTLAND

England will play in White Shirts and
Scotland in Navy Blue Jerseys an

Referee: W. BEL
Linesmen: S. F. RO
J. L. M

PLAYER'S CIGARETTES

ALEX JACKSON.

THE FOOTBALL ASSOCIATION
INTERNATIONAL MATCH

Stadium Wembley
March 31st 1928

ENGLAND
v
SCOTLAND

The valve with the wonderful Mullard P.M. Filament.

Mullard
THE · MASTER · VALVE

OFFICIAL PROGRAMME

PRICE SIXPENCE

PRODUCED & PUBLISHED BY FRED. E. BLOWER & CO. 152, HIGH ST. WATFORD

Home Again! See the Pets on page 13

Daily Mirror
THE DAILY PICTURE NEWSPAPER WITH THE LARGEST NET SALE

No. 293

SCOTLAND'S FOOTBALL TRIUMPH AT WEMBLEY GIVES ENGLAND THE WOODEN SPOON

A lively struggle for possession of the ball close to the Scottish goal.

Hufton, the English goalkeeper, fisting out in face of a Scottish attack.

Gallacher, Scotland's centre forward, does his utmost to score his team's first goal.

The Duke of York shaking hands with the Scottish players.

A Scottish defender baulking an Englishman with a fine leap to head the ball.

Scotland gave England's supporters an overwhelming shock at Wembley on Saturday, when the visitors were victorious by five goals to one in the struggle to escape the inter-national wooden spoon. The Scottish team showed marked superiority throughout the game, which was played under wretched weather conditions.—(Daily Mirror.)

Printed and Published by THE DAILY MIRROR NEWSPAPERS, LTD., at Geraldine House, Rolls Bldgs., Fetter-lane, London, E.C.4.—Monday, April 2, 1928. Tel. Holborn 4321.

1929: CHARLES BUCHAN

I went to Wembley expecting to collect my admission ticket at the main entrance. When I got there the commissionaire knew nothing about any ticket for me. He had strict orders that no one could get in without a ticket. I pleaded hard but, though he knew me, it was of no avail. There I stood, outside the stadium, wondering how on earth I was to get in. Right in front of me was a flaming yellow poster which said: READ CHARLES BUCHAN ON THE CUP FINAL ON MONDAY. This was my first Final as a reporter and it looked as though I would miss it.

Minutes flew past until I heard a roar from inside which told me the teams had walked out on to the stadium. I could see no hope of ever seeing the game. Just then the King's carriage rolled past. I ran behind it into the courtyard. I seemed to be no better off but, after talking persuasively to several attendants, I managed to squeeze a way on to the grandstand. As soon as I sat down on the stone steps of a gangway the match started. I forgot the discomfort in the exciting exchanges.

A LIFETIME IN FOOTBALL, PHOENIX HOUSE, 1955

The

FOOTBALL ASSOCIATION
CHALLENGE CUP
COMPETITION

FINAL TIE
THE STADIUM, WEMBLEY
April 27th
1929

PRICE
Official Souvenir Programme
SIXPENCE

BAX.

Some Facts concerning the Greatest Stadium in the World.

The Stadium, like all other buildings in the Exhibition, is the work of Sir Robert McAlpine & Sons, of 50 Pall Mall, London, S.W.1.

It is the largest undertaking of the kind in the world, and was erected at a total cost of £300,000.

It is over two and a half times larger than the famous Stadium at Rome, and covers an area ten times that of the Stadium at Nimes.

Twenty-five thousand tons of concrete have been used in its construction.

The weight of the structural steel work employed in the Stadium exceeds 1,400 tons.

Work on the Stadium was begun early in April, 1922, and was finished on April 25th, 1923—a feat which beats all previous records for work of this magnitude.

More than half a million rivets were used in its construction, involving the drilling of one and a half million holes!

It is constructed throughout of reinforced concrete, a method of building which was originated by Sir Robert McAlpine half a century ago.

250,000 steel rods, weighing 600 tons, have been used to reinforce the concrete, their total length being 500 miles.

The outside wall of the _____ _____ f a mile round, and apart from the _____ _____ _____ _____posed of 37 arches, each

_____ _____ _____ _____tretch from Westminster

_____ _____ _____ make the Stadium the

_____ _____ _____ining accommodation

The turf of the arena, which measures 390ft. long by 300ft. wide, was selected from the Golf Course, and was laid within an hour or two of its being cut.

The work of laying the turf was accomplished in September and October, 1922, so that the weather would knit the surface together.

There are 40 miles of terracing in the Stadium, ample accommodation being provided for 125,000 people.

Something like 150,000 tons of clay were dug up and redeposited for levelling up purposes, and to form part of the south terracing before the work on the superstructure was begun.

Two towers on the North front rise to a height of 160 feet—the same elevation as the Colosseum at Rome.

They are surmounted by concrete flagstaffs each capped by a concrete crown.

The floor of the banqueting hall has been specially constructed so that it may be used for dancing.

The Stadium is the only sports arena in Europe with a cinder track that provides a 220 yards straight.

An observation tower is situated at the top of the West Wall from which traffic will be controlled.

Modern accommodation is provided for 1,000 competitors under the stand in the East Wing—lockers, shower baths, hand basins, etc.

Nearly 100 turnstiles are provided at the various entrances to the Stadium.

The Stadium is an all-British creation—the combined work of an English Architect, a Welsh Engineer, and a Scottish Contractor.

R ROBERT McALPINE & SONS,
50 PALL MALL, LONDON, S.W.1.

Everybody Was Happy

1930-39

Thanks to a white horse, the Wembley Wizards and the patronage of royalty (our own and the likes, too, of the King and Queen of Afghanistan who witnessed England's humiliation in 1928), Wembley's reputation at home and abroad had been established within five years of the stadium opening. Its status as the home of world football's most glamorous fixture was assured: Wembley meant the Cup Final and, for Scots, a suitably impressive venue at which to pitch camp every other year in the hope of cheering the Old Enemy's undoing.

A reputation, though, was not going to pay the bills. Nor would a football match or two a year, however well subscribed. After Bolton had won their third Wembley final in 1929, goals from Butler and Blackmore seeing off Portsmouth in front of a crowd of 92,576, complaints were heard, not for the first time or the last, about the small ticket allocations awarded to supporters of the competing clubs.

A Mr Nicholls from Bolton Wanderers spoke at length on the subject at the club's victory banquet and was quoted in the following Monday's *Bolton Evening News*. In between blaming the Football Association and the Wembley authorities in equal measure for a situation which was 'rapidly developing into a national scandal', he suggested the Cup Final venue itself might be at the root of the problem: 'I understand from people quite competent to judge that Wembley will hold considerably more than 95,000. If it won't, then all I can say is that it was a terrific waste of money even to build it.'

For the 1929 Final Bolton and Portsmouth had received fewer than 8,000 tickets each. (Almost seventy years later, with clubs receiving nearly three times as many, trying to get a ticket to watch your team at Wembley can still be a frustrating proposition.) Supporters' complaints were noted with interest by the new company in control of the stadium. Arthur Elvin, perhaps for different reasons, was equally concerned at the limited attendance, and therefore limited income, at Wembley's showpiece game. For him the challenge was to prove that the stadium was not going to be that 'terrific waste of money'.

Arthur Elvin had an idea how he could make Wembley pay from day one. He had raised the money to buy the stadium from the official receiver, after all, not by promising his backers fistfuls of Cup Final tickets. The future for Wembley as a commercial proposition had been enshrined in the name of the organisation which took control in 1927 with the twenty-eight-year-old Elvin as managing director: the Wembley Stadium and Greyhound Racecourse Company Limited.

Above all, the timing was opportune. The company did not have to create an interest in greyhound racing; Elvin's gamble was just on whether the new craze would last long enough to justify the outlay needed to put Wembley on the dog-track map. Although greyhounds had been raced over a 400-yard straight course at the Welsh Harp, nearby at Hendon, back in the 1870s, the first circular track, complete with mechanical hare, had opened in 1926 at Belle Vue, Manchester, with 2,166 punters turning up for the first meeting. Within a year over 80,000 had jammed into a refurbished White City to watch the Greyhound Derby.

Though Wembley had not staged any sports events other than football since the Empire Exhibition closed, it had been built with more than just Cup Finals in mind. The stadium boasted Europe's only 220-yard sprint track.

There was no reason to suppose greyhounds could not run there, too, attracting the kind of crowds that were making the owners of the White City and a newly-built track at Harringay rich.

Elvin was in no doubt that greyhound racing had a part to play in Wembley's future and did not wait for the stadium to come under his control before taking matters in hand. Captain Arthur Brice, 'a man born and bred to country life' according to contemporary newspaper features, was already an expert on betting and dogs. As well as owning and breeding racehorses at Newmarket, Brice was a coursing buff, judge at the annual blue-riband event, the Waterloo Cup. He would later remember his introduction to Wembley: 'The editor of the *Sporting Life* remarked: "By the way, what about this new sport of dog-racing? A company is being formed in the city this afternoon to promote the Wembley track. May I get them on the telephone and say you are interested?" ... Within an hour I met the amazing Mr A J Elvin and some of his co-directors. They appointed me their director of racing.'

With other tracks already established, Elvin decided he had to give Wembley a distinct appeal and, during the course of 1927, the company threw £100,000 at turning the stadium into the 'Ascot of greyhound racing'. 'We badly overspent,' according to Elvin himself. The track was widened, lighting installed along with an electric hare, kennels built, additional seating put into the stands and a carpark laid out. With the necessary alterations complete, the overspending could begin in earnest on a cocktail bar, smoking lounges and a restaurant complete with dance floor.

Word got round and 50,000 customers turned up on the opening night, 10 December 1927. It turned out to be an evening as chaotic, in its way, as Wembley's first Cup Final afternoon. Elvin had invited five hundred VIP guests and arrived to find they had been joined by twice that many gate-crashers. 'What a shambles!' he wrote. 'I saw total strangers walking away with bottles of champagne in their pockets, and on my only visit to the kitchens I found the waiters fighting with knives and forks.'

Things were not much better ordered on the track. During the third race the leading dog caught and started to savage the mechanical hare, leaving off only when the other dogs passed him and he set off in pursuit. The stadium officials hurried to speed up the battered hare, which duly caught and bowled over a straggling dog named Big Attack. The stewards had experienced nothing like it before, but our man Brice decided the race would stand. Backers of Big Attack, presumably, were not best pleased, but most of the crowd had enjoyed the comedy turn during Wembley's first Big Night Out.

Three meetings later snowdrifts and frosts briefly brought down the shutters but within a couple of months greyhound racing at Wembley was operating at a profit and would continue to do so thereafter. The stadium held up to three meetings a week through the thirties. Football may have made Wembley famous; from 1928 onwards the dogs would pay the rent. Arthur Elvin himself described the rush to get the track ready for Saturday evening after a Cup Final afternoon: 'We only used to have a bare two hours to take up 20,000 seats, clear up the main enclosure and other equipment so that the first greyhound-racing spectators could enter the stadium at seven o'clock. In fact, the goal-posts had disappeared before the last football fan had got off the ground.'

Football, they say, is all about players. The Cup Final occasion, for those lucky (or determined) enough to get hold of a ticket, is all about the fans. The 1930 Final, however, which saw Arsenal beat Huddersfield Town 2-0 and become London's first Wembley winners, was all about one man, a man of whom the Arsenal and England winger Cliff Bastin was moved to remark: 'His qualities were worthy of an even better reward. He should have been prime minister ...'

Herbert Chapman, though, was a football man rather than a political animal; without doubt the greatest manager of the pre-war period and as significant a figure as any in the game's history. On the afternoon of 26 April 1930, the two clubs with whose fortunes Chapman had been memorably intertwined met at Wembley, an occasion which may be said to have marked the birth of football's modern era.

A miner's son, stocky, bluff and ambitious, Chapman joined Huddersfield as assistant manager in 1920. Taking charge in 1921 he quickly turned the club into the most powerful in the land, winners of three successive League Championships, a feat Arsenal would emulate in the 1930s. The offer of a £2,000 a year salary, however, was enough to persuade the man of the moment to take up the manager's job at Highbury in 1925. The change he wrought at Arsenal, then a mediocre club which had never won a trophy, has been often enough described. On the pitch and off he reshaped the image and substance of the club and, in effect, reinvented the professional game. In the words of Bernard Joy, Arsenal's famous amateur centre half: 'There are two kinds of visionary: those that dream of a whole new world, and those who dream of just one thing. Chapman's vision was of the greatest football team in the world. His genius was in actually creating something close to that.'

The 1930 Cup Final marked the end of a decade which had belonged largely to Huddersfield and ushered in one which would be dominated by Arsenal. It was fitting that Wembley should be the setting for such an historic encounter. The stadium's stature and reputation had already had a profound effect on football's most important fixture, according to the journalist Ivan Sharpe: 'In the beginning the Cup Final was an assembly of amateur players and public schools people. Then, as the provinces challenged and professionalism arrived, democracy entered the arena. Now Wembley, with its grand parade and VIPs and high-priced seats, has re-introduced the social touch of the early days at The Oval.'

Herbert Chapman, provincial and professional to his bootstraps, revolutionised the standing of the game as a whole in much the same way.

Once that first trophy was on the sideboard at Highbury, the man who had made Huddersfield Town great during the decade after World War I set about turning Arsenal into the 'Bank of England' club which would change the face of football in the decade before World War II.

To mark Chapman's contribution to the competing clubs the Huddersfield and Arsenal teams took the field together, the first to do so at Wembley, walking out in two lines behind the respective captains, Tom Wilson and Tom Parker. It had been agreed, too, that the two teams would meet again after the match for a joint Cup Final banquet.

It was Huddersfield's fourth Cup Final in eleven seasons and they started as favourites. But the game turned on the brilliance of Alex James. According to Cliff Bastin, James suggested on the coach bringing Arsenal to Wembley from their hotel in Harrow: 'If we get a free-kick in their half early on, I'll slip it out to you on the wing, you give it me back and I'll have a crack at goal.' Planned or spontaneous, the routine worked and Arsenal took the lead in the seventeenth minute courtesy of James's quick thinking. He laid on the pass, too, from which Lambert broke half the length of the pitch to score Arsenal's second seven minutes from time.

Between the goals Huddersfield had much the better of things without being able to take advantage of an eccentric display by Charlie Preedy in Arsenal's goal. The man from the *Daily Herald* could not remember a game in which he had 'seen more blunders by a goalkeeper prove so profitless to the opposing side'. Preedy played only because of an injury to the first choice keeper, the hapless Dan Lewis, who was thus denied the chance to make up for his error against Cardiff in 1927. Bastin was less than impressed with the stand-in's performance: 'I am all in favour of a goalkeeper who advances at the right time. On this particular occasion, however, Charlie was advancing all the time; whether it was the right or wrong time was purely incidental.'

Luck and, perhaps, history were to rest on Preedy's side, thanks in large part to the efforts of 'wee Alex' according to the *Herald*: 'It is difficult to estimate what Arsenal owed to James. He was magnificent throughout and, when the final whistle sounded, he revealed a little more of his cleverness by pouncing on the ball and carrying it off as a souvenir.'

James's performance ensured the game would live long in the memories of those at Wembley that day. The afternoon was marked, too, by the appearance of the German *Graf Zeppelin* over the stadium. Flying at well below its legally required 2,000 feet, the airship hovered like an enormous cloud over the arena, affording its passengers a unique bird's-eye view, but only briefly distracting the players and crowd from the drama unfolding below. Arsenal's Eddie Hapgood recalled it 'looking like a great lazy trout as it drifted in the sunshine'. The shadow it cast, however, was to lengthen during the coming decade, all but eclipsing football – and much else besides – come 1939.

Alex James, of course, was no stranger to the thrill of the stadium's big occasion. While a Preston North End player he had pulled the strings for the Wembley Wizards in 1928. He had turned out again for Scotland some three weeks before the 1930 Final. Although England won 5-2, the manner of their victory in no way compensated for the 1928 defeat. As the *Daily Mail* pointed out, 'even in that thrilling period – to Englishmen – in the first half, when three goals came to the home team in five minutes, there was no semblance of a rout'. The third of those goals, England's fourth, was scored by the captain, and James's new Arsenal team-mate, the debonair £10,000-man, David Jack.

The years between the wars saw Scotland hold the upper hand in fixtures between the two countries, endorsing in football terms at least the adage of the day: 'The English believe they are superior to everyone else. The Scots know they are superior to the English.'

England did not help themselves by inconsistent, if not haphazard, team selection, one XI often bearing no resemblance to that which preceded it.

Countless players emerged to play at Wembley once, then disappeared for years, if not for ever. The Arsenal winger Joe Hulme had no doubt as to the cause of the malaise: 'The selectors used to get together simply to try and talk their own club players into the side. It wasn't a question of who was best but rather "what about finding a place for one of ours?"'

In the early thirties, however, Scottish teams arrived at Wembley with problems of their own. Club versus country wrangles persist to this day. In 1931 the FA took the extraordinary decision to block the release of Scottish players based at English clubs for international duty, adding a new twist to the long-standing debate over the border about the relative merits of home-based players as against 'Anglos'.

In the midst of the furore, in 1932, the Scottish FA sent a 'tartan team', including only players from Scottish clubs, to Wembley. The *Athletic News* made clear that the team would not lack spirit: 'The match with England is the strong wine of the Scottish season. Old players have said how they saved their pennies to witness the enemy from over the border and to glory in his downfall ... Today's Scottish youth is fired with the same hope. I do not think it possible for English footballers to regard these matches in the same way.'

In the event, with the elegant Raich Carter making his England debut, the Scots were beaten 3-0, as they were again in 1934. On the latter occasion, however, a breathtaking half-hour's fight-back at the start of the second half, inspired by Hughie Gallacher, a veteran of 1928, salvaged Scottish pride. A new gate record for the fixture was established: 92,693 spectators, paid £19,400, a good third of them, by all accounts, cheering on Scotland.

The trip south itself was cause for celebration – the Wembley game had by now been invested with the ritualistic fervour of a biennial pilgrimage for Scottish fans. Workers at factories, mines and shipyards would subscribe a few pennies each week into a club fund to pay for the return journey to London every other spring. The expectation ensured that, whatever the result, the Tartan Army's day out never totally disappointed. The English, even when they had the upper hand on the pitch, did not stand a chance confronted by 30,000 Scots off it, as the *Daily Express* reported in 1934: 'Half the vast crowd seem to be wearing tartan. They urge on Massie and his men with warlike yells.' The urging and the yelling, thereafter, did the trick; Scotland would not lose again at Wembley in peacetime until 1955.

Since 1929 the stadium had become used to welcoming another friendly invasion from the North: supporters up for the Rugby League Challenge Cup Final. Although rugby league was played and watched almost exclusively in Lancashire, Yorkshire and Cumberland, there had been those working behind the scenes to bring its most prestigious fixture to London. It was seen as an opportunity for the sport to break out of its traditional constituency and establish itself on the national stage with what the rugby league historian John Huxley has called 'an unashamed propaganda exercise, as good behaviour and sportsmanship both on and off the field are demonstrated in front of the soccer-cynical audience of Britain's capital city'.

The Victorian era had brought an urban, industrial way of life to northern England, harsh, precarious but better paid and it was no coincidence, therefore, that professional sport in general, and rugby league in particular, had originated there. What better way for the Northern code to celebrate its identity, its rude economic good health and popularity, than to play in wealthy London's backyard, near enough to Twickenham for noses to be thumbed at strait-laced, amateur rugby union?

Those lobbying for the move to London received a boost in 1924, the year after the extraordinary scenes at Wembley's first FA Cup Final. Since 13,500 had watched Batley beat St Helens at Headingley in 1897, crowds at Challenge Cup Finals had increased steadily until the competition's popularity outstripped the northern grounds' capacity to accommodate them. The 1924 Final, at the Athletic Grounds in Rochdale, attracted 41,831 spectators, many of whom – not a white horse in sight – spilled on to the field of play. The minutes of the seventh annual conference of the Rugby League in 1928 record that, 'Mr John Leake moved that it be recommended to the Council that the final tie for each Challenge Cup be played each year in London'. The recommendation was carried by thirteen votes to ten.

What remained was to decide the choice of venue. The League's secretary John Wilson and chairman Fred Kennedy were packed off to London for a tour of inspection. The refurbished White City, laid out as a greyhound track, proved unsuitable. The choice was between the Crystal Palace and Wembley. The former, reputedly, demanded a third of the gate receipts and, really pushing their luck, all the money taken at the turnstiles before noon on the day of the Final. Arthur Elvin, meanwhile, saw beyond hard cash, ambitious as he was to broaden Wembley's horizons. The Rugby League Cup Final could enhance his and the stadium's reputations. He offered to settle for seven and a half per cent of the gate. In the last week of October 1928 the scouts reported back and, at an emergency committee meeting at the Trafford Arms in Wakefield, 'Mr Kennedy made a full report on his inspection to Crystal Palace and Wembley, after hearing which the committee unanimously decided to play the Cup Final at Wembley'.

To facilitate the switch-over of the stadium from football to rugby league the Challenge Cup Final was put back until May. The task now was to ensure a decent show, on and off the pitch, on the day. In April, the *Athletic News* reported: 'The intensive advertising campaign is being supported by many former Lancashire and Yorkshire supporters now residing in the metropolis and practically every big club in the League is sending a "special" . . . the organisers expressed themselves well satisfied with the results of the propaganda work undertaken to date.'

The game promised to be a David and Goliath affair, little Dewsbury, with a dozen local lads in the ranks, taking on the cosmopolitan might of wealthy Wigan. Half an hour before kick-off things looked bleak for the pro-London lobby, great swaths of the Wembley terraces all but deserted.

Unlike the FA Cup Final, however, spectators could pay at the turnstiles and last-minute customers arrived, swelling the crowd to a very satisfactory 41,500 by three o'clock.

The game lived up to expectations, too, Wigan winning comfortably with tries by Abrams, Brown and Kinnear. Dewsbury fans later contended, though, that the odds had been stacked in their opponents' favour. Dewsbury's reputation was as a dour, workmanlike team, taking the minimum of risks, worthy but, as an example of the game's appeal, less attractive than stylish Wigan. Before the Final, the story goes, the League chairman Mr Kennedy, who had staked his reputation on the move to Wembley, visited both dressing-rooms and stressed the need to provide an open attacking game which would reflect rugby league in the best possible light. That, Yorkshiremen claim to this day, was enough to put Dewsbury off their normal game and ensure Wigan's stars had room in which to play.

Whatever the truth of the legend, the record book reads: Wigan 13 Dewsbury 2. More significantly perhaps, the accounts showed gate receipts of £5,614, almost double the takings at any previous Final. Within five years Wembley was established as the Challenge Cup Final's natural home, as settled a fixture on the calendar as its football counterpart. In 1932 a Great Britain tour to Australia in the spring saw the Challenge Cup Final brought forward to 9 April. Wembley was unable to accommodate the earlier date and the match returned north. Only 29,000 turned up at Central Park, Wigan, to watch Leeds beat Swinton: those still unconvinced by Wembley had finally to concede the argument.

As if to set the seal on the Final's future there 1933's game was the first in the presence of royalty. George V, suffering from a heavy cold, was represented by Edward, Prince of Wales, who quickly made himself at home. While being presented to the Huddersfield and Warrington teams he recognised among the ranks of the latter the Australian international Bill Shankland. The pair had apparently met, and discovered a mutual interest in golf a couple of years previously and now they kept the rest of the world waiting as they discussed their handicaps. 'So Shankland, we meet again,' the Prince is reported to have said. 'How's your golf?' To which the Warrington captain replied: 'Fine, sir. How's yours?'

The match, watched by a record 41,874, was one of the best ever seen at Wembley. Huddersfield raced into a 9-0 lead against a visibly nervous Warrington (the stand-off Jack Oster, apparently, had to be helped on to the pitch), thanks to a Brindle try and two penalties and the conversion kicked by Bowkett. Back, though, came Warrington, Dingsdale and Davies touching down tries, converted by Holding, to lead 10-9 at the break.

Most of the second half went Huddersfield's way and converted tries from Mills and Richards helped them lead 21-12 with three minutes to go. In a grandstand finish, that margin was cut back first by a Davies try and then a Holding goal to leave Huddersfield hanging on at the end. The 21-17 scoreline added up to the biggest points total for a final, a record not broken until Wigan beat Hull 30-13 in 1959. There could have been more: the referee Fairhurst disallowed a second Dingsdale try which, with the conversion, would have won the game for Warrington.

The Prince of Wales duly handed the cup to the Huddersfield captain Les Bowkett, who had found the afternoon enjoyable enough to wave to the crowd each time he stepped up to kick for goal. The game and the Royal occasion had their impact well beyond the afternoon of 6 May. In the following months London outposts of the Northern game sprung up at Acton, Willesden, Streatham, Mitcham and White City. The London Broncos were a long way off but a start, at least, had been made.

Rugby league's popularity with its fans notwithstanding, Wembley in the thirties meant the last Saturday in April when England came to a standstill for the FA Cup Final. It is hard, at the end of the century, to appreciate how singular and climactic a football event the Cup Final was for supporters before satellite television brought the best from at home and abroad into every living-room. The trip to Wembley was considerably more glamorous than the battle at the top of the First Division and victory every bit as prestigious as the League title. For players and fans alike, the season built up towards football's big day. The long haul of the League Championship brought its own satisfactions, disappointments and rewards. International competition, with club or country, was as yet beyond, if not beneath, our little island's ambitions. England was, we were assured, the centre of the football world and the FA Cup Final was, definitively, what English football was about.

Year on year Wembley tradition became more firmly fixed in the national consciousness: the Cup Final was a day on which football, the lifeblood of the *aficionado*, was invested with a sense of romance which every man, woman and child in the country could understand. The headlines invariably told of stirring deeds, plucky heroes, tragic mistakes, unlucky injuries, breathtaking fight-backs, cruel turns of fate. And in 1931, this being England, they told of mucky weather.

It rained without interruption while West Bromwich Albion beat Birmingham City 2-1 to become the first Second Division team to win the Cup. Two goals by Richardson, the second scored less than a minute after Bradford had equalised for Birmingham, meant a victory for youth and enthusiasm over superior technique. Albion's virtues, indeed, won them promotion to the First Division in the same season.

The man from the *Daily Express* devoted most of his report to mud, puddles and drenched spectators but did capture a moment before kick-off which showed the degree to which the Cup Final had become invested with an almost religious significance beyond partisan interest in the match itself. 'The community singing', he wrote, 'ended with three verses of *Abide With Me* sung with a reverence that must amaze any person who encounters for the first time this paradox of England's greatest football event being preceded by the singing of the Church's most moving hymn'.

The high priest of Highbury and Arsenal's 1930 match winner Alex James made his headlines before the 1932 Final by breaking down with the recurrence of a knee injury. Newcastle deserved their 2-1 win on the balance of play but the game is remembered in Wembley's history for the most controversial of all Cup Final goals. With Arsenal one up, Newcastle's inside-right Richardson cut the ball back for Allen to stab in the equaliser. Arsenal's defenders and many in the crowd were convinced the ball had crossed the line for a goal-kick before being played in towards the goalscorer.

Sixty-odd years later we are used to refereeing decisions being criticized on the basis of intense scrutiny from every conceivable camera angle. Back in 1932, the seemingly clear proof of the referee Harper's error afforded by Movietone newsreel footage, was a novelty and the newspapers seized on it, devoting inordinate attention to the incident. In a very different age, however, Samuel Hill-Wood, the Arsenal chairman, remained admirably sanguine about the decision, no matter how the *Daily Herald* badgered for a newsworthy quote: 'If the film demonstrates the fatal point as clearly as you say, then we have had very bad luck. Of course, we can take no further action in the matter. The referee has made his decision and that is the end of it.'

Manchester City, in pre-war days the dominant Mancunian force, reached successive Cup Finals in 1933 and 1934. In the first, although the team included Jimmy McMullan, who had captained the Wembley Wizards, and a bright young talent at right half, Matt Busby (with whom Wembley's history would be intertwined for the next thirty-odd years), City were comprehensively outplayed by an Everton team who had been Second and then First Division champions in the two preceding seasons.

The second of Everton's three goals was scored by William Ralph 'Dixie' Dean whose reputation then as English football's greatest goalscorer has been threatened since only by Jimmy Greaves. Busby, however, was less impressed by Dean and company than he was dismayed by his own team's showing: 'Warney Cresswell, Dixie Dean, Cliff Britton and the rest of the Everton players were formidable foes but on that particular day I believe a Sunday School team would have stood an excellent chance of holding the City side.'

City gave a better account of themselves the following year. Sam Cowan, accepting commiserations from the Duke of York in 1933, had promised: 'We'll be back next year, Your Highness, to collect the winning medals.' Two late goals from Fred Tilson against Rutherford's opener for Portsmouth meant City proved as good as their captain's word.

Before the game Jack Tinn, the Portsmouth manager, had invited entertainer Bud Flanagan into the dressing-room to relieve pre-match nerves. After it, Frank Swift, the young Manchester City goalkeeper, experienced a spectacular release of tension himself, passing out as the final whistle blew. 'There's the whistle, it's all over,' he later wrote. 'I stoop into the net for my cap and gloves, take a couple of steps out to meet Sam [Cowan] . . . then everything went black.'

In the sense that 1934 was remembered, in Busby's words, 'as Frank Swift's big day', almost every Final has one man who, in the shorthand of the football fan's memory, stands out as the dominant and defining figure of the occasion. In 1935 Ellis Rimmer's two late goals for Sheffield Wednesday, to beat West Brom and maintain his record of scoring in every round, ensured that year's Final 'belonged' to him. The following year Ted Drake's heroics wrote the headlines, as he scored the only goal for Arsenal against Sheffield United while strapped with what the trainer Tom Whittaker described as 'the biggest bandage I've ever wound round a player's leg'.

The 1937 Final had its hero, too, in the Sunderland captain Horatio 'Raich' Carter, who inspired his side's fight-back to beat Preston 3-1 after being a goal down at half-time. In retrospect, however, the day's greatest significance lay, perhaps, in the pictures from Wembley transmitted by the BBC, the first time television had spied on football's great day. In 1938 the game was broadcast live, to the delight, no doubt of the estimated 10,000 viewers who were in a position to take advantage of this latest wonder of modern technology.

The lucky few, in fact, got more then they had bargained for, Preston versus Huddersfield turning out to be the first Wembley Final to run into extra-time. The decisive moment arrived late, in the last minute of the last half-hour. Alf Young, a stalwart in Huddersfield's defence, was controversially judged to have brought down George Mutch inside the area and referee Jewell awarded Wembley's first Cup Final penalty. (Eddie Hapgood, playing for England against Scotland, had conceded the first at the stadium two years previously.) Preston's right-half, a young Bill Shankly, was in no doubt about the decision: 'Of course it was a penalty. It's a terrible thing when a man has nothing left to do but bring another man down. I was standing next to Alf Young afterwards. Tears were running down his cheeks. I said to him: "Aye, and that's no' the first one you've given away!"' Mutch, though still dazed from Young's challenge, was equally ruthless from the spot and the whistle blew on the narrowest of 1-0 victories for Preston.

The twenty-one-year agreement signed by the FA to stage football at the stadium had been a crucial factor in realising the Prince of Wales' dream of 'a great national sports ground' at Wembley. The Cup Final was no longer the only profitable event regularly staged by what was now a successful commercial operation under Arthur Elvin's control. It was, though, without doubt the one afternoon each year which underlined the stadium's prestige, an occasion which defined Wembley in the public's imagination.

Much had been done through the decade to broaden Wembley's appeal: the building of the Empire Pool next door in 1933-34; the construction of a grandstand restaurant to cater to the demands of greyhound racing's high society crowd. Meanwhile, the stadium's attitude to the Cup Final hordes was the same as that of club chairmen all over the country in an era when football's popularity seemed boundless: all you had to do was open the gates, count the money and send them home again.

That complacency was disturbed in 1937. With Wembley's contract with the FA due to expire in 1944, the owners of the White City stepped in with a proposal to increase their stadium's capacity to 150,000 and lure away the Cup Final, for which tickets always seemed in short supply. The FA was wary: the White City scheme would involve an investment of half a million pounds on the part of football. Instead the idea of a move was used as a lever in renegotiating terms at what was now the Cup Final's natural home. Wembley promised and completed improvements at a cost to the stadium of some £50,000, to be recouped by adding four further years to the FA's contract and allocating a larger share of gate receipts to Arthur Elvin's company.

As a result of the works undertaken in 1938 the crowd for the 1939 Cup Final was the biggest since 1923: 99,370 paid a record £30,000 to watch the 5-1 on favourites Wolverhampton Wanderers play 1934's beaten finalists Portsmouth. Wolves, second in the League and managed by the fearsome Major Frank Buckley – he of the strict fitness regime, energy injections and team psychologist – were so confident that they did not bother to travel to Wembley until the Saturday morning. Portsmouth, struggling against relegation, relied on their manager Jack Tinn's 'lucky' spats, the comedian and Pompey fan Albert Burdon's wisecracks on the team coach and the mood of a goalscorer with a point to prove: Bert Barlow had been sold to them two months earlier by Wolves.

Jimmy Guthrie, the Portsmouth captain, would later claim he knew it would be their day when the autograph books came round the dressing-rooms. The Wolves players' signatures were shaky to the point of illegibility; the war of nerves, Guthrie reasoned, was already won. And so, a couple of hours later, was the game, two goals from the Buckley reject Barlow helping Portsmouth to a 4-1 victory. A young Wolverhampton boot boy, fifteen-year-old Billy Wright, watched from the touchline as Guthrie received the Cup for Portsmouth from King George VI. It was a sight which, before the gaze of a young man who would have much to do with Wembley's post-war renaissance, was to be the closing image of the first, pre-war episodes in the stadium's history.

One of Wright's jobs that day had been to clean and prepare the Wolves captain Stan Cullis' boots. Ten years later Cullis would manage a Wanderers' Cup-winning side with Wright as its captain. On the afternoon of 29 April 1939, however, there was only the frustration of the cup being carried off to Portsmouth, where it would remain for longer than even the most partisan of Pompey fans could have imagined or desired. Speaking after World War II, Cullis would remember that pre-war moment all too well: 'As we walked off Wembley's pitch, bitterly disappointed, we consoled ourselves with the time-honoured thought of the losing side: there is always next year. But in 1939 there was no next year in the football sense. When next April came around, most of the twenty-two players who fought out that memorable Final found themselves in services camps far removed from Wembley.'

THE DAILY MIRROR. Monday, April 28, 1930.

Wilfred at the Zoo: See page 14

Daily Mirror

THE F.A. CUP COMES BACK TO LONDON—GRAF ZEPPELIN OVER WEMBLEY

Parker and other Arsenal players taking the Cup away.

The King with the Duke of York and Mr. Snowden.

Preedy, out of goal, hard-pressed by Huddersfield forwards.

Turner, of Huddersfield, stops a high shot, with Lambert jumping.

The giant German airship, Graf Zeppelin, passing low over the Wembley Stadium during the Cup Final in which Arsenal beat Huddersfield Town by two goals to nil and thus brought the Cup to London for the third time since 1882. The airship was booed by some of the crowd who regarded its presence as likely to distract the players. Arsenal won the match on their merits, but Huddersfield played hard throughout and did not lose their form. The King presented the trophy and medals.

Printed and Published by THE DAILY MIRROR NEWSPAPERS, LTD., at Geraldine House, Rolls Bldgs., Fetter-lane, London, E.C.4.— Monday, April 28, 1930. Tel. Holborn 4321.

Capt A.E. Brice

1931: CAPTAIN A.E. BRICE

I've seen some fine races, but perhaps the greatest of all of them was Mick the Miller's last race. It was on 3 October 1931 – the final of the 700-yard classic, the Greyhound St Leger. Mick was now six years old and the public were beginning to regard him as 'an old man'. That year, however, he won both his heats and the semi-final and an enormous crowd came to the final to see him run what they knew would be his last race. It was a four-dog final, and the atmosphere was electric.

As the lights in the stand were dimmed all eyes turned towards the start. Round came the hare, up went the traps, and the sudden hush was broken by a tremendous cheer as it was seen that Mick had leapt straight into the lead which he held round the first and second bends. Up the home straight, first time round, Seldom Led began making up ground on the outside and you could almost see Mick's brain working as he forced his rival further out as they came to the fifth bend. It was here that Virile Bill made a great effort cutting inside both of them on the rails. Again Mick showed his superb track craft; he came sharply across the track to the left, making Bill check, and so he held his lead into the sixth bend and the home straight. From here on it was full tilt for the finish and the old warrior gamely held his own and flashed over the line a fraction ahead of Virile Bill with Seldom Led third, less than six inches away.

What a marvellous reception Mick got from the crowd, and what a scene that was, everybody shouting, yelling, cheering, waving, for nearly five minutes after. Everybody was happy and the happiest of all: Mick the Miller. The louder the cheers the more he wagged his tail. I'm sure he knew they were for him.

BBC RADIO INTERVIEW, 1944

The Ascot of
GREYHOUND RACING

RACING ALL THE YEAR ROUND
Admission : B/, 4/, 2/, (including Official Race Card)

UNEXCELLED AMENITIES
- First-class racing.
- Seats in all enclosures.
- Full Totalisator facilities.
- Easy access from all parts.

EMPIRE STADIUM
WEMBLEY

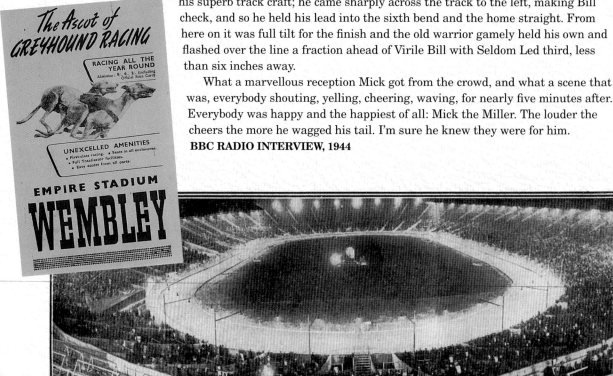

1932: EDDIE HAPGOOD

The luck doesn't always run smoothly, even for Arsenal, much as many people would have us believe, and it went against us in my second Final, against Newcastle United, in 1932. I still think their first goal should have been disallowed, but there's nothing I can do about it now. You remember the famous 'over-the-line' incident? Here's how I do.

Boyd, the Newcastle right-winger, cut inside to chase a long ball from Sammy Weaver, but I was there first and hit it upfield in the direction of Jack Lambert, our centre-forward. Meanwhile Richardson had run out to the wing, when Boyd cut inside. Davison, the Newcastle centre-half, intercepted my clearance and banged it down the right wing. Richardson chased after the ball.

It was a long ball and I could see that it would be a desperately close thing if he were to catch it. Richardson, travelling at top speed, drew up to it and centred first time. But, by that time, we were appealing for an 'over-the-line' ball. At the same time Allen cracked the centre into the net. But, although we protested strongly to the referee (Mr W P Harper of Stourbridge), he allowed the goal to stand. Allen got another later on, and we only scored one, through Bob John. But that's the luck of the game.

FOOTBALL AMBASSADOR, SPORTING HANDBOOKS, 1945

WILLS'S CIGARETTES

E. HAPGOOD (ARSENAL)

1933: MATT BUSBY

The Everton match was lost in the dressing-room – of that I am convinced. There are ways of combating big-match jitters: unfortunately Manchester City employed none of these methods. On the contrary in fact. We turned up at Wembley one hour and three-quarters before kick-off time, a manoeuvre which, although enabling the team to miss the rush, was not only unnecessary but a tactical blunder of the first magnitude.

The players took a stroll on to the delightful green turf, surveyed massive terraces on which only a handful of spectators had by then taken up their stations, returned to the dressing-room and began to wonder how they could fill in the best part of two hours. Stripping was delayed for as long as possible but eventually, to relieve the boredom, a few ties were loosened, an odd shoe kicked off here and there. The entire Manchester City team was ready to start the match at 2.15 . . . three-quarters of an hour before the referee was due to blow his whistle.

To this day I cannot remember how we passed those forty-five minutes, but I do know with each moment of passing time the nervous tension increased, and by the time our captain, Sam Cowan, was summoned to lead us out to meet the Duke of York (later King George VI), we were as unprepared for a game of football as any team could be.

MY STORY, SOUVENIR PRESS, 1957

THE KING'S REPRESENTATIVE
The Duke of York shaking hands with the Manchester City players.

CITY ROUT FOLLOWS THE STEIN SONG

Manchester Men Outplayed After Rivals' First Goal

DEAN AND DUNN ALSO SCORE

EVERTON (1) .... 3 | MANCHESTER C. (0) 0
Stein, Dean, Dunn.

OFFICIAL ATTENDANCE, 92,390. GATE RECEIPTS, £24,831 6s.

EVERTON triumphant! Superior in practically every phase from the first kick to the last, the famous Goodison organisation scored a magnificent victory over their great Lancashire rivals, Manchester City, by three clear goals in the final for the English Cup at the Wembley Stadium yesterday—the biggest win in the final stage of the great knock-out competition since Sheffield United beat Chelsea at Old Trafford in 1915.

Against the classic Everton side Manchester City . . .

1934: FRANK SWIFT

The next thing I realised was that I was lying on the turf, with somebody pouring cold water on my face. Sam was holding my head and Alec Bell was dabbing water on me from the sponge. I had fainted, I still think it was because of the tremendous nerve strain, through the mounting tension and excitement, as those photographers, helpful as they were, ticked away the dying moments of the game.

Sam helped me to my feet and I limped across to where the other players and officials were waiting for our skipper to lead the parade up to the royal dais. I still felt a bit woozy, which is probably why I didn't turn and run away instead of slowly climbing what seemed to be an endless number of stone steps up to the Royal Box.

I can still recall it vividly. A long, gawky lad of nineteen-and-a-bit stands alone in front of a bearded gentleman with kind eyes. Two minutes previously the boy had lain unconscious on the sacred turf at Wembley. The buzzing in his brain beats against the crowd noises. Then the kindly face of this much-loved man crystallises from the dizzy mist.

How are you feeling now, my boy? says a deep voice. It is the King speaking.

Fine, Sir, says the lad.

That's good. You played well. Here is your medal, and good luck.

FOOTBALL FROM THE GOALMOUTH, SPORTING HANDBOOKS, 1948

The King presenting the Cup to Sam Cowan, captain of the Manchester City team, after their victory over Portsmouth at Wembley, yesterday. Sir Frederick Wall is seen in the background.

"AS COOL AS ICE"

But Young Goalkeeper Went Dizzy When City Won

1936: TOM WHITTAKER

On the Saturday morning the party travelled out to Hendon by coach, to have lunch at the house of a friend of the manager's. The travelling schedule I had worked out was rigidly followed and we arrived in nice time at Wembley. The secret is not to get your players to the match too early. Some of them can fret if they've too much time to think about the ordeal ahead. By the time the lads had popped outside to the main entrance to hand over last-minute tickets to friends, there was just time for them to change so as to be ready when the FA official put his head inside the door at 2.45. For four of the players, Hapgood, Male, Crayston and Bastin – as well as myself – entering the No.1 dressing-room was like coming home again. Only a fortnight previously we had been there with the England team for the international match with Scotland. The four lads used the same pegs on which to hang their clothes when they changed for the Final. That is, bar Cliff Bastin, who played inside-left for England and outside-left for us.

TOM WHITTAKER'S ARSENAL STORY, SPORTING HANDBOOKS,1958

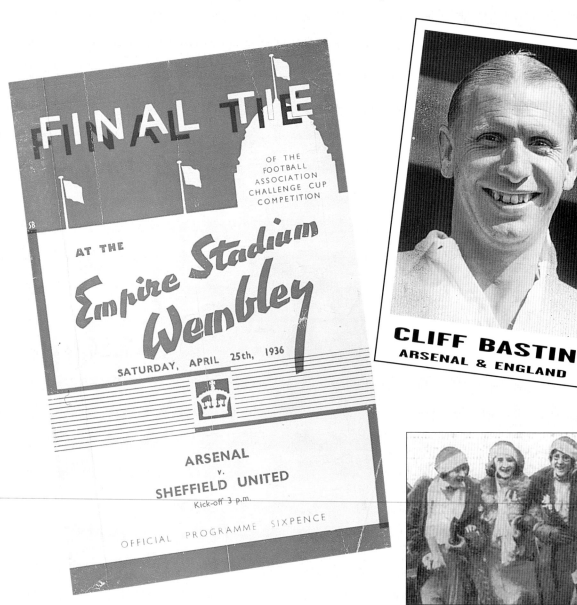

FINAL TIE

OF THE
FOOTBALL
ASSOCIATION
CHALLENGE CUP
COMPETITION

AT THE

Empire Stadium
Wembley

SATURDAY, APRIL 25th, 1936

ARSENAL
v.
SHEFFIELD UNITED

Kick-off 3 p.m.

OFFICIAL PROGRAMME SIXPENCE

CLIFF BASTIN
ARSENAL & ENGLAND

1937: RAICH CARTER

I shall never forget that first sight of the Mecca of footballers. The ground was still half-empty with people crowding in and swarming into the stands like ants. Everywhere there was a mass of movement, and the noise of movement, and the noise of the crowd. There was singing and catcalling, and the barking of programme sellers. It was the noise of excitement, a mingling of a thousand and one different sounds, that set my stomach aswirl. And yet it was distant and unreal and I seemed curiously detached from it all. There was the noise, and there was the pitch. The pitch looked like a bowling green. The grass was so very green and well cut, and the white lines so precise and very white. So this was Wembley! I had never seen a football pitch like that one. It looked perfect for football.

FOOTBALLER'S PROGRESS, SPORTING HANDBOOKS, 1950

FINAL TIE

OF THE FOOTBALL ASSOCIATION CHALLENGE CUP COMPETITION

AT THE

EMPIRE STADIUM WEMBLEY

SATURDAY, MAY 1, 1937

CORONATION YEAR OF THEIR MAJESTIES KING GEORGE VI AND QUEEN ELIZABETH

PRESTON NORTH END

v.

SUNDERLAND

Kick-off 3 p.m.

OFFICIAL PROGRAMME

WILLS'S CIGARETTES

H. CARTER (SUNDERLAND)

Wembley Spe...

Thursday, July 25t...

ASK HERE

SPECIAL
CONCESSIO...
TICKET

Which if presented at Turnstile
will entitle you to admission to th...

1/2 ENCLOSURE for 6d...

993

THE EMPIRE STADIUM,
WEMBLEY.

BASEBALL

SATURDAY, JUNE 16th, 1934.
At 3.30 p.m.

U.S.S. "NEW ORLEANS" "A"
versus
U.S.S. "NEW ORLEANS" "B2"
With one or two London players assisting.

Under the patronage of
His Excellency Hon. Robert Worth Bingham
The American Ambassador
who will welcome the Officers and Men of the U.S.S.
"NEW ORLEANS" on behalf of the American Colony
in London.

Match by arrangement with
The Anglo-American Baseball Association, c/o Cosmo Club,
33, Wardour Street, W.1.
Charlie Muirhead, Secretary

All enquiries during the game to Bud Munro, A.A.B.A.

PROGRAMME

THREEPENCE.

DIAGRAM OF FIELD OF PLAY

Left Field   Center Field   Right Field
2nd Base

3rd Base   Short Stop   66.3   Base

FOUL GROUND 90   Pitcher   90 FOUL GROUND

60.5

Home Plate

Catcher

A FEW BASEBALL TERMS EXPLAINED

"That's the Boy"—a general term of
encouragement.
...id player.
...nety foot square bounded by the bases.
...on which batsman reaches 2nd base.
...y a fielder which allows a runner to
...just ticks the bat and passes behind.
...nthusiast.
...high into the air a "skier".
...which batsman gets to home plate.
...ng a weak pitcher's arm.
...t ball that travels on a level line.
...that gets away from catcher with
...n bases.
...to the air.
...ally to a player.
...a player.
...the infield.
...ch batsman is put out but which
...nner to advance.
...hit.

"Safety"—A safe hit on which batter gets to first base or
further.
"Steal"—To gain a base without aid of batsman.
"Southpaw"—A left handed pitcher.
"Slugger"—A batsman who specialises in long hitting.
"Solid Ivory"—What a "fan" thinks a stupid player's head
is made of.
"Three Bagger"—A hit on which batsman gets to 3rd base.
"Wild Pitch"—A throw by pitcher that catcher has no
chance of getting.
"The Ball Player's Dream"—To make home run with
the bases full.
"The Ball Player's Nightmare"—To strike out with the
bases full.
"Snap Out of it"—Pull yourself together.
"Hit the Dirt"—An exhortation to play safe by sliding.
"Slide Kelly Slide"—Mike Kelly was the first player to
develop sliding into a base. Everybody is a
Kelly when he slides.
"Stick it on him"—An exhortation to touch out the runner
with the ball.
"Kill the Umpire"—A mild form of disagreement with the
umpire's decision.

IF you have an ODD numbered programme RO... ..." Team.
" " " EVEN " ROOT ..." "2"

THE SCORE BY INNINGS.

	1	2	3	4	5	6	7	8	9	TOTAL
"A" TEAM										
"B2" TEAM										

U.S.S. "NEW ORLEANS" "B2" TEAM.

Manager—Chief Yeoman A. V. Boutin.

A.A.B.A., c/o Cosmo Club, 33, Wardour St., W.1.

PLEASE SEND NOTICES OF FUTURE FIXTURES

Name.................................. Address.........................

Phone Number Gerrard 2342

THE RUGBY LEAGUE GAME.

HOW IT DIFFERS FROM THE FIFTEEN-A-SIDE CODE.

The formations on the field in the Rugby League game are exactly the same as those of the Rugby Union, but in the case of the Northern code there are two less men in the scrum.

There are a number of differences in the rules of play, all of which have been framed with the idea of making the game faster and more spectacular.

There is no " line out " in Rugby League football. In its place a scrum is formed five yards from the point where the ball bounced over the touch line. It is important to note that except in the case of a penalty, the ball MUST bounce from the field of play into touch, otherwise a scrum is ordered at the point from which the ball was kicked. It will be appreciated that this rule helps to keep the ball in play, as it gives the defending side an opportunity to gather the ball and start a run.

The half back rule is another important alteration. In the thirteen-a-side game the scrum half must stay behind his scrum, even though the opposing side obtains possession. In this way a great deal of the scrummaging which takes place in the Rugby Union game as the result of an alert scrum half pouncing on a slower rival the moment the latter gets the ball from the scrum is eliminated.

The " play the ball " rule is possibly the most interesting difference of all. When a player is tackled he must be allowed to rise with the ball in his possession. At that moment only one player on the opposing side may " mark " him, and the ball can only be played with the feet. Other players must not stand within five yards of this area.

The formation of the scrum is three, two, one, the player in the back row being more of a " loose head " than anything else.

" Marking " the ball may only be used for defensive purposes, and no goal can be scored from a mark.

Simplicity is the key-note of the method of scoring. A try counts three points, while a goal of any kind counts two points. It should be noted, too, that a try converted counts as a try and a goal, or five points, and not as a goal—five points—as in the Rugby Union game.

ROYAL CONGRATULATIONS

The Prince of Wales presenting the cup to the captain of team after their victory over Warrington in the Rugby Le Wembley yesterday,

THE SPORTS CENTRE OF THE EMPIRE

The Rugby League Challenge Cup Final

HUDDERSFIELD v. WARRINGTON

The Empire Stadium, Wembley

Saturday, May 6th, 1933

70,000 EXPECTED AT RUGBY LEAGUE FINAL

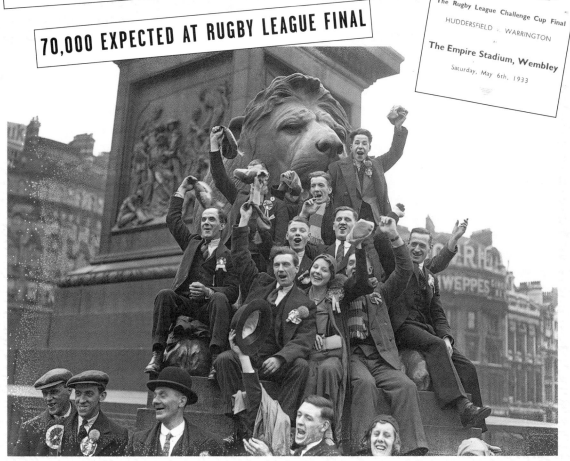

Monday, September 4, 1939

"I KNOW YOU WILL PLAY YOUR PART WITH COURAGE"—PREMIER

peneu,
which were re...

ce to
ions,
cked
ntry
ld be
come

"I trust I may live to see the day when Hitlerism has been destroyed and a restored and liberated Europe has been re-established."
With Mr. Chamberlain is a secretary carrying the Premier's gas mask and his own.

..."right," It is the evil things that we shall be fighting against—brute force, bad faith, injustice, oppression and persecution — and against them I am certain that the right will prevail.

As Far As War Conditions Permitted

1939-45

EMPIRE STADIUM WEMBLEY
MAY 26th, 1945   Kick-off 3.0 p.m.
INTERNATIONAL ASSOCIATION FOOTBALL MATCH
ENGLAND V FRANCE
OFFICIAL PROGRAMME SIXPENCE

The Second World War did not exactly 'break out'. Conflict in Europe, if not at home, had seemed increasingly likely at least since 1932 when the controversy surrounding Newcastle's 'over-the-line' goal in the Cup Final had shared the front pages with news of Hitler's success in that weekend's German elections. During the summer of 1939 nearly two million people were evacuated from Britain's cities to be billeted in safer, rural areas. The time had come to fear the worst.

During World War I sport in general, and football in particular, had misjudged the national mood. Although many players and, of course, many more spectators found 'in the service of the nation a higher call than in playing football' (the words of a Football League directive), the professional game had carried on well into 1915 in the face of mounting criticism and dwindling gates. The same mistake would not be made again. War was declared on 3 September and with it came implications hinted at in King George's address to the nation on the same day: 'There may be dark days ahead and war can no longer be confined to the battlefield.'

Barbed wire rolled out across Britain's beaches; streets and homes were plunged into darkness; and families gathered in the gloom to listen to the BBC's first emergency broadcasts. In 1914 the war had seemed like something happening at a distance while life continued at home. Now Britain prepared for conflict in her own backyard.

On 8 September the Football Association suspended all competition until further notice and other sports followed the lead of the national game if they had not pre-empted it. Wembley shut down at once and staff joined thousands who had played and watched at the stadium in signing up for national service.

Wembley's kennels, too, were closed in the first few days of war. Some hundred greyhounds were evacuated; others were not given that opportunity. Jack Tetlow, a post-war racing manager, was at the stadium in early September, 1939, before leaving to join the RAF: 'When racing temporarily ceased at Wembley, a number of dogs had to be destroyed because there was no use for them. I had to identify them before they were put down. It was the saddest experience of my life.'

During the eerie autumn of 1939, however, the threat of imminent invasion seemed to recede and the country drifted into the strange, enervated interim of the 'Phoney War'. The War Office gave careful consideration to what role organised sport might play during the long period of conflict now being envisaged. Football was, in effect, put at the nation's disposal.

Hundreds of players, trainers and masseurs were whisked off to Aldershot to be prepared for service as the spine of the Forces' physical training corps. At the same time a programme of friendly matches got under way, the game being perceived as an important way of sustaining civilian morale. Wembley's doors reopened almost as suddenly as they had closed, and not just for football.

After the cancellation of only nine meetings greyhound racing returned to the stadium, although the blackout and restrictions on mass gatherings meant crowds were small and the single card each week was run in daylight. The Spring Cup meeting on Easter Monday, 1940, was the first ever to be broadcast live by the BBC.

That April, too, saw the first wartime football fixture. The crowd was restricted to 40,000 and the practicalities of players travelling from their service units meant that twelve of the twenty-two were London-based.

A sense of unreality in the air, Wales took the opportunity to mark their first Wembley fixture with a win. Hall missed a penalty for England while Bartram let Bryn Jones' shot squirm out of his hands for the only goal.

Although the FA's original contract enabled them to stage the Cup Final and any other games they saw fit at Wembley, Wales were the first international team other than Scotland to play there. While Cardiff's 1927 victory over Arsenal had proved a false dawn for Welsh football, the national team's victory in 1940 earned them, in the public's mind, the right to return to Wembley in future seasons.

Two games in 1943 would serve rather to undermine what Wales had achieved on first acquaintance with the stadium: England won 5–3 in February and 8–3 in September. The latter occasion demonstrated the informality and good humour which often marked arrangements during wartime. Although substitutes were still a thing of the distant future, when the Welsh half-back Ivor Powell was injured early in the game, it was hurriedly agreed that a reserve might take his place. As the visitors were without a twelfth man, an uncapped youngster, Stan Mortensen, who would go on to score twenty-three goals in twenty-five England appearances, made his international debut for Wales.

That sort of fun seemed a long way off as autumn froze into winter in 1940. The spring, though, saw a return to something like organised football, albeit regional and sparsely attended, with the prospect, unlikely a few months previously, of a Wembley Cup Final at the end of the first wartime season. On 1 March 1940 the clubs sought and were granted an extension to their schedule in which to contest a War Cup, complete with medals and its own trophy and for which players could be paid £1 win bonuses and 10s a draw. The tournament, it turned out, coincided with some of the most difficult weeks of the entire war.

Denmark had already been invaded and Norway fell as Chamberlain's cabinet fumbled in response to Hitler's blitzkrieg. Churchill had formed a war government by the time the Cup rounds kicked off on 13 April. As the competition proceeded, Europe fell: Holland, Belgium, then France. These were ominous days: defeat at the front, shattered morale at home. Many shell-shocked Dunkirk evacuees were admitted to Wembley free. Others had already been billeted in and around the stadium in the course of returning to camp, hospital or home.

This early in the war both teams were able to call on their own players and nearly 43,000 were at the stadium, restricted to a 50,000 capacity, to watch a single Sam Small goal for West Ham beat Blackburn. The game, though, was remembered by Ted Fenton of West Ham as being 'as hilarious as a wet Sunday in Cardiff'. If hope is football's defining emotion, this was surely no time to be playing or watching the game. As Jack Rollin remarks in *Soccer At War*, his exhaustive history of the era, 'The first wartime season ended and coincided with England's darkest hour.'

Still football, like the country, survived. In the five years of conflict which remained the game muddled through, even briefly flourished. Although one could never be sure, because of the movements of enlisted players, quite who would be playing where or for whom, there were plenty of games to be watched and to play in, as Arsenal's Denis Compton would later recall: 'Cup Finals, League South matches and Army representative games followed one on top of each other in a seemingly endless stream.'

Apart from uncertainty as to the availability of players, wartime put other, sometimes bizarre, obstacles in the way of a semblance of normal competition. Clubs had to husband rations of clothing coupons to ensure there would be kit to turn out in come Saturday. The fall of Singapore meant a shortage of rubber and, therefore, bladders for balls. Thus the theft by a spectator of the one used in the 1942 London War Cup Final was cause for serious concern.

In some respects, however, football and those who played it thrived. Though not all spectators would have agreed with the Arsenal manager George Allison's judgement, passed in the afterglow of a 7–1 victory at Wembley, that the wartime game was 'better in quality than pre-war League Football', many players would have agreed with Joe Mercer (later to captain and manage Cup-winning teams) in his estimation of his own form while serving as an Army PT instructor between 1939 and 1945: 'I suppose I was at my peak during the War years. I could call on stamina and never feel tired. You get tired when you are young and when you are old. There are five or six years in between when you don't. The Army made me fitter than I had ever been before.'

If the results of wartime matches between the two countries are anything to go by, Mercer and his England team-mates kept in better shape than their Scottish counterparts. As well as inflicting humiliation on them elsewhere – an 8–0 hiding at Maine Road, for example – England beat Scotland at Wembley four times in the early 1940s: 2–0 in 1941, 3–0 in 1942 and 6–2 twice in 1944.

There were reasons other than superior fitness for the lop-sided scorelines. In many respects the wartime England team was like a club side; the players played together regularly. Forces representative sides were often, in effect, international teams. The England set-up, for administrative reasons, had to dispense with the formality of a board of selectors. Stanley Rous, FA secretary and former Cup Final referee, took charge of the side and he was first to point out that his job and the team's were made easier by the goodwill of those serving alongside the likes of Matthews, Cullis, Finney and Lawton: 'Picking the team was no problem. The hardest part was . . . getting their release from their army units . . . we relied a lot on the help of people I never met and whose names no one will ever know: the soldiers and sergeants who agreed to switch duties, or do an extra guard or something, so that these players could get away to play.'

Gathering a side was far trickier for the Scots and the other home countries because, without a national base within the Services, the players were more widely and randomly scattered. Before the October 1944 Wembley fixture, for example, when the redoubtable Bill Shankly went down injured at the last moment, the only replacement to hand was a Darlington centre-half, Bob Thyne, who was in London on convalescent care, recovering from shock and shrapnel wounds sustained when his trench took a direct hit on D-Day plus six. Insensitively, if unsurprisingly, Tommy Lawton helped himself to three of England's six goals that afternoon.

With the war well on the way to being won, a **90,000** crowd took advantage of the removal of restrictions on Wembley's capacity to watch that England win. A significant proportion of the gate receipts (after deduction of entertainment tax) was donated to war charities, as they were from all fixtures played at the stadium during the conflict. Wembley recorded record profits over the six-year period and distributed nearly £150,000 to a long list of war charities including the Red Cross, the St. John Ambulance Brigade, King George's Fund for Sailors, the Forces Benevolent Fund, the Civil Defence Welfare Fund, the Merchant Navy Comforts Fund, the Soldiers', Sailors' and Airmen's Families Association, St. Dunstan's, the YMCA Services Appeal and War Services Fund, the Salvation Army, the National Children's Home, the Newspaper Press Fund, the Aid to China Fund, Wings For Victory and the Spitfire Fund.

The cause with which Wembley – and the England versus Scotland games, in particular – would be most closely associated, however, was Mrs Churchill's Aid to Russia Fund. Churchill himself was well aware of the truth of the opinion recorded in 1940's *Mass Observation* that 'sports like football have an absolute major effect on the morale of people'. So were the Nazis: one wartime propaganda broadcast promised the proper re-organisation of

English football after a German invasion. It was no surprise, therefore, that the prime minister and seven cabinet ministers were on hand to be introduced to the players before 1941's England versus Scotland game during the war's most dispiriting phase.

The following January all proceeds from the fixture, watched by a crowd limited to 64,000, were given to the Aid to Russia Fund. Mrs Churchill, therefore, was the guest of honour to watch England win 3–0 thanks to a goal after only fifty seconds by Jimmy Hagan and two from Tommy Lawton, who enjoyed himself against the Scots during the war but failed to score in the game at Wembley that October, a 0–0 draw which, as he would later remember it, was as straitened as its wartime setting: 'The 75,000 crowd were asked, in a note in the programme, to be waste salvage collectors by disposing of their tickets and programmes after the game in one of the receptacles provided; and escorts of Spitfires constantly circled over the ground.'

Though Wembley came through the Blitz unscathed, an incendiary in 1944 scorched the pitch and a V2 narrowly missed the Twin Towers, landing instead in a car- park near the kennels. Only two greyhounds were killed, although dozens fled the stadium to be retrieved, disoriented, from Wembley High Street and surrounding areas the following day. Wartime made its mark on the stadium, of course, but change was embraced rather than enforced and would prove to be profound, beneficial and long-term.

Arthur Elvin's imaginative and expansive attitude to the arena's use made good business and public relations sense and saw Wembley, in the difficult and exceptional circumstances of 1939–45, develop an international and talismanic appeal. Home Internationals and War Cup Finals there were occasions to celebrate at least a semblance of life somehow carrying on, however grim the wider picture. The size and the mood of Wembley crowds – 40,000 in 1940 rising to 90,000 in 1944 – were tangible evidence of the turning tide of the war.

In 1940 Wembley's corridors and dressing-rooms were occupied by hundreds of returning Dunkirk evacuees. During the early years of the conflict the arena was central to the 'Fitness for Service' campaign, opening its doors to reservists and the public for regular programmes of training and organised games. Football matches between Forces teams enjoyed the prestige and accompanying national attention of Wembley as a venue, as did exercises to boost the morale of the London public such as a Pageant of Youth staged in 1942. Christmas parties held in the stadium restaurant – who knows where, with rationing, the turkeys came from? – welcomed by open invitation any serving members of the Forces who could get to Wembley on the day. Hundreds did.

The stadium's profile as a symbol of national resistance during the conflict made Wembley an obvious setting in which to mark the Allies' eventual victory: 5,000 civil defence workers were stood down with due ceremony; six days after VE Day a thanksgiving service was held with the Cup Final's Man in White, T P Ratcliffe, conducting a 500-strong choir and a capacity crowd. Before a victory review and service of commemoration were celebrated the following month, England met France in a victory international, on 26 May 1945, playing host to foreign opposition at Wembley for the first time. The 2–2 draw was a resounding success both as a football match and as an exercise in diplomatic relations.

Wembley's part in sustaining morale was not restricted to its effect on the domestic population. During the first years of war thousands of foreign Forces' personnel escaped to England as Europe fell. In 1942 a friendly international between teams of Dutch and Belgian refugee players, though attracting a crowd of only 7,000 to Wembley, had a propaganda value of far wider significance: the match was broadcast live by radio throughout Occupied Europe. When the United States joined the war they brought their own sports with them: in 1943 a baseball game between US Ground Forces and the US Air Force featured teams composed entirely of professional players and a running commentary to enlighten English spectators sitting alongside Wembley's GI guests in the stands.

Wembley was energetic and conscientious in its contribution to the war effort, endorsing a growing reputation around the world which would find its fullest expression in the first post-war Olympiad. In the spring of 1945 the Wembley offices received a letter from five Londoners serving in Burma: 'For the past fourteen months we have been fighting the Jap with the magnificent 14th Army. We can assure you that amusements have been limited but football has been played whenever possible ... As we sit here in the jungle we are thinking of dear old Wembley and the 1945 Cup Final.'

The goodwill earned by Wembley during wartime presented opportunities of which Arthur Elvin was ready to take advantage and obligations he was equally eager to fulfil. Broadcasting on Forces radio in 1944, Wembley's managing director sounded every bit as sincere and sentimental as his Burmese correspondents: 'Sport will undoubtedly play a great part in the resettlement of the world when hostilities cease, and nowhere will people turn to sport more eagerly than our own sports-loving country ... When peace is with us again and the lads and lasses return home, they may rest assured that Wembley will give them as good sport and entertainment as they can get anywhere in the world.'

The FA Cup spent the war years in Portsmouth, making an occasional appearance, in the manner of a holy relic under police guard, when a school or hospital held a fund-raising charity event. The old pot's nearest brush with active service was on the night of a blitz on Portsmouth which destroyed the bank in which the club had placed it for safe-keeping. Purely by chance the Cup was in Jack Tinn's possession that evening and the Portsmouth manager spent the duration of the bombing raid with it clutched to his chest beneath the stairs at home.

Wembley, however, would stage a Cup Final of some description each season through the war years. The 1940 War Cup Final between West Ham and Blackburn had proceeded despite the desperate circumstances of the week of the Dunkirk retreat. The following season saw the competition better organised along regional lines up to the semi-final stage. The Final itself was a resonant affair: Arsenal, the dominant team of the thirties, took on Preston who, but for the war, might have inherited their mantle.

In September 1939 forty of the forty-two professionals on Arsenal's playing staff had joined up while Highbury itself was turned into a civil defence headquarters. Based in London, however, the club could easily assemble a side comprising their own players, stationed within travelling distance, and 'guests' brought in to fill any spaces on the team sheet. Preston's left-back in the 1941 Final, Andy Beattie, for example, had guested for Arsenal against Millwall in a League game the previous week.

Preston, meanwhile, fielded a relatively inexperienced side, including a young Tom Finney among players developed by the club's exceptional youth programme in the late thirties and given their chance by the unique circumstances in which football now found itself. The crowd was limited to 60,000. Interest was sufficiently intense for the 40,000 available terrace tickets to be snapped up in twenty-four hours.

Three minutes into the game Arsenal were awarded a penalty which the hefty Leslie Compton struck against a post with such force that the ball bounced back nearly to the centre circle. Finney then laid on a goal for McLaren before the other Compton, Denis, equalised for Arsenal. To the crowd's surprise and disappointment, no extra-time was played and the savings certificates which were to be presented in place of medals stayed under wraps. The replay was at Blackburn's Ewood Park and won 2–1 by Preston. Restrained celebrations were enjoyed, in the words of Tom Finney, 'as far as war conditions permitted'.

Although the country was responding to Churchill's exhortation to pull together, the football authorities fell prey to internal divisions and in the autumn of 1941 disagreements over players' pay and administrative arrangements saw the formation of a breakaway London League competing in the South-East. For the next four years Wembley's Final was, in effect, a semi-final, with the winners of the League South Cup going on to play their northern counterparts at Stamford Bridge.

In the Wembley showpiece Brentford beat Portsmouth 2–0 in 1942, Pompey's FA Cup-winning captain of 1938, Jimmy Guthrie, missing a penalty. The following year Arsenal, fielding eleven of their 'own' players, beat Charlton 7–1, a young Reg Lewis scoring four. Then, with the war turning decisively in the Allies' favour, restrictions on Wembley's capacity were lifted in 1944 and 85,000 watched Charlton beat Chelsea 3–1. Watching from the Royal Box – 'always crowded', according to Eddie Hapgood, during the war – was General and future US President Dwight D Eisenhower, who seemed to enjoy the spectacle while managing, in all innocence, to miss the point: 'I started cheering for the Blues but when I saw the Reds winning I had to go on cheering for the Reds,' he explained while presenting the Cup.

The last League South Final, in 1945, was perhaps the strangest in the series. After a week of bickering between the clubs over which borrowed talent might turn out for each team, Chelsea won what was dubbed the 'Lend-Lease' Final 2–0 with eight 'guests' in their side. Millwall perhaps felt themselves at a disadvantage, fielding seven of their own players. Their goalkeeper, though, borrowed from Charlton, was the England international Sam Bartram, who was as surprised as anyone to find himself back at Wembley for a third successive year: 'I had not anticipated playing in the Final but, as I was able to get leave and Millwall were still without a regular goalkeeper ....'

Ad hoc as the arrangements and teams may have been, Wembley's wartime finals retained their own distinct sense of occasion. In many respects who was playing and how well they played seemed less pressing a concern, for those able to get to Wembley, than it had been on those partisan afternoons at the stadium in the 1930s. What was important was that a Cup Final, of some description, was being played at all.

What mattered, too, of course, was that the stadium and all it had come to stand for was still there. When war finished and it was time to come home, football after all would be an integral part of the world that people came home to, just as it had been an integral part of the world that they had left. In 1945, like Britain, after six years of war Wembley began to prepare itself for peace.

1940: JOE MERCER

In one way I ought to be sick when I think back to these years. For certainly the best years of my career were used up during the war. Like Lawton, Hagan and perhaps Stan Matthews, I wasn't as good a player before or after as I was during this time. When I look back and see the number of caps I am credited with, then remember the number of times I actually played, it does seem a bit sad. But on the other hand this was a wonderful bunch to play with. I was lucky to be around at the same time. I have never played with a team so eager to do well. In these matches everybody fancied himself a bit, everybody wanted the ball. Every time you gave a pass, you made nine enemies. The spirit was as keen as that.

ENGLAND V SCOTLAND, BRIAN JAMES, PELHAM BOOKS, 1969

WILLS'S CIGARETTES

J. MERCER (EVERTON)

Daily Mirror

No. 11,152 · · ONE PENNY
Registered at the G.P.O. as a Newspaper.

BRITAIN'S FIRST DAY OF WAR: CHURCHILL IN NEW CABINET

BRITAIN and Germany have been at war since eleven o'clock yesterday morning. France delivered an ultimatum, similar to that sent by Britain. It expired at five o'clock yesterday afternoon.

A BRITISH WAR CABINET WAS SET UP YESTERDAY. MR. WINSTON CHURCHILL RETURNS TO THE POST OF FIRST LORD OF THE ADMIRALTY, THE OFFICE HE HELD WHEN BRITAIN LAST DECLARED WAR TWENTY-FIVE YEARS AGO.

Full list of the War Cabinet is—

PRIME MINISTER: Mr. Neville Chamberlain.
CHANCELLOR OF THE EXCHEQUER:
   Sir John Simon.
FOREIGN SECRETARY: Viscount Halifax.
DEFENCE M... ...d Chatfield.
FIRST LORD

SECRETARY FOR WAR:
   Mr. Leslie Hore-Belisha.
SECRETARY FOR AIR: Sir Kingsley Wood.
LORD PRIVY SEAL: Sir Samuel Hoare.
MINISTER WITHOUT PORTFOLIO:
   Lord Hankey.

KING'S SPEECH

BROADCASTING to the Empire last night, the King said: "In this grave hour, perhaps the most fateful in our history, I send to every household of my peoples, both at home and overseas, this message, spoken with the same depth of feeling for each one of you as if I were able to cross your threshold and speak to you myself.

"For the second time in the lives of most of us we are at war. Over and over again we have tried to find a peaceful way out of the differences between ourselves and those who are now our enemies.

But it has been in vain. We have been forced into a conflict. For we are called, with our allies, to meet the challenge of a principle which, if it were to prevail, would be fatal to any civilised order in the world.

It is the principle which permits a State, in the selfish pursuit of power, to disregard its treaties and its solemn pledges, which sanctions the use of force or threat of force against the sovereignty and independence of other States.

Such a principle, stripped of all disguise, is surely the mere primitive doctrine that might is right; and if this principle were established throughout the world, the freedom of our own country and of the whole British Commonwealth of Nations would be in danger.

Bondage of Fear

But far more than this—the peoples of the world would be kept in the bondage of fear, and all hopes of settled peace and of the security of justice and liberty among nations would be ended.

This is the ultimate issue which confronts us. For the sake of all that we ourselves hold dear, and of the world's order and peace, it is unthinkable that we should refuse to meet the challenge.

It is to this high purpose that I now call my people at home and my peoples across the seas, who will make our cause their own. I ask them to stand calm, firm and united in this time of trial.

The task will be hard. There may be dark days ahead, and war can no longer be confined to the battlefield. But we can only do the right as we see the right, and reverently commit our cause to God.

If one and all we keep resolutely faithful to it, ready for whatever service or sacrifice it may demand, then, with God's help, we shall prevail.

May He bless and keep us all."

team.

THEY ARE NOT ONLY FOOTBALLERS!

By OUR NORTH-EASTERN CORRESPONDENT

A FEW MONTHS AGO LITTLE ATTENTION WAS PAID TO WHAT FOOTBALLERS WERE CAPABLE OF DOING OFF THE FIELD, BUT IT IS NOW EVIDENT THAT THOSE WHO WERE WISE ENOUGH TO SERVE APPRENTICESHIPS TO TRADES ARE GOING TO BE OF ... ...LE ASSISTANCE TO THE THE PRESENT WAR

1941: GIL MERRICK

There are not many people perhaps who can say that their first representative match was at Wembley, but that was the way it was with me. I was twenty-one years old then and had gained a regular place in Birmingham's war-time first team. The Wembley match was between the Civil Defence, for whom I played, and the Combined Services.

These were the teams: Civil Defence - G. Merrick (Birmingham); C. Bicknell (West Ham), F.W. Dawes (Crystal Palace); W.M. Owen (Newport County), D. Affleck (Southampton), D. Magnall (Q.P.R.); R. Spence (Chelsea), A Dawes (Crystal Palace), G.A.Foreman (West Ham), L.Goulden (West Ham), E. Thorley (Huddersfield).

Combined Services - E. Ditchburn (Spurs); G. Male (Arsenal), H.Ferrier (Barnsley); R.White (Spurs), J. Oakes (Charlton), R. Burgess (Spurs); F.Kurz (Grimsby Town), M.Edelston (Reading), E. Drake (Arsenal), A. Tennant (Chelsea), L. Smith (Brentford).

It was an evening game watched by about 40, 000 people, the biggest crowd I had played in front of up to that time. Looking back I think I must have been scared stiff. We lost by five clear goals and I'm sure I couldn't have looked a very impressive figure. Three of the goals were scored by Ted Drake, running on to through passes down the middle.

I SEE IT ALL, MUSEUM PRESS, 1954

1941: TOM FINNEY

The first time I played at Wembley was the 1941 War Cup Final against Arsenal. I'd signed part-time professional with Preston by then, on the basis that if you played, you got paid and if you didn't, you didn't get paid. We won the League up here and Arsenal won it down there: it was very much north versus south at Wembley.

It was a wonderful occasion for me, a young boy of eighteen. I walked out in awe of this huge stadium. Of course, it was wartime: there were bombs dropping on London at that time. We stayed overnight at Northampton and then went down to Wembley in the morning for the game.

Arsenal were the great name in football, all great players, and I found myself, a young lad, lining up against Eddie Hapgood, who was captain of England at the time. Even though the stadium wasn't full, there were restrictions on how many could watch the game, the amosphere was fantastic. It still seemed a great thing to walk out of the tunnel at Wembley.

Useless Eustace

A lot of the lads in that team were the same age as me, juniors at the club who were too young to be called up. There were five or six of us: myself, Bill Scott, Andrew McLaren, Cliff Mansley, young lads who'd come through the youth system and went on to play League football for Preston after the war. It was us and the nucleus of the side that had played at Wembley in 1938. I suppose the young lads got their chance so early because of the conditions of war.

We played very well and drew 1–1, then won the replay 2–1 at Blackburn Rovers. I got a Cup Winners medal but that was from the club, a bronze medal with a gold cup in the centre. After the replay, we were presented with £15 in War Bonds for the two games, which seemed like a lot of money at the time; I think we got £2.50 a game during wartime.

INTERVIEW, 1998

"Put a skylight in the top! We can't see what we're doing inside!"

1942: TOMMY LAWTON

I was selected for England in January 1942 in the side to meet Scotland at Wembley. It was my first appearance in the national side for about eleven months, and I was glad to wear the white shirt once more. It was a memorable occasion. Although we didn't know it. Mrs. Churchill (for whose Aid to Russia Fund the match was being played) intended to be present. But all the week it looked as if the match might be postponed as it snowed heavily for about four days. But Wembley ground staff did a grand job of work and when we walked out on to the snow-covered pitch, it was quite easy to see the side-lines. The snow had been swept from these and instead of the familiar white lines, they had been repainted blue. Looked for all the world like a larger edition of an ice rink.

We lined up in front of the stand for the usual inspection. And then Mrs Churchill appeared, to set up a novel record. It must be the first time in soccer history that a woman has come out to be introduced to international teams. She greeted us all pleasantly, and then walked over to the microphone to say a few words to the crowd. The teams broke away to their respective goalmouths for the kick-in, and I couldn't hear what she said, but a sudden roar of excited cheering made me figure it must have been something other than mere thanks for coming along and helping the Fund.

Later we learned that Mrs Churchill was rather dramatically announcing the return of her famous husband, who was flying from the Bermudas to Plymouth after signing the Atlantic Charter. Pity the drama of the moment was tinged with comedy as a Scotch (by absorption) sailor attempted to help Jerry Dawson repel the trial shots of the Scottish forwards.

FOOTBALL IS MY BUSINESS, SPORTING HANDBOOKS, 1946

An Hour Of The International

SATURDAY'S England v. Scotland match at Wembley is to be given an hour on the air. The interest in this game has aroused the B.B.C. so much that they will broadcast the last 30 minutes before half-time and the last half-hour of the second half.

By the way, all tickets for the match have been sold, and the Wembley staff is working overtime in an effort to have them dispatched by Tuesday. Handling these tickets is one of the biggest tasks the Stadium people have had to deal with during the war.

Give all you can on Mrs. Churchill's RED CROSS 'AID TO RUSSIA' FLAG DAY

'Let us remember the measureless services which Russia has rendered to the common cause through long years of measureless suffering, by tearing out the life of the German military monster.'
Mr. Winston Churchill, The House of Commons, Sept. 28th, 1944

(Registered under the War Charities Act, 1940)

LONDON TOMORROW TO BE HELD SHORTLY IN ALL DISTRICTS

1943: STANLEY MORTENSEN

In one of the war-time international matches I was chosen as reserve for England against Wales at Wembley. Not expecting to be called on, as all the players reported fit, I sat on a bench on the touch-line and settled down to watch the game. Within a few minutes Ivor Powell, that fine little Welsh half-back, was hurt. A swift examination showed that his collar-bone was fractured, and there was no hope of his being able to return to the field.

In many of those war-time games, staged not in a strict competitive spirit but as entertainment to keep up the morale of the people, substitutes were allowed. There were whispered consultations between officials, and it was agreed that Wales should be allowed to put a man on the field to replace Ivor. There was no twelfth man with the Wales party, however. Being the only player ready to hand, they told me I was to play - for Wales! I was so excited that I stood up on the touch-line and started to pull off my R.A.F tunic in full view of the huge crowds. Just how far I should have gone I don't know, but there were people less excited and I was gently led away to a much more secluded place. I simply tore off my clothes and jumped into playing gear.

FOOTBALL IS MY GAME, SAMPSON LOW, 1949

1944: SAM BARTRAM

It was in 1944, and it was a war-time League South Cup Final, with Chelsea as our opponents. Maybe it was only a war-time Final; maybe the Cup, the 'little tin idol' itself, was not at stake; maybe there were no medals to be won, and only rewards of £5 in savings certificates for the winners and £3 for the losers to be gained. But it was still Wembley - and it was still a Cup Final.

SAM BARTRAM, BURKE, 1956

1945: TOMMY LAWTON

Little more than twenty-four hours before England played France at Wembley, Saturday, May 26th, 1945, I was elected captain of the national side for the first time in my life. Before the game M. Gaston Barreau, the selector of the French team - he had had sole charge of the national team since 1935 - told me 'It will be a privilege to be beaten by such distinguished opponents.' Whether he was joking or not I don't know, but we had to pull out all we knew at Wembley, and even then were held to a 2-2 draw. Only three players, Da Rui, Jordan and Aston were known to me by name, they looked a useful side when we lined up for the presentation to General Koenig, the hero of Bir Hakeim, who had flown over from Paris especially for the game.

WILLS'S CIGARETTES

T. LAWTON (*EVERTON*)

Da Rui, the goalkeeper, although a bit on the small side, had a great reputation as a goalkeeper. Captured at Dunkirk, he was a prisoner for only three weeks before escaping to Lille. Right-back Maurice Dupuis had a thrilling war-time story to tell. After the collapse of France he became a policeman at Versailles, and joined the underground movement. During the battle of Paris he was a roof-top sniper. Jean Swiatek, a powerfully built left-back, who was to give Stanley Matthews a gruelling afternoon, was like Siklo, the inside-left, born in Poland. He had escaped from the Germans during the war after doing six months' forced labour. Jean Samuel, who was a last-minute choice, was only twenty and served in the French Air Force. Gusty Jordan, the centre-half, was an old favourite among British touring teams, but Jasseron, the left-half, was new to us. A sergeant in the French Air Force, he had served in Algeria, Tunisia and Italy.

FOOTBALL IS MY BUSINESS,
SPORTING HANDBOOKS, 1946

LIVELY FRENCHMEN SHOCK ENGLAND

ENGLAND 2, FRANCE 2

THERE may have been a touch of sentiment in the welcome the English crowd gave the French team at Wembley yesterday and the cheers for the players at the end were purely from admiration.

This French eleven, more or less derided as a chopping block for the miracle England team, appreciated the compliment that had been paid them by the F.A. in choosing such a strong eleven, and they proceeded to show it, for a large part of the game, how to play football.

Some of the work between wing halves and forwards was beautiful. Unexpected cross-passing from Samuel, at right half, to Vaast, on the left wing, nearly brought about the downfall of the England defence.

We even had centre-forward Bihel starting moves by tricking Franklin with a dance that must have made Stanley Matthews jealous.

Carter gave England an early lead with a first-time shot round one of the best moves in the match, and not long afterwards da Rui saved Leslie Smith's penalty kick, awarded for a foul on Lawton. A minute later still he fisted round a red-

not effort from Brown, standing within a couple of yards and intending to finish off a great movement between Smith and Carter.

Vaast equalised following a defensive blunder which gave him the ball and a clear way to goal. He took it. Lawton headed England's second goal early in the second half, and in the last seconds Heisserer shot another beautiful goal.

That is the record, but it doesn't matter much. What does matter is that, on this showing England's supremacy over Continental sides is in jeopardy.

The French backs and halves kept on top of their men, and gave the England attack little room to move and no time to work.

Staggered HOLIDAYS 1945

The capacity of holiday resorts and transport services will still be strictly limited this summer. You will help yourselves and others if you can take your holiday in

JUNE, SEPTEMBER OR OCTOBER

RAILWAY EXECUTIVE COMMITTEE

PLAN OF THE FIELD OF PLAY

□

FRANCE

COLOURS : Blue shirts, white knickers, red stockings

1. *Goalkeeper*
J. DA RUI
(Lille O.S.C.)

2. *Right Back*
M. DUPUIS
(R.C. Paris)

3. *Left Back*
J. SWIATEK
(Girondins, Bordeaux)

4. *Right Half-back*
J. BIGOT
(Lille O.S.C.)

5. *Centre Half-back*
G. JORDAN
(R.C. Paris)

6. *Left Half-back*
L. JASSERON
(R.C. Paris)

7. *Outside Right*
A. ASTON
(Red Star O.)

8. *Inside Right*
O. HEISSERER
(R.C. Paris)

9. *Centre Forward*
R. BIHEL
(Lille O.S.C.)

10. *Inside Left*
L. SIKLO
(R.C. Lens)

11. *Outside Left*
E. VAAST
(R.C. Paris)

11. *Outside Left*
L. G. F. SMITH
(Brentford and R.A.F.)

10. *Inside Left*
R. A. J. BROWN
(Charlton and R.A.F.)

9. *Centre Forward*
T. LAWTON
(Everton and Army)

8. *Inside Right*
H. S. CARTER
(Sunderland and R.A.F.)

7. *Outside Right*
S. MATTHEWS
(Stoke City and R.A.F.)

6. *Left Half-back*
J. MERCER
(Everton and Army)

5. *Centre Half-back*
N. FRANKLIN
(Stoke City and R.A.F.)

4. *Right Half-back*
F. SOO
(Stoke City and R.A.F.)

3. *Left Back*
G. F. HARDWICK
(Middlesbrough and R.A.F.)

2. *Right Back*
L. SCOTT
(Arsenal and R.A.F.)

1. *Goalkeeper*
B. F. WILLIAMS
(Walsall and R.A.F.)

ENGLAND

COLOURS : White shirts, dark blue knickers

F. DAMBACH (F.C. Rouen), J. SAMUEL (R.C. Paris)
S. MORTENSEN (Blackpool and R.A.F.), F. HALL (Blackburn Rovers and R.A.F.)

...DER
...ire)

LINESMEN : Cmdr. G. CLARK and Capt. A. P. RAE
(Royal Navy) (Army)

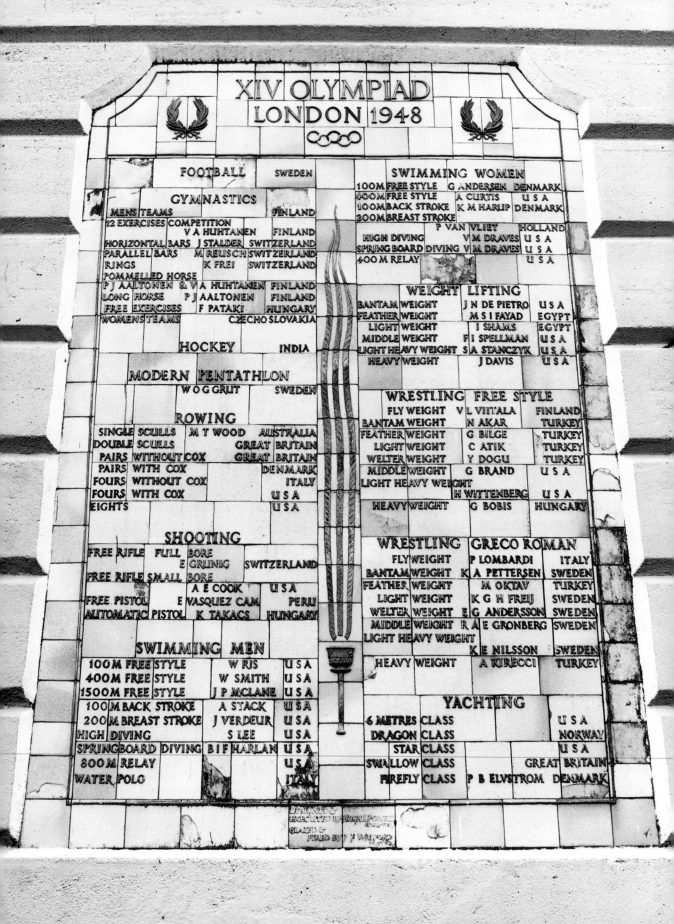

Just Glad To
Be There

1946-53

Peace in 1945 was celebrated fervently at Wembley, as elsewhere, but the sense of optimism generated at thanksgiving services and victory internationals at the stadium was soon tempered by the realisation that an end to fighting would not bring with it an end to austerity. Rationing and other hardships made the first years after victory as hard to bear, from day to day, as the later stages of war which had at least been illuminated by a sense of common purpose and a belief that an end to conflict was in sight.

A return to anything resembling normal life still seemed a long way off and the fulfilment of the country's aspirations – the desire for change which swept Atlee's Labour government into power – even more distant. Anything which could remind people of Britain before the war or offer relief from the privations victory had brought in its wake was seized upon. Fans poured into football grounds in unprecedented numbers in the first months of peace. And what better occasion than an FA Cup Final at Wembley to remember stirring times past and to imagine better days to come? Football's big day now more than ever offered a chance to hope even as it offered the opportunity to bask in the warm glow of a great British tradition.

Peace came too late for league football to return to the national competition abandoned in September 1939 and it continued on the regional basis established during the war years. The FA Cup, replacing the ad hoc knock-out tournaments which had stood in for it between 1940 and 1945, took on added significance. Recognising the Cup's role as the season's sole national competition – and mindful too, no doubt, of the gate receipts which might be generated as a result – the FA arranged for the 1945–46 tournament, up to the semi-finals, to be played on a two-leg, home-and-away basis.

The public responded in huge numbers: more than 80,000 packed Maine Road to watch Derby County beat Birmingham City in their semi-final replay; tragically, thirty-three died and four hundred were injured in the crush to watch Bolton play Stanley Matthews' Stoke City at Burnden Park. The Manchester crowd remains a record for a midweek game at an English club ground. The disaster at Burnden Park, however, would not be the last before football learnt its harshest lessons.

Nonetheless, 27 April 1946 was grasped as a day for looking forward rather than back by the 98,215 squeezed into Wembley for the FA Cup Final. Special as it was for supporters of the opposing teams, Derby County and Charlton Athletic, the occasion expressed, too, a sense of national unity: the men and women in uniform everywhere in the crowd, the wait for King George VI to arrive for the presentation of the players, the tears shed in memory during a passionate rendition of the Cup Final hymn:

> *Abide with me; fast falls the eventide;*
> *The darkness deepens; Lord, with me abide;*
> *When other helpers fail, and comforts flee,*
> *Help of the helpless, O, abide with me.*

Over the years anxiety, fatigue or individual fallibility has seen many Cup Finals disappoint, crushed under the weight of expectation. In 1946, however, with both teams fielding many players recently demobbed and others waiting for their release papers to come through, Derby and Charlton produced a spectacle worthy of the Wembley setting and the day's emotional charge.

For Charlton the stadium had become something of a second home after appearances in war-time finals in two of the three preceding seasons. It was Derby's first Wembley fixture, albeit some in their ranks were making welcome returns: Raich Carter, for example, had captained Sunderland's 1937 Cup-winning team.

Carter, indeed, and his partner at inside-forward, the mercurial Peter Doherty, were expected to dominate proceedings, which they did during a goalless opening half. Their opposite numbers, Don Welsh and Albert Brown, then engineered a Charlton recovery after the break. Four of the era's great stylists, however, much as their talents had illuminated an overcast afternoon, were unable to break the deadlock. The day's drama turned instead on the efforts of two lesser lights.

With five minutes of normal time remaining the Charlton left-back Bert Turner sliced the ball into his own net in attempting to clear a shot from the Derby winger Dally Duncan. A minute later, sparing his own and his team's blushes, Turner's free-kick from twenty-five yards was deflected past goalkeeper Woodley by Peter Doherty to take the game into extra-time.

The additional half-hour would hinge on fitness and physical strength. In Jack Stamps Derby had a centre-forward who had both to spare, despite having been told in 1942 that, as a result of injuries sustained during the retreat from Dunkirk, he would never play again. In the closing moments of normal time Stamps had hit a shot of such force that the ball burst and all but deflated on its way to the Charlton keeper Sam Bartram – this after referee Smith had dismissed the possibility of such an occurrence as a million-to-one chance in a radio broadcast on Cup Final eve – and two minutes into the extra period he sent in another which Bartram could only parry to the feet of Doherty, who scored.

Thereafter the Charlton manager Jimmy Seed watched as his players were over-run: 'For ninety minutes they had given just as much as they had taken but now they were like a groggy boxer being punched around the ring by an opponent who had found his second wind.' Stamps himself was on hand to deliver two further knock-out blows.

The quality of the play in normal time had been all a football-hungry crowd could wish for on the FA Cup's return to Wembley; the power of Stamps' final flourish provided, in the words of Arsenal's pre-war hero Alex James, reporting for the *News of the World*, 'a glorious finish to a memorable game'.

For a nation craving release from wartime tension and relief from post-war austerity, football was just one diversion available. Cinemas and dance halls boomed, the long hot summer of 1947 saw millions cram on to Britain's beaches, and sport, in general, was played and watched insatiably. In 1946 attendances at greyhound racing reached forty-five million and at Wembley, as elsewhere, the quality and quantity of cards gradually returned to the pre-war standard. Rugby league, too, returned to the stadium and the Challenge Cup, like the FA Cup, produced a classic in its first season after the war: the underdogs Wakefield Trinity squeezed past Wigan 13–12 thanks to an enormous Bill Stott penalty ninety seconds from time, struck from just a few feet inside the Wigan half.

The 1946 Final, watched by 54,730, generated record gate receipts of £12,014. Like their footballing counterparts, however, the players enjoyed little by way of financial reward for their contribution. Derby's players, whose maximum weekly wage was to rise from £8 to £10 that summer, got a £25 bonus for beating Charlton. Rugby league players got an even smaller slice of the cake. Wakefield's scrum-half Herbert Goodfellow, like many of his team-mates, worked as a miner during the week and was in trouble for missing shifts to play first at Wembley and then in a league game three days later: 'We got £15 for winning at Wembley. That wasn't bad money but I lost £7 10s in four days' lost wages. And worse than that I almost lost my job ... the [pit] manager spoke up for me. He said that he'd been at Wembley for the day and I deserved to keep my job because it had been great entertainment.'

Whoever reaped the rewards, fans continued to pour into Wembley for the Challenge Cup final: in 1949 a Yorkshire derby, Bradford Northern beating Halifax 12–0, would attract a capacity crowd to Wembley for rugby league for the first time. Huge crowds continued to come to watch football and enjoy a flutter on the dogs. More surprising, perhaps, with the 'teenager' phenomenon still a generation away, was the popularity with a younger audience of dirt-track racing, speedway and Wembley's enormously successful home team, the Lions.

Arthur Elvin's alacrity in bringing a new sport, greyhound racing, to Wembley in the late 1920s paid off virtually overnight. Unsurprisingly, within a couple of years the attention of the stadium's managing director had been drawn to the next craze, speedway, which was already successful in other parts of the world, its stars attracting big crowds at the dirt-tracks opening around Britain in 1928.

Gambling on the success of a domestic league in which Wembley could compete, Elvin appointed Johnnie Hoskins, one of the sport's Australian pioneers, as Wembley's speedway racing manager in 1929. An amateur football team, Pegasus, had provisionally booked the stadium as a venue in what turned out to be an unsuccessful application for Football League membership the previous year. Speedway would, therefore, be Wembley's first venture as a 'home ground' with its own team, the Wembley Lions.

It seemed, initially, as though the venture would not be a roaring success, according to Hoskins: 'We expected 20,000 crowds and only got three or four thousand. International speedway had all the top riders under contract. They would not permit any of their riders to appear in the newly formed league. It was a tough start.'

While Hoskins began finding promising youngsters and luring established riders away from other teams, Elvin set about developing an audience for speedway at Wembley. Crucial to long-term success was the establishment of a Lions supporters' club with concessionary rates for members. Wembley nights out were spiced with gimmicks: women's races, stunt displays, the acquisition of a pair of lion cubs as mascots.

By the mid-thirties it had all fallen into place. The national league had established itself, nowhere more so than at Wembley. Early losses of £500 per week were soon turned round: the supporters' club had over 20,000 members by the time the Lions won their first title in 1930. Rather than beat the international circuit, Wembley joined it, staging World Championship rounds and England versus Australia Test matches. In 1936 the Wembley Lions' captain, Lionel van Praag, won the first official individual World Championship. The following year the title went to an American, Jack Milne, in front of a world record speedway crowd of 85,000 at the stadium.

The Second World War came with speedway having reached a remarkable peak and, although fuel rationing meant the sport shut down for the duration of the conflict, its fans simply held their collective breath before returning to Wembley to pick up where they had left off in 1939. A new generation of riders came in to replace the likes of van Praag (who won a George Medal for exceptional bravery during the war): Bill Kitchen, Freddie Williams, Tommy Price, Split Waterman, Brian Crutcher. By 1948 the supporters' club had over 60,000 members; one League meeting against West Ham was watched by 85,000 fans, with 20,000 more locked out and listening to a broadcast relay of the action inside.

The organisation of the crowd, the wearing of club colours by large numbers of young fans, the chanting and clapping routines which were a part of the speedway scene would be taken over by football crowds within a generation. The sound of 'England!' echoing round Wembley, as it would memorably at the World Cup Final twenty years later, was first heard at international speedway matches just after the war.

In fact, the late forties and early fifties were to be the high-water mark both for the Wembley Lions, who won seven of the first eight League titles contested after the war, and for the sport which, in racing and economic terms, the team had come to dominate. During the mid-fifties entertainment tax (at 45 per cent) and internal squabbles hit speedway hard. As fans saw it, too, breakneck competition was giving way to predictable processions. The crowds fell away and shareholders at the Wembley AGM in 1957 were first to hear the bad news: 'Speedway racing has been disappointing for the past few years and by reason of the losses suffered your board have already taken the decision not to stage speedway racing at Wembley during 1957.'

Thereafter the stadium continued to be let out for the World Individual Championship Final and the occasional international, and fans continued to turn up for those major events in huge numbers. Rumours would surface, from year to year, that the Lions were about to re-emerge from the Wembley shadows and, briefly and unsuccessfully, they did so in 1970 and 1971. But the sport's golden era, at the stadium at least, was over. Speedway had nonetheless helped to put Wembley on the map in the 1930s and a nostalgic refrain, familiar to an older generation of fans, echoes the impact made on the sport by those years of competition at the stadium: 'It's not the same without Wembley.'

In the years after the war the passion for football was by no means restricted to the professional game: enthusiasm swept along those who played and watched at youth and amateur level, too, until the schoolboys and Corinthians came knocking at Wembley's front door.

Stanley Rous, the secretary of the FA, had supervised the England team with some success during the war. After it, he appointed a new man to the job. Walter Winterbottom became England's first 'team manager' in the autumn of 1946. Sadly the intense, thoughtful Winterbottom did not have the freedom to manoeuvre which Rous had enjoyed between 1939 and 1945, when a club spirit and common sense of purpose had emerged under the unique circumstances of wartime. Team selection became, once more, a matter for diplomatic transaction with an International Committee whose agenda was often determined by partisan interest or an attempt to gauge the drift of public opinion. Winterbottom would later describe those as 'difficult years ... there was this tremendous resistance to change'.

More satisfying, perhaps, was his role in the FA's programme to develop junior football. During his time in office Winterbottom oversaw a gradual but profound change in the way coaching was taught, deployed and structured, which would continue to benefit the game at all levels long after he had been replaced as England manager by Alf Ramsey in 1963.

Schoolboy football had, by and large, lacked the incentive of organised competition until the introduction, after the war, of county championships, international matches at schoolboy, youth and under-23 levels and, later, the FA Youth Cup. Full use was made of a small army of fitness instructors and coaches, trained for a very different challenge in the years from 1939, who were employed by the FA to work in schools and youth organisations.

The professional clubs were naturally interested in the opportunity to keep track of developing talent. So, too, was the football-watching public: the first schoolboy international between England and Scotland at Wembley in 1950 was played in front of 53,000. Both the game and the setting suggested a path to guide England's international future. The day's brightest talent, a fifteen-year-old Johnny Haynes, would be back at Wembley four years later as Winterbottom sought to rebuild a new generation's full England team.

These were promising years, too, for the amateur game. Apart from schools and Forces football, by the end of the 1940s there were over 30,000 registered clubs. Of these, only 500 were paying their players. The eagerness of the rest to play amateur football was matched by spectators' eagerness to watch. Attendances for amateur games grew at the same heady pace as those at League matches in the post-war era.

Amateur football, of course, had its own blue-riband occasion to match the FA Cup Final and, for three years after the war, attendances at the Amateur Cup Final doubled those of the late 1930s. The Football Association responded to the groundswell of enthusiasm by moving the game to Wembley. In April 1949 Bromley beat Romford 1–0 and the success of the day was duly noted in Arthur Elvin's speech to Wembley shareholders the following March: 'It is pleasing to note that the newcomer to Wembley attracted a record crowd for that event of over **94,000**.'

Bromley's historic victory was not the first time a capacity crowd had filled Wembley to watch amateur football. Indeed, the spirit of the 1949 Amateur Cup Final offered spectators the chance to enjoy again something of the extraordinary mood with which the stadium had been suffused the previous summer when it was the centrepiece of the Olympic Games, staging the opening and closing ceremonies, the track, field and hockey events, as well as the final games of the football tournament.

For a generation of young fans today Wembley's significance will always find its clearest focus in images of Euro '96. Their parents, when thinking about the stadium, will conjure memories first of the World Cup summer of 1966. For a generation old enough to remember the trials of life in post-war Britain, however, the bright, fragile optimism of the 1948 Games is a recollection as inspiring as any brought to mind by those more recent tournaments enjoyed in easier times.

In 1908, before Wembley was built, London had staged an early Olympics, based at White City. So crucial was the stadium in making the whole thing possible forty years later that the 1948 Olympics would come to be remembered as the Wembley Games. It was a summer of sport, in setting and character, unlike any before or since, and, despite shaky economic foundations, it stands out perhaps as Wembley's finest hour.

The last pre-war Games, in Berlin in 1936, had been a supremely well-organised exercise in chest-beating on the part of Nazi Germany and by 1940 the symbolism of Hitler's version of the Olympics had given way to the fact of a world at war. Before the conflict began, however, the 1944 Games had been provisionally allocated to London. When peace came in 1945 and the possibility of staging a post-war Games was first discussed, the International Olympic Committee turned to Britain once more.

The chairman of the British Olympic Association, Lord Burghley, was approached as early as October 1945 and agreed to set up a working group to look into the practicalities of a London Games. Three years later the writer of the official Olympic Report was still trying to work out how they had pulled it off: 'The organisation of the Olympic Games under ordinary circumstances is a tremendous undertaking; to carry through what promised to be the largest gathering ever held, in a country which had been torn and racked by warfare, and for which the problems of housing, feeding, equipment and the like had thereby been increased a hundred fold, was indeed a Herculean task.'

The commitment of Wembley, under the direction of Sir Arthur Elvin (newly knighted for his contribution to the efforts of War Charities), was decisive. The stadium and the services of its staff were made available without charge: everything from preparing the arena for the various track and field events, through engineering the opening and closing ceremonies, to handling tickets for the entire Olympiad (which included competition at sites all over Southern England) in the Wembley box-office. Wembley undertook improvements – the construction of Olympic Way, new dressing-rooms, renewal of terracing, extra seating and the provision of hospitality facilities – at its own expense, a figure which eventually ran to some £200,000.

Room had to be made in the arena itself ahead of the seventeen days in July and August when Wembley would be the focus of the Games. Greyhound racing was suspended for six weeks and speedway meetings were transferred to Plough Lane, Wimbledon, perhaps explaining why 1948 was the one year in eight after the war when the Lions failed to take the League title. The resulting operating losses were to be made up from Games gate receipts.

The existing track was ripped up and soil and turf removed to expose the old running track which had been used for Empire Exhibition events in 1924 and 1925. This was then treated by the application of some 800 tons of 'special dressing', ash from fireplaces in Leicester — why Leicester's cinders should be preferred remains an Olympic trade secret if, that is, anyone ever knew — which was levelled to within one-thousandth of an inch. A platform was erected, behind what is now the players' tunnel, to accommodate the Olympic Flame and, above that, a wooden scoreboard, with 3,000 individual letter and number boards, constructed from timber donated by the Finnish and Swedish governments.

Finally Elvin offered the Games a guarantee against loss of £100,000 which was used by the BOA to fund their preparations for the summer. Altruistic as Wembley's contribution appeared and, to some extent, doubtless was, the real incentive for the stadium's involvement lay, perhaps, in the long term, as Sir Arthur explained to Wembley shareholders understandably concerned about the threat to their dividends: 'Shareholders will readily recognise the many advantages to Wembley in being the venue for the main events of this world's athletic festival. The holding of the XIVth Olympiad in this country should be very helpful to Britain's prestige at this difficult time in our history, and we are very proud that Wembley should be so closely identified with its organisation.'

Sir Arthur Elvin was in no doubt as to the benefits which an Olympic Games could offer the stadium and the country. Twenty years in charge of Wembley had led him to understand the importance of investment in tradition and prestige, intangible qualities which could not be reckoned on a balance sheet but which nonetheless underwrote the stadium's continuing and profitable existence.

The British public, on the other hand, was not much impressed. An Olympic Games in austere times seemed a frivolous way to spend money when so many were without jobs or homes or both. With rationing at its most stringent during 1947, food became a dominant issue for those who took exception to Britain's commitment to the Games. Some felt that well-fed American athletes would hold so comprehensive an advantage over hungry Allied counterparts that competition would be rendered meaningless. Others questioned the point of Britain staging an Olympics she could barely afford when her rationed athletes, 'scarecrows in running shoes', stood no chance of winning anything.

Whatever the scepticism during the build-up, the Games of the XIVth Olympiad won the battle for hearts and minds from day one. A packed stadium watched the opening ceremony in brilliant sunshine on the afternoon of 29 July: 4,500 competitors from fifty-nine countries and 82,000 spectators were present; 7,000 pigeons (fanciers all over Britain having responded to the call) flew skyward; a twenty-two-year-old medical student from Surbiton, John Mark, jogged round the track to light the Olympic flame; the King did what kings do on such occasions and declared the XIVth Olympiad open; and finally, on behalf of the assembled athletes, the British team captain, the hurdler Wing Commander Donald Finlay, took the Olympic Oath, the words breathing a sincerity which, with today's Games dominated by television, sponsorship and hype, makes fifty years seem a very long time ago:

> We swear that we will take part in the Olympic Games in loyal competition, respecting the regulations which govern them, and desirous of participating in them in the true spirit of sportsmanship, for the honour of our country and for the glory of sport.

Though the weather did not hold – it rained for most of the second week before clearing for the closing ceremony – the sentiments did, and nowhere more intensely or fulfillingly than at Wembley during the eight days of track and field competition. Predictably the United States dominated, taking twelve of the thirty-three athletics gold medals. Honours, though, and the Games' most abiding memories were more evenly spread among the competing countries.

The athlete who was to define, in spirit and in fact, the 1948 Games embodied also the Corinthian ideal to a degree unequalled, perhaps, in all Olympic history. The Dutchwoman Fanny Blankers-Koen was a thirty-year-old mother of two who cheerfully listed her hobbies as 'housework'. A healthy lifestyle, drinking three pints of milk a day and training for a couple of hours each morning, Blankers-Koen, even in less cynical times, seemed almost too good to be true. She was certainly far too quick to be caught.

Though she was world record-holder at high jump and long jump, Blankers-Koen withdrew from both to concentrate on sprints and hurdles. She then set new Olympic records in the 100m and 200m and inspired Holland's 4x100m relay team to victory, thereby securing her own third gold medal. Between times her race with Britain's Maureen Gardner – a crowd favourite herself who, amid great fanfare, married her trainer later in the year – in the 80m hurdles had proved as breathtaking a contest as any that summer: both women finished in 11.2 seconds, only for Wembley's new photo-finish equipment to decide the gold in Blankers-Koen's favour.

Another of the all-time greats of Games history, a Czech army officer Emil Zatopek, had arrived at Wembley a relative unknown. On 30 July, the first day of athletics competition, he left a distinguished 10,000m field for dead to take gold in a new Olympic record time, after which he was made favourite for the 5,000m later in the week. In the event, on a rain-sodden track he again broke the existing Olympic record but in a desperate sprint finish, was held off by the Belgian runner Gaston Reiff.

The marathon, too, featured a dramatic finish, a reminder of the 1908 London Games when the little Italian Dorando Pietri collapsed before reaching the White City finish line. Forty years later a twenty-one-year-old

Belgian paratrooper named Etienne Gailly led the field into Wembley Stadium but, half a lap short of the gold medal, ran out of gas in spectacular fashion ('gallant but practically insensible,' read the official assessment in the Olympic Report) to be caught on the line by Delfo Cabrera of Argentina and Tom Richards of Great Britain. Bizarrely, on the day of the race an impostor, an Italian from Birmingham, turned up at Wembley claiming to be the 1908 hero Pietri and convinced enough people to get himself into the Royal Box for a few hours and on to the front pages of the papers the following day.

The warmth and enthusiasm for which the XIV Olympiad is remembered were generated as much by the Wembley crowd as by the competitors they came along to cheer. The fortnight's fiercest controversy provoked one of its defining moments. In the 4x100m men's relay the United States team was disqualified over a mix-up at a baton change, giving Great Britain her first athletics gold medal. Then, after close inspection of the race film, the judges reversed their decision. According to the *New York Times*, however, the Wembley audience had already taken their opportunity to enter into the spirit of the 1948 Games: 'The judicial victory awarded the British sprinters was the first time the British crowd had had an opportunity to cheer a triumph by their own countrymen. But the Britons disagreed with the judges. They did not want to win even one victory in that way. They gave their loudest cheers to the disqualified Americans, three of whom, incidentally, were Negroes. That is sportsmanship at its best. That will be remembered, we believe, long after many other incidents of the Olympiad are forgotten.'

Wembley's Olympics saw Britain cast in the role of gallant loser. Gold medals were won in 1948 but at events held away from the stadium's spotlight. Apart from disappointing in the track and field events, in the men's hockey final (there was, as yet, no women's event) Great Britain lost to India at Wembley. A silver medal and the enthusiasm of the crowd were enough, though, to pave a way for the sport to find a place on the stadium's calendar. Three years later a women's international between England and Ireland attracted a 30,000 crowd.

Sweden, coached by Englishman George Raynor, won gold in the football tournament. The British team, meanwhile, in finishing forth exceeded even their own optimistic expectations given that the amateur game in many countries was run along all but professional lines. The Yugoslav team, for example, which beat Britain 3–1 in their semi-final at Wembley was effectively a full international side.

The British team, too, exploited a degree of professional expertise, albeit applied to the talents of genuinely amateur players. The honorary, and therefore unpaid, team manager was Matt Busby, by now in charge at Manchester United, who co-opted his club trainer Tom Curry on to the Olympic team's staff and talked his senior pros into sacrificing part of their summer break to coach their amateur counterparts.

Led by Bob Hardisty from Bishop Auckland, who would later grace Amateur Cup Finals at Wembley on more than one occasion, the team responded to Busby's enthusiasm in kind and, after defeating the favourites Holland and then France in the qualifying rounds, were disappointed not to have given a better account of themselves in the semi-finals. The manager himself would later wonder 'how different the result might have been had Harry McIlvenny not missed two excellent scoring chances when he was through and the score stood at 0–0 ... soccer's full of ifs and one should not dwell on what might have been'.

Busby, though, could be forgiven for dwelling on what had already been. A few weeks before the Olympic football tournament he had guided Manchester United to victory in a marvellous FA Cup Final. After appearances with Manchester City as a player in 1933 and 1934 the 1948

Final was Busby's first visit as a manager. Bombed out of Old Trafford during the war, United had been playing home games at the Maine Road ground of Busby's former club. Nothing about the Cup run was easy, therefore, and victory in the Final was due, if far from routine, reward.

Their opponents Blackpool had the Footballer of the Year, Stanley Matthews, and England centre-forward Stan Mortensen in their attack and twice took the lead during a breathtakingly open and adventurous game, only for three goals in fifteen minutes towards the end to give Busby's United a 4–2 win.

The game made up for a poor Final the year before which had been memorable only for the half-volley and subsequent manic celebration by Charlton's Chris Duffy which proved enough to beat Burnley. 'He jumped into the air, whirled round like a top and then, with his arms above his head, careered crazily down the pitch like a madman,' remembered his goalkeeper Sam Bartram.

Victory for Matt Busby's first great United team – built around a nucleus of home-grown talent, thereby establishing what has continued to be an Old Trafford tradition – opened a remarkable sequence of classic matches at Wembley which, in retrospect, seem to build towards the climax of 1953 and the greatest Cup Final of all, when Matthews and Mortensen, losers in 1948, returned to inspire Blackpool in their finest hour.

In 1949 Billy Wright, a boot boy at the stadium a decade earlier, was back at Wembley as Wolves – and England – captain to lead his team to a 3–1 victory over Leicester. In 1950, with ground improvements enabling a 100,000 crowd to watch at Wembley for the first time since 1923, two goals from Arsenal's Reg Lewis accounted for a Liverpool team appearing in their first Cup Final.

Both those games featured goals described in contemporary reports as 'Wembley's finest ever' – Sammy Smyth's fifty-yard dribble and low drive sealing Wolves' victory against Leicester, Lewis first rounding off an intricate passing movement. Those finishes were quickly set aside, however, in the fuss made about the shot, 'blurred by the speed of its flight' according to the *Sunday Express*, which settled the Final in 1951.

The No. 9 shirt has a unique significance for the players and fans of Newcastle United. Malcolm Macdonald, Andy Cole and Alan Shearer have been more recent Geordie icons, inheriting a tradition established by the greatest centre-forward in the club's history, Jackie Milburn. In Newcastle's first Wembley appearance for nearly twenty years two Milburn goals accounted for Blackpool, leaving Matthews and Mortensen disappointed again. Both sides were managed by heroes from the stadium's earliest days: United's Stan Seymour had scored Newcastle's second in the 1924 Cup Final and Blackpool's Joe Smith had captained Bolton in 1923 and 1926.

Milburn's first goal stemmed from a mistake made in Newcastle's penalty area (and remembered only too well) by his England team-mate Stanley Matthews: 'I gave them the first goal, a terrible pass of mine. One of the Newcastle United players picked it up, went forward and then Jackie went through and scored.' The second, though, was very much Wor Jackie's own work, as the next day's headlines – 'Wonder Goal by Milburn' – proclaimed: a first time shot from outside the area which flew past George Farm in the Blackpool goal. What a fluke! thought Milburn, apparently, as he fell to the ground. 'Well played, Jackie. That goal deserved to win any game,' muttered Stan Mortensen as the players made their way back to the centre-circle.

The following year Newcastle were back again. Their goalscorer in 1952 was Milburn's room-mate, the Chilean George Robledo, with a header six minutes from time to beat Arsenal. The No. 9, however, was involved in the game's crucial incident when a collision with Walley Barnes saw the Arsenal full-back limp off with torn knee ligaments and, in the days before substitutes, leave his team with ten men for three-quarters of the match. The shine was thus taken off Newcastle's achievement in becoming the first team this century successfully to defend the FA Cup. As their manager Seymour admitted: 'Newcastle won the Cup but Arsenal won the honours.'

The 1953 Cup Final will always be remembered as the greatest chapter in the career of the most enduringly popular figure in the history of the English game. Despite a hat-trick from Stan Mortensen, a perfect ninety minutes from the inside-right Ernie Taylor and the goalscoring heroics of Bolton's injured left-half Eric Bell, the day belonged to Stanley Matthews, focus at thirty-eight for a sentimental nation's goodwill, whose display in a heart-stopping last twenty minutes turned the Cup Final Blackpool's way.

The gifted individualist, whose ball control, balance and trickery can illuminate one-on-one confrontations between attacker and defender – within the context of a team game in which the quality of passing will more usually prove the decisive factor – has a particular place in the heart of the English football fan. Matthews, perhaps the greatest example of that old-fashioned strain of footballing talent, was a national figure: his ability, his age, his capacity for hard work, his characteristic modesty and his role in two previous Cup Finals as plucky loser had combined to cast him as the definitively English sporting hero.

The Wembley setting was perfect, 100,000 spectators basking in clear May sunshine and Queen Elizabeth II watching from the Royal Box. For the first time League fixtures had been rearranged so as to avoid clashing with the Cup Final broadcasts; attendances at other games on football's big Saturday had suffered in previous years. The overall audience, therefore, was by far the biggest ever for a Final: ears pressed to radios, families gathered round TV sets bought in readiness for the Coronation a month later.

While the whole country looked on or listened in, willing Matthews to get his winner's medal at last, the game itself set out at first to confound expectations and best wishes. Thanks to a typically forceful performance from Bolton Wanderers' centre-forward, the Footballer of the Year Nat Lofthouse, and some nerve-rackingly inept goalkeeping by Blackpool's George Farm, the hour mark passed with Bolton sitting comfortably on a 3–1 lead. Our hero's time had come: 'It's mostly the last twenty minutes that wins matches,' Matthews said later. 'You keep plodding on and plodding on.

You never think you're going to lose anyway, you just keep going,' which is just what Matthews did. With Bolton's left flank weakened by injuries to Bell and Ralph Banks, Taylor laid a steady stream of passes to the feet of Blackpool's right-winger.

First his cross was touched down to the feet of Stan Mortensen who scored his second goal of the game. Then, after a succession of Matthews-created chances had been passed up by Bill Perry, Jackie Mudie and even Mortensen, the centre-forward at last equalised from a free-kick with a minute of normal time remaining. As the game drifted into injury-time, a few seconds remained for Matthews to find room in which to improvise his own historic finale. As Desmond Hackett described it for the *Daily Express*: 'Matthews is gliding down the wing with all the menace and smoothness of a snake. There is the brave music of cheers rising, rising in salute to this slight, balding man with the ball. There is the sudden shock of hushed silence as Matthews smooths over his pass, leaning widely over on his left ankle before he falls. And he is still leaning on his elbow on the ground when Perry sweeps the ball past the frantically reaching foot of John Ball.'

Blackpool's supporters inside the stadium erupted, 'crazily happy'. Moments later their cheers, as Matthews was hoisted on to his team-mates' shoulders with a Cup-winner's medal grasped tight in his right hand, echoed those of fans all over England listening on the wireless or watching on TV. The man himself, meanwhile, would remember private, contemplative moments in the midst of the hurrahs: 'I just kept on playing ... on and on. It was only when it was all over that I spoke aloud to myself, "I've done it at last." '

1946: REG HARRISON

Raich Carter was the master, a great bloke. He was the gaffer, aloof but a great bloke. Raich was that confident. We drew 2-2 at Charlton the Saturday before the Final, Raich and Peter didn't play. We came into the Imperial Hotel in Russell Square for a meal. Raich met the bus, stood on the steps, looked around and announced: *Cup winners in town!*

On the day, we went for a walk in the morning, had a little lunch. I was twenty-two and I think the nerves had started to hit us the evening before, especially the older players: they knew what a privilege it was to be playing in a Cup Final. I know I was pretty knotted up in the dressing-room before we went out.

Once you kicked off, of course, you were just concentrating on what was going on there and then. The crowd was just a roar that you put out of your mind, really. Raich had a goal disallowed early on but it was pretty even, two even sides, until extra time when they crumbled; once you get a goal behind in extra time, that can deflate you. Me, I didn't see much of the ball first half, but second I thought I had a good game and had a hand in our second goal. Jack Stamp was big and strong, took the buffeting for Peter and Raich, and he did it for us in extra time, even though he hadn't really played in the ninety minutes. It was a good, balanced game, but once the second goal went in we knew we'd done it.

When the whistle went, I couldn't really believe it. I welled up, you know. You fight it back because men don't cry, but it's that emotional. And going up the steps, six seats in, there was my wife, all my family there, too, all sat there as we went up to get the Cup. No lap of honour though, in them days, we just got the Cup and walked off! It was the best day of my career. To be at that first Cup Final after the war was a new start. When we came out of the tunnel, everything felt different. Everyone sang the national anthem and we were just glad to be there.

INTERVIEW, 1997

OFFICIAL PROGRAMME · *SIXPENCE*

THE FOOTBALL ASSOCIATION CHALLENGE CUP COMPETITION

Final Tie

at the

EMPIRE STADIUM
WEMBLEY

Managing Director A.J. ELVIN

CHARLTON ATHLETIC
v
DERBY COUNTY

SATURDAY APRIL 27TH 1946

1946: MARTIN EASTERBROOK

My first Wembley memories are all to do with speedway, just after the war. My ambition was to be a speedway rider: I'd sit on the loo pretending it was a bike. My dad started taking me. I think the home league matches were on a Thursday and the crowds were enormous: 70,000 or something if we were riding against Wimbledon or West Ham.

Those riders were heroes to us, Wembley were my home team. They always did things a bit special at Wembley. I remember they used to suddenly play a record, *The March of the Gladiators*, and the tractor would come out which used to sweep the shale on the track. That would be followed by a team of sweepers, very smart in black berets and wearing white polo neck sweaters with a big red lion on the front. They did a sort of lap of honour behind the tractor which sort of built up the atmosphere.

Before each heat, there'd be a bugler who'd blow his bugle to say the riders had to get ready. They'd race the regulation four laps; there was a guy who had a gun, a sort of starters' pistol, which he worked with his foot and, when the first rider crossed the line, he'd fire it off to say the race was over. There was a real atmosphere, a real sense of occasion about it all. I used to love the smell of the ether, or whatever it was they mixed in the petrol, standing by the corners where the shale would fly up as the bikes came round.

INTERVIEW, 1997

1948: STANLEY MORTENSEN

I cried after the Cup Final of 1948 . . . but it wasn't because I had been on the losing side at Wembley. The picture will remain with me while memory lasts. The game was over, the medals had been presented to both sides, and the Cup itself to Johnny Carey, the Manchester United captain. The Blackpool players had stood in a group, talking of this and that, while the victorious team walked up to the Royal Box to receive their mementoes and handshakes from the King and Queen. Then our turn had come, and we had filed past the Royal Family with their warm smiles, their words of sympathy for the losers coming just as sincerely as their earlier words of congratulations for the winners.

In accordance with tradition, the United players had chaired their captain off the pitch, all the way to the dressing-room. We Blackpool players walked off slowly behind the victors . . . I happened to glance up to the crowd, loath to go away, staying on to see the curtain rung down on the drama of the Cup Final. There, standing over the tunnel which led to the dressing-rooms, was a party of Blackpool supporters. Beribboned and bedecked in our famous tangerine, with caps, streamers, rosettes, scarves, they stood, silently surveying the last moments of a memorable day. In the spring sunshine I could see almost every individual plainly. They stood there, mute in their disappointment, gazing down as their favourite team walked off – without the Cup which they had hoped we would carry back to the seaside.

Their silent sympathy with us, their regret at the result, was obvious; and across the intervening space, from crowd to players, there seemed some link, some bond of fellowship. Hardly thinking what I was doing, I waved to that silent crowd. The effect was magical. They responded with a shout which seemed as mighty as anything we had heard during the pulsating struggle of the match itself. With a thunderous roar they let loose all their hot fanaticism for us and for the game of soccer.

**FOOTBALL IS MY GAME,
SAMPSON LOW, 1949**

1948: FANNY BLANKERS-KOEN

The race that will forever stand out clearly in my mind when I think back to the Wembley Games will be my struggle in the 80 metres hurdles with Maureen Gardner. For one of the very few times in my career, I was off to a late start. Just when I was thinking that there was going to be a 'flier' the pistol shot rang out and I was left standing. The rest of the field were a yard ahead of me. *You are beaten, Fanny. You'll never catch them.* That's what I was thinking, but then I realised that the finishing tape still loomed a long way ahead. I could make up that lost ground.

By the time we reached the fifth hurdle I was level with Maureen, but I was going so fast that I went too close to the hurdle, hit it, and lost my balance. What happened after that is just a blurred memory. It was a grim struggle in which my hurdling style went to pieces. I staggered like a drunkard.

Even so, I was fairly confident that I had passed Maureen before the finish ... it was quite a jolt for me to hear the British national anthem being played. Had Maureen, then, won after all? No – the band were saluting the Royal Family, who had just arrived at the stadium.

I breathed again but the suspense was still not over. It was a photo-finish and we had to await the camera's judgement. As the programme continued, Maureen and I glanced continually at the scoring board. Then, at last, the result came up. The first two ciphers of the winner's number appeared on the board ... a six ... then a nine. I jumped for joy. My number was 692.

OLYMPIC ODYSSEY, MODERN ATHLETE PUBLICATIONS LTD, 1956

1948: LORD BURGHLEY, CHAIRMAN OF THE ORGANISING COMMITTEE

In 1946, the clarion call went forth to the athletes of the world, inviting them to gather in London in 1948 to celebrate the XIV Modern Olympiad. Here to-day, in this vast arena, are assembled 6,000 competitors, the cream of the Youth of the world drawn from the fifty-nine assembled nations, who have answered this call. Here is the proof of the inherent strength and vitality of the Olympic Movement.

For the next two weeks, these young men and young women will be engaged in keen but friendly rivalry, competing together in the highest traditions of our Olympic ideals and of Amateur Sport. The eyes of the world to-day, and for the next fourteen days, will be on London. Not only will they be turned towards this ancient City to follow the fortunes of their champions and those of other countries, but also, I believe that in the hearts of millions of men and women in every corner of the earth, that warm flame of hope, for a better understanding in the world which has burned so low, will flare up into a very beacon, pointing a way to the goal through the Fellowship of Sport.

SPEECH, OPENING CEREMONY, 1948

Daily Round By JOSS

OLYMPIC CAMP

KEEP OUT !

" May we watch the athletes at feeding time ? "

Ticket (left)

XIV OLYMPIAD
EMPIRE STADIUM

Friday
July 30, 1948
at 2.30 pm

ATHLETICS

By Lift to
Entrance 81

PRIVATE BOX
ROW   SEAT

COMPLIMENTARY

JULY
30
AFTERNOON

EMPIRE STADIUM

Friday, July 30, 1948
at 2.30 pm

ATHLETICS

By Lift to
Entrance 81

PRIVATE BOX
ROW   SEAT

COMPLIMENTARY

This ticket is Morning
(TO

XIVth OLYMPIAD — COMPLETE LIST OF — LONDON, 1948 — GOLD MEDALLISTS

ATHLETICS

100 metres	Dillard (U.S.A.)
200 metres	Patton (U.S.A.)
400 metres	Wint (Jamaica)
800 metres	Whitfield (U.S.A.)
1,500 metres	Eriksson (Sweden)
5,000 metres	Reiff (Belgium)
10,000 metres	Zatopek (Czecho.)
110m. Hurdles	Porter (U.S.A.)
400m. Hurdles	Cochran (U.S.A.)
Marathon	Sjöstrand (Sweden)
10km. Walk	Cabrera (Argentina)
50km. Walk	Mikaelsson (Sweden)
4 × 100m. Relay	Ljunggren (Sweden)
4 × 400m. Relay	U.S.A.
Long Jump	U.S.A.
High Jump	Steele (U.S.A.)
Pole Vault	Winter (Australia)
Hop, Step & Jump	Smith (U.S.A.)
Weight	Ahman (Sweden)
Discus	Thompson (U.S.A.)
Javelin	Consolini (Italy)
Hammer	Rautavaara (Finland)
Decathlon	Nemeth (Hungary)
	Mathias (U.S.A.)

WOMEN

100 metres	Blankers-Koen (N'lands)
200 metres	Blankers-Koen (N'lands)
80m. Hurdles	Blankers-Koen (N'lands)
4 × 100m. Relay	Netherlands
Long Jump	Gyarmati (Hungary)
High Jump	Coachman (U.S.A.)
Weight	Ostermeyer (France)
Discus	Ostermeyer (France)
Javelin	Bauma (Austria)

BASKETBALL

Winners	U.S.A.

BOXING

Fly-weight	Perez (Argent.)
Bantam-weight	Csik (Hungary)
Feather-weight	Formenti (Italy)
Light-weight	Dreyer (South Africa)
Welter-weight	Torma (Czecho.)
Middle-weight	Papp (Hungary)
Light-Heavy-weight	Hunter (S. Africa)
Heavy-weight	Iglesias (Argent.)

CANOEING

Single Kayak 10,000m.	Fredriksson (Sweden)
Single Kayak 10,000m.	Akerlund-Wetterström (Sweden)
Canadian 10,000m.	Capek (Czechoslovakia)
Canadian 10,000m.	Lysac-Macknowski (U.S.A.)
Single Kayak 1,000m.	Fredriksson (Sweden)
Single Kayak 1,000m.	Berglund-Klingström (Swed.)
Canadian 1,000m.	Holecek (Czechoslovakia)
Canadian 1,000m.	Brzak-Kudrna (Czecho.)
Single Kayak 500m.	Hoff (Denmark)

CYCLING

	Dupont (France)
	Ghella (Italy)
	Teruzzi, Perona (Italy)
Pursuit	France
	Beyaert (France)
	Belgium

EQUESTRIAN EVENTS

Dressage Test (Individual)	Moser (Switzerland)
Dressage Test (Team)	Sweden
Three Days' Event (Individual)	Chevallier (France)
Three Days' Event (Team)	U.S.A.
Prix des Nations (Individual)	Cortes (Mexico)
Prix des Nations (Team)	Mexico

FENCING

Foil (Individual)	Buhan (France)
Foil (Team)	France
Epee (Individual)	Cantone (Italy)
Epee (Team)	France
Sabre (Individual)	Gerevich (Hungary)
Sabre (Team)	Hungary
Women's Foil (Individual)	Elek (Hungary)

FOOTBALL

	Sweden

GYMNASTICS

12 Exercises combined— Individual	Huhtanen (Finland)
Team	Finland
Horizontal Bars	Stalder (Switzerland)
Parallel Bars	Reusch (Switzerland)
Rings	Frei (Switzerland)
Pommelled Horse	Aaltonen (Finland)
Long Horse	Aaltonen (Finland)
Free Exercises	Pataki (Hungary)
Women—Team	Czechoslovakia

HOCKEY

Winners	India

MODERN PENTATHLON

Winner	Grut (Sweden)

ROWING

Single Sculls	Wood (Australia)
Double Sculls	Burnell and Bushnell (Great Britain)
Coxwainless Pairs	Wilson and Laurie (G.B.)
Coxed Pairs	Denmark
Coxwainless Fours	Italy
Coxed Fours	U.S.A.
Eights	U.S.A.

SHOOTING

Free Rifle 50m.	Cook (U.S.A.)
Free Rifle 300m.	Grünig (Switzerland)
Free Pistol 50m.	Cam (Peru)
Rapid Fire Pistol 25m.	Takacs (Hungary)

SWIMMING

100m. Free-style	Ris (U.S.A.)
400m. Free-style	Smith (U.S.A.)
1,500m. Free-style	McLane (U.S.A.)
4 × 200m. Relay	U.S.A.
100m. Back-stroke	Stack (U.S.A.)
200m. Breast-stroke	Verdeur (U.S.A.)
Springboard Diving	Harlan (U.S.A.)
High Diving	Lee (U.S.A.)
Water Polo	Italy

WOMEN

100m. Free-style	Andersen (Denmark)
400m. Free-style	Curtis (U.S.A.)
4 × 100m. Relay	U.S.A.
100m. Back-stroke	Harup (Denmark)
200m. Breast-stroke	Van Vliet (N'lands)
Springboard Diving	Draves (U.S.A.)
High Diving	Draves (U.S.A.)

WEIGHT-LIFTING

Bantam-weight	de Pietro (U.S.A.)
Feather-weight	Fayad (Egypt)
Light-weight	Shams (Egypt)
Middle-weight	Spellman (U.S.A.)
Light-Heavy-weight	Stanczyk (U.S.A.)
Heavy-weight	Davis (U.S.A.)

WRESTLING

FREE-STYLE

Fly-weight	Viitala (Finland)
Bantam-weight	Akar (Turkey)
Feather-weight	Bilge (Turkey)
Light-weight	Atik (Turkey)
Middle-weight	Dogu (Turkey)
Light-Heavy-weight	Brand (U.S.A.)
Heavy-weight	Wittenberg (U.S.A.)
	Bobis (Hungary)

GRECO-ROMAN

Fly-weight	Lombardi (Italy)
Bantam-weight	Petersen (Sweden)
Feather-weight	Octav (Turkey)
Light-weight	Freij (Sweden)
Welter-weight	Andersson (Sweden)
Middle-weight	Grönberg (Sweden)
Light-Heavy-weight	Nilsson (Sweden)
Heavy-weight	A. Kirecci (Turkey)

YACHTING

Dragon Class	Norway
Swallow Class	Great Britain
Firefly Class	Elvström (Denmark)
Star Class	U.S.A.
6-metre Class	U.S.A.

RECORD OLYMPIC ENTRY

59 countries, a record entry, sent competitors to the XIVth London Olympic Games.
The countries represented, in alphabetical order, were :

AFGHANISTAN	CZECHOSLOVAKIA	KOREA	PORTUGAL
ARGENTINA	DENMARK	LEBANON	PUERTO RICO
AUSTRALIA	EGYPT	LIECHTENSTEIN	SINGAPORE
AUSTRIA	EIRE	LUXEMBURG	SOUTH AFRICA
BELGIUM	FINLAND	MALTA	SPAIN
BERMUDA	FRANCE	MEXICO	SWEDEN
BRAZIL	GREAT BRITAIN	MONACO	SWITZERLAND
BRITISH GUIANA	GREECE	NETHERLANDS	SYRIA
BURMA	HUNGARY	NEW ZEALAND	TRINIDAD
CANADA	ICELAND	NORWAY	TURKEY
CEYLON	INDIA	PAKISTAN	URUGUAY
CHILE	IRAN	PANAMA	U.S.A.
CHINA	IRAQ	PERU	VENEZUELA
COLOMBIA	ITALY	PHILIPPINES	YUGOSLAVIA
CUBA	JAMAICA	POLAND	

The XVth Olympiad has been awarded to Helsinki, the capital city of Finland, and will take place in 1952 in the modern Stadium which can accomodate a 70,000 crowd.

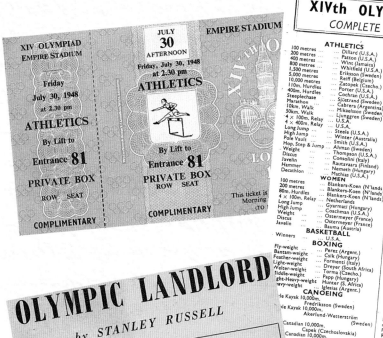

OLYMPIC LANDLORD

by STANLEY RUSSELL

He's no athlete, yet he's staging the biggest athletic show in history ; takes months to make a decision, yet works to hair-spring timing. Success slogan of the man who began in a kiosk and now owns a great stadium: "Look Ahead. Never Stand Still"

John Bull colour photograph by William Kemp

The Elvins at home. Their devotion to each other is foundation of success

---

Pass card (right)

ALL ARENAS
FOR
EMPIRE STADIUM, WEMBLEY
Enter at Stadium Office Entrance or Turnstiles F.
(See plan on back).

LONDON
1948

G.P.O.

1948: MATT BUSBY

By this time I was gradually getting to know the lads, and what is more important, they were getting used to me – and appreciating my requirements. I handled them as I would professionals, worked them like slaves, and not once did I hear a word of complaint. They deserved a lot of credit for the spirit and enthusiasm with which they tackled a strenuous routine, especially when it is taken into account that they were not accustomed to training, concentrated training, that is.

There were some fine characters in my squad. Bobby Hardisty whose successes in amateur soccer between 1947 and 1957 earn him the right to be classed as one of Britain's greatest-ever unpaid footballers, Eric Fright, a veritable terrier of a wing-half, Tommy Hopper, one of the most courageous players with whom I have ever been associated, Denis Kelleher, the Irish doctor from Barnet who had enough ability to command a place with most clubs in First Division football, Harry McIlvenny and Eric Lee, 'comedians' of the party but both excellent footballers, Peter Kippax, Bill Amor, Doug McBain, Gwyn Manning, Jack Neale, Ronnie Simpson, and the rest. It was a pleasure to work with such men.

MY STORY, SOUVENIR PRESS, 1957

1950: DAVE MACKAY

First time I played at Wembley was for Scotland schoolboys. Clement Atlee presented each of us with a little plaque: I didn't know who he was, I don't think, but he was about the same size as me. I've still got the plaque at home. In those days, you were allowed a sub in schoolboy games. They had more sense than the professionals. Think of all the Cup Finals spoilt by a player getting injured and one team being down to ten men. I came on at half-time – any substitute had to be made before the start of the second half – and we got slaughtered 8–2! The whole thing, the train journey, coming to Wembley, though, was like a fairy tale. Can you imagine? A little fourteen-year-old coming out of that tunnel. Johnny Haynes played for England that day.
INTERVIEW, 1997

1951: CHARLIE CROWE

I don't know about a Cup team but in the fifties Newcastle had a lot of Cup players who raised their game for one-off occasions. In 1951 we should have been the club that did the Double. Before the Final we played about fourteen matches and never won one and finished about fourth in the League.

The Football Association Challenge Cup was the attraction, you see. The League was mundane, your bread-and-butter stuff. There was no real incentive for us in the League, there was no European Cup; the glamour was at Wembley and so were the bonuses! Mind you, in 1951 the bandsmen of the Coldstream Guards got more money for playing at the Cup Final than we did.

The team in '51 we all got on well together. I had little Ernie Taylor, always available in the centre of the park. You might play a one-two with him and he'd set off the speedsters in the front line, Milburn and Tommy Walker, who was almost as fast as Jackie. Behind them we had Joe Harvey, who took no prisoners, and Bob Cowell. On my side of the field we had Bob Mitchell and then there was George Robledo who was the poacher. He'd make for the far post as soon as Bob got the ball. Those were our attacking moves: simple, really, but we had two centre-forwards before anybody else had thought of doing it.

INTERVIEW, 1998

1952: WALLEY BARNES

How does it feel now, Walley?
Not so good.
Billy Milne sighed and shook his head.
Well, that's it, I'm afraid. Better make up your mind that you've had it this time.

There was no doubt that trainer Billy Milne was right. That was the end of the 1952 Cup Final for me. Billy helped me off the field and into the dressing-room, and the thought uppermost in my mind was that I had let the rest of the lads down. How could they possibly avoid defeat now, with only ten men and an hour still to play?

Later, as I lay on the table in the dressing-room with Billy Milne to comfort me, messages from the field of play bolstered our hopes slightly. And when there were only seven minutes left to play, and still no score, we even started to think that the boys might after all achieve the 'impossible' – hold out and force a replay. Then we heard a roar from the crowd, and Billy and I exchanged a glance. There was something awfully conclusive about that cheer.

We heard slow, hesitant footsteps approaching down the tunnel and, after a pause, the door opened to reveal the figure of a very dejected-looking dressing-room attendant. He seemed at a loss for words to tell his news. At length, *We're one down* he said. Quite unconsciously he had employed the personal pronoun. That dressing-room attendant must have seen dozens of Cup Finals and big international matches. Great dramas were everyday events in his life, and one team was like another. But obviously this match was affecting him like no other had done: all his emotion had become entangled in it, and there was no doubt on which side his sympathy lay.

**CAPTAIN OF WALES,
STANLEY PAUL ,1953**

1953: STANLEY MATTHEWS

You know Stan Mortensen was a great player, like a whippet, he was so quick. He scored three goals: a hat-trick in a Cup Final, now that is something. He was the man of the match. I don't know why they called it the 'Matthews' Final: perhaps because of my age; I was thirty-eight, what they call a veteran, in 1953. I never thought of it as 'my last chance'. You never do. You concentrate on the game.

On the day, you've got to be lucky. You've got to make fewer mistakes than they do. Well, our goalkeeper, George Farm, made mistakes but so did theirs. And most games are won in the last twenty minutes and that's when we came good. On my wing, Eric Bell was injured and, even though he scored to make it 3-1, later on it meant I had more room, no-one chasing back at me.

Football is riddled with 'ifs', isn't it? The fourth goal: Ian Fenton, our wing-half, got the ball. I was on the halfway line. I shouted to give it to me but he didn't. He tried to beat Hassall but he couldn't and the ball broke to Ernie Taylor. In the meantime, I'd been running forward. If Ian had given me the ball earlier, the goal might never have happened.

To win football matches you've got to have wingers, even today. A winger's cross tries to get the goal-keeper in two minds. Now, Stan Mortensen and I had a great understanding. When I received the ball from Ernie Taylor, only Banks was in front of me. I knew I had to beat him quickly and on his left side. I looked up and saw Mortensen running to the nearest post and, in the gap he'd left behind him, there was Bill Perry who deserves credit, too: it wasn't an easy chance, he had to hit it first time from about ten yards. But it was Morty's run had pulled the centre-half away. That was great thinking, wasn't it? Three goals and that little run to create the fourth goal: I've always said it was 'Morty's' Final.

INTERVIEW, 1998

Langton Hassall Lofthouse Holden Bell Barrass Wheeler Banks, R. Ball Har

SPORT PICTORIAL Page 3

Crippled Bell is Bolton hero

Page 18 SUNDAY PICTORIAL, May 3, 1953

Blackpool hit 2 in 3 minutes

END OF A PERFECT DAY

MORTENSEN TAYLOR PERRY

NORTH GRAND STAND

ENTER AT TURNSTILES
(See Plan on back)

ENTRANCE
(LEFT)

E 85

Row 15 Seat 38

EMPIRE STADIUM, WEMBLEY
THE FOOTBALL ASSOCIATION
CUP COMPETITION

FINAL TIE

SATURDAY, MAY 2nd, 1953

Kick-off 3 p.m.

Price 25/-
(Including Tax)

CHAIRMAN AND
MANAGING DIRECTOR,
Wembley Stadium Limited.

THIS PORTION TO BE RETAINED
(See Conditions on back)

Moir BOLTON ★ BLACKPOOL Johnston Farm Shimwell Garrett Fenton Robinson Matthews Taylor Mortensen Mudie Perry

PLAN OF THE FIELD OF PLAY

ENGLAND
(White Shirts, Dark Blue Shorts)

Goal
G. MERRICK
(Birmingham City)

2
Right Back
A. RAMSEY
(Tottenham Hotspur)

3
Left Back
W. ECKERSLEY
(Blackburn Rovers)

5
Centre Half
H. JOHNSTON
(Blackpool)

6
Left Half
J. W. DICKINSON
(Portsmouth)

4
Right Half
W. WRIGHT (Capt.)
(Wolverhampton Wanderers)

8
Inside Right
E. TAYLOR
(Blackpool)

Centre Forward
S. MORTENSEN
(Blackpool)

10
Inside Left
J. SEWELL
(Sheffield Wednesday)

7
Outside Right
S. MATTHEWS
(Blackpool)

11
Outside Left
Z. CZIBOR

10
Inside Left
F. PUSKAS (Capt.)

9
Centre Forward
N. HIDEGKUTI

8
Inside Right
S. KOCSIS

4
Right Half
M. LAN...

6
Left Half
J. ZAKARIAS

5
Centre Half
J. BOZSIK

2
Right Back
J. BUZANSZKY

3
Left Back
G. LORANT

Goal
G. GROSICS

Referee
L. HORN
(Holland)

HUNGARY
(Red Shirts, White Shorts)

<u>INJURED PLAYERS</u> :—The goalkeeper may be changed at any time during the match and substitutes will be allowed for any other players up to the 44th minute.

Reserves for England : B. WILLIAMS (Wolverhampton Wanderers) J. KENNEDY (West Bromwich Albion) H. HASSALL...
Reserves for Hungary : I. KOVACS, L. CSORDAS, P. PALOTAS, S. GELLER, K. SANDOR, M. TOTH.

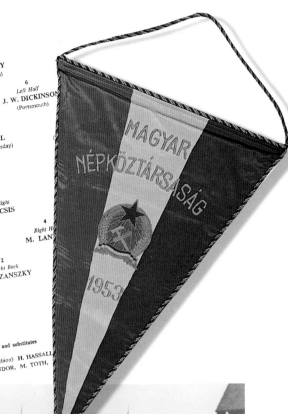

A Right Way Of Winning

1953-61

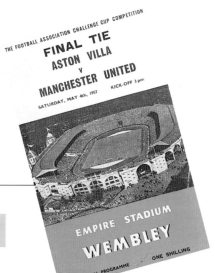

Perhaps we were dazzled. The years after the war were brilliant enough for the English domestic game: massive crowds flocked to grounds up and down the country and descended on Wembley for showpiece games each season; the stars of the day were national figures whose reputations still glow, undimmed by partisan interest or the passage of time: Swift, Finney, Matthews, Mortensen, Mannion, Milburn, Lawton, Lofthouse, Franklin and Wright, life peers in English football's upper house.

Only in the last few years have we experienced anything like the enthusiasm generated for football by those players and the club sides they played for, a sense of the whole country enraptured by the excitement of breakneck league campaigns and the heroics of Cup Final afternoons. Wembley, of course, was the perfect setting for some of a golden era's most intense and memorable dramas, the place to celebrate in style the thrilling hurly-burly that was – and is? – English football at its thrusting and competitive best.

The same decade, however, which saw the stadium illuminated by the entrances and exits of the domestic game's brightest talents, leading actors in the melodrama of the FA Cup, witnessed too the all but complete (and largely unforeseen) eclipse of English football on the international stage. During the course of a single year, 1953, Stanley Matthews would first delight a nation, tapping history bewitchingly from foot to foot, in the greatest of all Cup Finals and then look on helplessly as he and his England team-mates were left chasing red-shirted shadows by Hungary, the greatest team in the world, across the unforgiving expanse of Wembley's perfect surface the following November.

In 1942, Belgium had been the first foreign side to win at Wembley, in an international against Holland, a game arranged for its propaganda value between teams of exiled players. It needed, perhaps, the unique circumstances of wartime to bring about a break with the tradition which had seen Wembley, thus far, host only England versus Scotland international games. After Wales had played three times at the stadium during the early 1940s a Victory International against France in 1945 began the process which would lead to Wembley becoming the natural home not just of the Cup Final but of the English national team.

In a second Victory International Belgium returned in 1946, this time to play England. Though the result was a routine 2–0 victory for the hosts, hindsight endows the occasion with a certain resonance. Albert Brown and Jesse Pye scored during a first half dominated by England and played in brilliant sunshine. As the game wore on, however, a thick January fog descended and, with it, what the goalkeeper Frank Swift described as 'an eerie gloom' in which 'although we could hear the crowd we couldn't see them and they couldn't see us, except for the isolated glimpse they got of a man sprinting down the touchline'. A debutant that day, Billy Wright of Wolves, would go on to enjoy one of the most distinguished of all international careers, winning 105 caps, ninety of them as captain, but during an era which saw England drift inexorably towards the fringes of the world game.

During the late forties internationals were played once more at club grounds around the country and results – seventy-two goals scored and only one defeat in nineteen games – did little to disrupt the complacent assumption that the inventors of football remained its masters. The run pulled up short at Wembley in April 1949. Scotland's 3–1 win, achieved after a brave and athletic display in the game's opening period by the goalkeeper Jimmy Cowan, was celebrated by the Scots fans who streamed on to the pitch at the end with a delight matching that which had greeted the Wembley Wizards' victory back in 1928.

While less individually gifted than their illustrious predecessors the class of '49, all of whom save Derby's Billy Steel played their football at home, had combative spirit and a sense of purpose to spare. Jackie Milburn scored England's goal and his analysis of his side's shortcomings was accurate enough on the day and prescient, too, as regards what lay ahead in the international arena: 'England were beaten by a much better and more purposeful side. The Scots played as a team. Unfortunately we were eleven units who never moved at all after our early burst of unsustained brilliance.'

The vagaries of the selection process which preceded each international fixture undermined team manager Walter Winterbottom's best efforts to establish a consistent team pattern for an England side that was not without its talented individuals: 'It was hopeless to try to build quickly the club spirit and understanding I knew we must have.' At the 1950 World Cup, the first England deigned to participate in, Winterbottom's unsettled team came unstuck in spectacular fashion. The 1–0 defeat by the United States in Belo Horizonte remains one of world football's most celebrated upsets.

The game, though, took place on the other side of the world, in hot weather, on a bumpy pitch, after all, and didn't we hit the woodwork half a dozen times? The embarrassment was keenly felt but it would be another three years before the lessons hit home. Wembley, rather than a stadium in a small mining town in Brazil, would be the stage on which the insularity, the arrogance and the amateurishness of the English attitude to international football would at last be exploded for ever.

Regular matches against foreign opposition at Wembley began in earnest with a sequence of games organised in 1951 as part of the Festival of Britain. The first of these, in May, was against Argentina, a country taking a first step back into international football after years of isolation imposed by the Peronist regime. The novelty of a South American side playing in this country stirred enormous interest. Britain was still rationed and there was a degree of xenophobia in the air – England v Argentina, then as now, a fixture fraught with political undertones – as the referee, Mervyn Griffiths, would later remember: 'Fantastic stories were told of the food brought from the Argentine as the visitors did not intend to suffer because of rationing in this country. Excitement was intense in the stadium and feelings were a little high because at that particular time the Old Country was getting a raw deal in the meat negotiations with the Argentine.'

Poor finishing and a bravura display from the goalkeeper Rugilo, who would thereafter be celebrated as 'The Lion of Wembley' at home in Buenos Aires, kept the score blank until Argentina took a shock lead. England's reputation, resting as it now did on a still formidable home record, was rescued by goals from Milburn and Mortensen in the last ten minutes. According to Griffiths, 'when the final whistle went there were remarkable scenes. Caps and hats went sailing into the air and friends told me that many cried with joy. "You can keep your meat," said one gentleman sitting near my wife.'

The visit of Austria, too, in November attracted considerable attention in the press and at the Wembley box-office. Built around the talismanic figure of the centre-half Ernst Ocwirk, the Austrians were considered the strongest team in Europe at the time. The England right-back, Alf Ramsey, recognised 'there was something different about the atmosphere' at Wembley and the players, if not the 100,000 crowd, were only too aware that 'England had never been beaten on home soil and that Austria supplied probably the biggest threat of all time'.

Ramsey himself scored from the penalty spot and sent in a free-kick which Lofthouse met with a header for England's second goal. Melchior's cross-shot and a Stojaspal penalty, however, earned the Austrians a deserved draw. The sense of relief at a preserved unbeaten home record against continental opposition was understandable; Ramsey's judgement of what England's performance had proved was less so: 'We had only to keep this form to put England back on top of the soccer world again.' Tottenham's right-back would, fifteen years later, be manager of an England team which achieved that ambition. In the short term, however, for Ramsey and his international team-mates, things were to get worse before they got better.

In any catalogue of the great teams in the history of world football – alongside the Wembley Wizards of 1928, Brazil in 1958 and 1970, Holland in 1974 and, if we're being sentimental, England's boys of 1966 – the Hungarian team of the early 1950s is automatically included.

Hungary arrived at Wembley in November 1953 as Olympic champions and in the middle of a run which would see them beaten only once between 1950 and 1956. Although only George Robb, a member of England's amateur side at the Helsinki Olympics, had seen the Hungarians play, the reputations of the likes of Bozsik, Koscis, Hidegkuti and Puskas and the unprecedented publicity they received from the English press were such that, as Billy Wright would remember, 'by the time the great day arrived for the Wembley match I'd seen so many photographs of the Hungarians and read so much about them I felt I was going to play against very old friends'.

Little good did the sense of familiarity do him. Wright and his colleagues were comprehensively undone before the 100,000 spectators who had crowded, expectantly, into Wembley. Among the fans were knots of players from English professional clubs, as eager as the punters to see what all the fuss was about. Peter McParland was in the Aston Villa party and remembers a team-mate turning towards him before kick-off to assure him: 'They'll be all possession and no shots.'

Within ninety seconds Hidegkuti had put the Hungarians ahead. McParland's colleague was, presumably, as chastened as the England captain Wright who later wrote: 'All I can remember was a flash of white as the ball whined into the far corner of the net for a goal which stunned everybody. It was some seconds before even the crowd realised what had happened – and, with the Hungarians dancing about patting Hidegkuti on the back, it was just like watching a soccer match on television with the sound switched off. Then followed some of the most magnificent football I have ever seen.'

Optimistically, England equalised through Jackie Sewell but they were then destroyed by three Hungarian goals in an eight-minute burst which shook English football to its foundations. The highlight was a sleight of foot from Ferenc Puskas, his dummy setting him up to finish past Gil Merrick in goal, while Wright, his victim, in the words of Geoffrey Green reporting for the *Times*, 'carried on with the intended tackle like a fire engine going to the wrong fire in a hurry'.

The Hungarians apparently had everything, and too much of it for England to do more than struggle manfully to keep the score down: pace, speed of thought, precise short and devastating long passing, perfect first touches and relentless support play, clinical finishing. As McParland remembers, 'for anyone who loves football, watching them that day was El Dorado'. The Hungarians, 4–2 up at the interval, had eased up long before they ran out 6–3 winners.

Puskas, the Hungarian captain, thought the match had turned on the fact that 'throughout the game we demonstrated the golden rule of modern football, and that is: the good player keeps playing even without the ball'. Watching as eleven great Hungarian players dismantled what remained of England's pretensions that November afternoon, Geoffrey Green was in no doubt that the Wembley crowd had witnessed a chapter in the game's history being brought to a dramatic close: 'English football can be proud of its past, but it must wake up to a new future.'

The Cup Final the following May proved as disappointing as 1953's had been memorable. The build-up cast Tom Finney in the central role played by Matthews the previous year. Finney, like Matthews a splendid, traditional winger, vied with the Blackpool man for a decade: the 'Preston Plumber' was held in the same high esteem by his peers and had almost as secure a place in the nation's affections. West Bromwich Albion, however, were in no mood to provide the supporting cast, according to their goalkeeper Jim Saunders: 'The Albion manager, Mr Buckingham, said that George Lee must stop Finney. Then Ray Barlow must stop Finney and then Len Millard would have a go at him. In other words, the idea was that if you stopped Finney, you stopped Preston.'

The plan to contain 1954's Footballer of the Year worked and West Brom won 3–2 with a goal two minutes from time by the right-winger Frank Griffin. Finney was not alone in describing the game as 'one of the most disappointing finals ever to be played at the famous Empire Stadium'; indeed, it was doubly disappointing for him – 'my own performance was awful' – in that, public expectation having focused on him before the game, he took the blame for the sense of anticlimax after it.

Perhaps it was for the best that the Cup Final did not distract from the home truths delivered to the Wembley crowd by the Hungarians six months previously and that, in the words of the official FA Year Book, '1953/54 saw the eclipse of England's supremacy and will be remembered as the season in which she suffered the first home defeat in her history'.

The reference, of course, was to defeat in games against continental opposition and the FA summary tried to cushion the blow with a reminder 'that eclipses are more frequently partial than total and that even the latter, however full of omens, are normally of short duration'. This one was at least long enough to see England dumped out of the 1954 World Cup by Uruguay in Basle, as well as lose a return match against Puskas and company 7–1 in Budapest.

At home, though, at least one club player had picked up something from the Hungarians' Wembley masterclass. In that match nobody had given the England defence more trouble than Hungary's centre-forward Nandor Hidegkuti, whose mobility – dropping off into midfield to begin attacks – had pulled Wright and his colleagues out of position time and again. In Don

Revie Manchester City enjoyed the services of a player with the intelligence and technical ability to fulfil the same withdrawn role.

Sadly the 1955 Cup Final turned not on Revie's anticipated contribution but on an early injury to City's full-back Jimmy Meadows. Newcastle, as in the 1952 Final against ten-man Arsenal, went on to win, 3–1 this time, against depleted Manchester City. Indeed, the man Meadows had been detailed to mark, the winger Bobby Mitchell, scored the decisive second goal.

City and Revie were not to be denied, although the centre-forward played in the 1956 Final only because Billy Spurdle was missing, reportedly 'the hapless victim of boils'. Revie would return to Wembley as a manager, with Leeds United and England, but this, perhaps, was his finest hour, as described by H D Davies in the *Guardian*: 'His skilful assortment of long and short passes, timed and measured to perfection, probed ceaselessly into the Birmingham defences while his shrewd positioning in deep midfield enabled him to collect, re-label and re-dispatch Trautmann's constructive throws and clearances to his fellow conspirators lurking upfield.'

Although Revie's contribution was crucial in his team overturning the form book to beat Birmingham City 3–1, much attention focused also on Manchester City's German goalkeeper Bert Trautmann, who was injured late in the game but, helped by covering defenders, made it through to the final whistle. Trautmann himself had no idea what had happened: '[At] the official banquet, although I could hardly move my head because of the pain, I did not let that interfere with my enjoyment.' Within forty-eight hours, however, he was in bed at Manchester Royal Infirmary. His continuing discomfort was eventually diagnosed and Wednesday's *Manchester Evening News* carried the headline by which the 1956 Final is best remembered: 'Trautmann: Neck Broken'.

It was a critical year in the fortunes of the stadium, too. The immediate post-war period had been a boom-time for Wembley, as for sport in general. By the mid-fifties, however, the financial situation had become straitened and in 1956 net profits for the year reached a low ebb at £11,755.

Sir Arthur Elvin, in his report to Wembley shareholders, outlined details of a share issue during 1955 that had raised funds for improvements to the stadium. He also re-iterated the circumstances which had led to a continuing slide in the company's profitability. A ten per cent tote tax had bitten into Wembley's bread-and-butter income from greyhound racing, while entertainment tax at forty-five per cent made it almost impossible to make speedway pay. Not even the Cup Final was exempt. While Test matches and the Wimbledon tennis championships were free from any liability a third of the gate receipts from football's biggest pay-day were swallowed up in tax.

It had been company policy for some time to try to bolster the balance sheet by other events at the stadium. Amateur international football, American gridiron, the Oxford v Cambridge match all appeared on the calendar for the first time, along with schoolboy internationals, hockey and the Amateur Cup Final. Wembley, of course, was already football's high church and the setting of the stadium attracted bookings from religious organisations, too: the Jehovah's Witnesses, Dr Billy Gaham and a Catholic rally, the Family Rosary Crusade.

Each was held over several days and brought enormous crowds to the stadium. The Catholic crusade saw a banner hung between the Twin Towers proclaiming 'The Family That Prays Together, Stays Together'. An American priest, Father Patrick Peyton, was introduced to 83,000 believers as 'that great international, that prolific goalscorer, who has brought his team ... the greatest team in the world, Family United ... to Wembley today'.

Barring divine intervention, however, Wembley's economic decline appeared inexorable, reflecting cultural trends which professional sports — football in particular — were struggling to come to terms with, as Elvin explained to the 1955 AGM: 'Television, both as a competing influence and as a charge on the family budget, likewise continued to be a serious competitor to our various activities, and the much wider range of consumer goods on which the public can spend their money, particularly during the period when the Hire Purchase restrictions were raised, are other factors which helped towards the disappointing results for the year.'

Negotiations with the Football Association, to be concluded in 1956, were already under way to allow Wembley to keep a greater proportion of gate receipts and to enable evening games to take place under newly installed floodlights. The latter investment was underwritten by the 1955 share issue and, after considerable bureaucratic wrangling with Lancaster Gate and a programme of tests which gave two amateur teams from Hendon the opportunity to live out every Sunday footballer's dream, the first floodlit game, between a London XI and a Frankfurt team in a forerunner of the Uefa Cup, took place on 22 October 1955. Elvin was delighted: 'Those of you who saw our first floodlit match will, I am sure, agree with me that it is an exceedingly fine installation, and it will be remembered that press comments after the match were most emphatic in their praise of this outstanding addition to our amenities.'

Much to Wembley's frustration, evening games would not become a regular feature until the 1960s. The lights, though, stood as a last testament to the contribution of Sir Arthur Elvin during thirty years in charge of the stadium. Already unwell, Sir Arthur sold a large number of his shares to the Arsenal chairman Sir Guy Bracewell Smith during 1956. In January, 1957, the Wembley MD set sail on board the SS *Winchester Castle*, on a cruise intended to improve his health. After four days on board, with the ship off Madeira, the fifty-seven-year-old Elvin died and was buried at sea.

Sir Guy took over as Wembley chairman and appointed John Connell as general manager. The new regime made immediate economies, cutting directors' emoluments, staff pension fund contributions and the share dividend. The event schedule, too, was rationalised, which meant the end, for example, of league speedway at the stadium. As a result, profits showed immediate, if slight, improvement. Three years later, at the end of a decade during which television had emerged as a real threat to Wembley's future, Associated Rediffusion, the broadcasting arm of the British Electric Traction group of companies, acquired a majority shareholding in a stadium which was once more a going concern. 'Our future prospects are fairly good,' claimed an optimistic Sir Bracewell Smith.

Manchester City's Revie-inspired victory in the 1956 Cup Final completed a double of sorts in a season which saw their neighbours United win the First Division Championship. Matt Busby's new team, rebuilt since winning at Wembley in 1948, went on to appear in successive Cup Finals in 1957 and 1958, two matches as emotionally charged as any in the stadium's history.

The Busby Babes were, without question, the most exciting team of the era. The darkest of tragedies was to ensure they would remain, for very different reasons, the most famous of all time. After winning the League title in 1952 Busby had wasted no time in giving youth its head, blooding a generation of talented home-grown youngsters while they were still in their teens. His foresight was rewarded with successive Championship wins in 1956 and 1957, the latter the first step towards what the football world confidently expected would be the century's first League and Cup Double.

The team's combination of power and grace was exemplified across United's half-back line: the incisive Eddie Colman and cultured centre-half Jackie Blanchflower alongside a youngster who had the potential, it seemed, to become English football's most complete player: Duncan Edwards. Ahead of them, leading the line, was Tommy Taylor, the finest centre-forward, according to Nat Lofthouse, of a decade which was blessed with great players in that position, Mortensen, Milburn, Allen and Lofthouse himself among them.

United arrived at Wembley in 1957 looking like the perfectly balanced team. Only the injured Dennis Viollet was missing, his place taken by a promising youngster by the name of Bobby Charlton. Nothing but the most extraordinary of circumstances, it seemed, would stop them overwhelming mid-table Aston Villa. But this was a football match and the unlikely duly took place. After six minutes, what contemporary accounts referred to as 'a collision' between the Villa winger Peter McParland and United's keeper Ray Wood rewrote the script. In fact, McParland deliberately charged Wood, whose only mistake, perhaps, was to seek to evade the impact rather than meet it head on: 'I saw him run in and I sort of swayed to one side but he caught me with his head. It was diabolical, really. That cost us the Double.'

The referee Frank Coultas took no action and described the incident afterwards as 'just one of those things in a Cup Final' but the upshot was that Wood had a fractured cheekbone and United only ten men. To McParland's credit, he proved sufficiently strong-willed, after weathering Duncan Edwards' attempts to exact retribution, to emerge as the game's outstanding performer, scoring both Villa's goals in a 2–1 win. The stand-in goalkeeper Jackie Blanchflower – 'I didn't have to go in but I was volunteered without getting a vote' – and his United team-mates were the day's heroes. Aston Villa were happy to make do with winners' medals and the dual satisfaction of remaining the last team to have achieved the Double and becoming the first to win the Cup seven times.

Few would have doubted, after the drama of that May afternoon, the possibility of Busby's Babes returning to Wembley the following year. No one could have imagined the circumstances in which they would do so. In February 1958, returning from a European Cup quarter-final against Red Star in Belgrade, United's charter plane crashed on the runway after stopping in Munich, leaving the heart, if not the soul, of one of the finest club sides in history dying in the snow. As tributes delivered in 1998 on the occasion of the fortieth anniversary of the Munich air disaster made plain, memories of the Busby Babes and their tragic fate have remained crystal clear, poignant and yet somehow inspirational ever since.

Just three months after the crash United, under the guidance of Busby's assistant Jimmy Murphy – Busby himself was still recovering from his injuries – found their way to Wembley once more, this time to face Bolton. Only Bill Foulkes and Bobby Charlton were left of the side which had lost so gallantly in the previous year's Cup Final: Roger Byrne, Eddie Colman, Duncan Edwards, Liam Whelan, Tommy Taylor and Dave Pegg all lost their lives at Munich (as did a thirties Cup Final hero, the goalkeeper-turned-journalist Frank Swift) while Johnny Berry and Jackie Blanchflower sustained injuries so severe they were never to play again.

Murphy had assembled in their place a side composed of youngsters from the reserves and old campaigners, like Ernie Taylor who had won finals with Blackpool and Newcastle and Stan Crowther who had played for Villa in 1957, acquired by transfers after the crash and before United's fifth-round tie against Sheffield Wednesday. The team's own courage, buoyed by a nation's goodwill, swept them into the Final that May. The appearance of Busby, still frail, alongside Murphy on the touchline was a poignant reminder, if any were needed, of what the club had been through. Bill Foulkes, United's right-back, found the build-up to the game all but impossible to bear: 'The Boss insisted on coming to the Final, although he had only just got on his feet again, against all expectations. The fact that he appeared to be in a pretty bad state – he looked grey and very, very old – upset me for a start. We could hear from the dressing-room the crowd singing *Abide With Me* and this just about finished me off.'

As they had in 1953, therefore, Bolton Wanderers went into a Cup Final as 'the other team', carrying the best wishes of only their own supporters. This time, though, they refused to be upstaged once the game had kicked off. The 1958 Final capped a marvellous career for their local hero Nat Lofthouse. Fittingly, the Bolton and England centre-forward scored both goals, the first gifted to him by a deflection off a United player, the second a shoulder charge – a battered United goalkeeper again – which took Harry

Gregg and the ball into the back of the net. Few begrudged hardworking and homespun Bolton their victory. For United, as Bobby Charlton would later point out: 'I don't think it was the end of the world that we didn't win the Cup Final. People were pleased to see business was carrying on.'

The Munich air disaster not only dealt Manchester a terrible blow but also undermined Walter Winterbottom's continuing attempts to rebuild England's fortunes. A gradual changing of the guard had been nowhere more in evidence than at Wembley in April 1955 when an eighteen-year-old Duncan Edwards made his debut for England in a 7–2 defeat of Scotland. The day's star, though, was an old hand by the name of Matthews. 'He even had the Scots rooting for him; everyone was sorry he did not get a goal,' said the referee, Mervyn Griffiths.

Experience, braced by an infusion of fresh talent like Edwards and his United team-mates Roger Byrne and Tommy Taylor, helped England qualify in some style for the 1958 World Cup Finals. Indeed, in November 1957 after a friendly against France won at Wembley by four goals to nil, the *France Soir* journalist Jean Eskinazi assured England's trainer Harold Shepherdson: 'There is no need for France to go to Sweden for the World Cup. We cannot win it, England surely will.'

Russian referee Nicolai Laychey would remember the occasion because his wallet and passport were stolen from the Wembley dressing-rooms during the game. Of more general significance, however, was the evidence on display to suggest that Winterbottom's programme of youth and technical development was beginning to bear fruit. Six of the winning team had graduated from representing England at under-23 level. Sadly Winterbottom would be denied the services of Edwards, Byrne and Taylor in Sweden. The game against France was their last for England before they lost their lives.

The 1958 World Cup, and early elimination from it, were a reminder that England still lagged behind a football world celebrating the emergence of Brazil as its new super-power. Worse, the following season a team featuring Brian Clough in his only appearance at the stadium as a player lost 3–2 to Sweden, the second time England had been beaten at Wembley by foreign opposition.

In retrospect, however, the game marked the international team's lowest ebb. In 1960 Fifa announced that England would host the 1966 World Cup Finals. By way of celebration, perhaps, Winterbottom's team, now playing a 4-2-4 formation based on the Brazilian model, embarked on an inspired run of form which treated the Wembley crowd to four consecutive victories and twenty-six goals, including a victory over Scotland which went some way to laying the ghost of the Wembley Wizards.

Johnny Haynes, the era's most gifted English player and a shining example of the continuity Walter Winterbottom sought – Haynes had played for England Schoolboys at Wembley in 1950 – scored twice in a 9–3 mauling for which the Scottish goalkeeper Frank Haffey took much of the blame. Winterbottom claimed that 'the home internationals, for me, obviously had less importance than the bigger picture'. The team, though, were as heartened as the Scots were distraught. Dave Mackay had faced Haynes in 1950, when Scotland Schoolboys had lost 8–2, which made this latest scoreline all the harder to swallow: 'It was a total disaster, a suicidal job. Everything England hit went in. Every one of us played badly. Games like that happen; but not in an international, not Scotland playing England!'

Mackay, though, was back at Wembley to make up for his disappointment in spectacular fashion three weeks later. The Tottenham Hotspur side of 1960/61, in which the barrel-chested midfielder played such a crucial role, stands comparison with any club side in the history of the English game.

Two years previously the captain Danny Blanchflower had boldly announced to the football world that 'the Double will be done and Spurs are the team to do it'. At Wembley, on 6 May 1961, boast became fact, and fact history: Tottenham became the first club since Aston Villa in 1897 to win League and Cup in a single season.

Spurs had already galloped away with the First Division title. Bill Nicholson, according to a later recruit Jimmy Greaves, 'was a great manager. It was his firm belief that we should pay Tottenham for the privilege of playing for them'. Certainly it was a privilege to watch as the team won their first eleven games of the season. Dave Mackay remembers it as a one-horse race: 'No one could get near us and we won the League with 66 points and games to spare.'

Mackay himself, the centre-half Maurice Norman and centre-forward Bobby Smith were the steel, Blanchflower and the wingers Cliff Jones and Terry Dyson the engine; the Scottish international John White, who was to die young in a freak accident, struck by lightning, lent vision and creative impetus. The team blended with an athletic passing game, (Liverpool would thrive on a comparable style two decades later) which at last proved that an English side had learnt Puskas's lesson: Spurs relied on players without the ball continuing to play.

The match, if not Spurs' achievement, proved an anti-climax. Since the early fifties a succession of injuries had ruined or, at least, unbalanced Cup Finals. The two which preceded Spurs v Leicester in 1961 had seen a player break his leg in each: in 1959 Roy Dwight had scored Nottingham Forest's first goal before mistiming a tackle on Luton's Brendan McNally, leaving ten men to hang on for a 2–1 win; in 1960 Blackburn Rovers, already rocked by a transfer request from their centre-forward Derek Dougan delivered an hour before kick-off, lost their left-back Dave Whelan during a 3–0 defeat by Wolves. The calls for substitutes to be allowed in Cup Finals were heard every May but went unheeded until 1967.

Sure enough, after seventeen minutes of the 1961 Final, during which the underdogs Leicester had promised to make a game of it, their right-back Len Chalmers came off worse in a clash with Les Allen. As Alan Hoby described in the *News of the World*: 'A crack of legs, a split-second mingling of blue-and-white shirts and then a silence spread around the stadium.' With Chalmers a limping non-contributor thereafter, the result was never in doubt and second-half goals from Smith and Dyson secured Spurs the victory their season, if not their anxious performance on the day, had deserved.

For Mackay and his team-mates, of course, the details of the afternoon mattered less than the fact that posterity would remember victory over Leicester as the realisation of a dream, 'the Double which had become an obsession for us all'. It was a momentous day for English football, too. The Double side fashioned by Bill Nicholson set a new standard for combination play by an English team. The historian A J Ayer, a staunch Spurs fan, celebrated the secret of his heroes' success in the *New Statesman* a few days later. His summary foreshadowed the strength which would take England, five summers later, back to the pinnacle of the football world: 'It is not so much to the individual merits of the players as to their teamwork that the Spurs owe their extraordinary success.'

WEMBLEY SCRAPBOOK

1949: GEORGE YOUNG

Aye, and when referee Mervyn Griffiths blew up for time I felt a little moist about the eyes and am not ashamed to mention it. So, too, were quite a number of fellows I knew to be in the crowd. The old country had once again been hoisted to the top of the soccer ladder.

What of Jimmy Cowan, the man who had contributed so much towards our victory? After we had struggled through masses of tartan-wearing fans to the dressing-room, and were entering the plunge bath, someone asked: *Where's Jimmy?*

Then it dawned upon the rest of us that our goalkeeper was not in the dressing-room; he had literally disappeared when surrounded by hundreds of excited Scots. A number of us had changed and were ready to board our coach to the banquet when finally Cowan limped into the dressing-room and fell back on the bench next to me, muttering: *O Lord, save us from our friends!*

**CAPTAIN OF SCOTLAND,
STANLEY PAUL, 1951**

1954: TOM FINNEY

There was a fuss made in the media because Stan had had such a good game against Bolton in 1953. There was never any rivalry between Stan and myself but the press always tried to build something up. So in 1954 they were talking about the Finney Final, like they had the Mathhews Final.

It was just one of those games you go into physically drained. As a professional footballer you're like any working man. There are days you go to work and you feel you could work all day. There are others when you just don't feel up to it. The unfortunate thing for a footballer is there are tens of thousands of people watching you. That Final, the spark was missing somehow. I felt drained before the game even started.

I think you tend to look on a Cup Final as a one and only chance - there are so many great players who never play in one - and I wanted to play the game of my life. Instead, it was one of the worst games I ever had in a Preston shirt. I was never in the game, really. I'd played against the left back before, so it wasn't that. It was one of these days you have: it just happened to be the Cup Final.

INTERVIEW, 1998

IT'S HAPPENED! WE'VE HAD IT! THAT'S THAT!

Even the weather let us down — it kept fine

BEATEN BY A BETTER TEAM ANOTHER DATE HAS TO GO DOWN IN OUR HISTORY BOOK.

1066 The Normans 1953 The Hungarians

AS WE WENT DOWN IN A FLOOD OF SIX GOALS — BUT WITH OUR COLOURS NAILED TO THE MAST.

Sewell Mortensen Ramsey

EACH OF THEIR GOAL-SCORERS WAS KISSED ALL ROUND BY THE TEAM.

NO FURTIVE LITTLE GOOD-NIGHT PECKS

BUT REAL FULL BLOODED BANGERS!

THEIR CENTRE-FORWARD SCORED 3 TIMES SO HE'S PROBABLY IN BED WITH SORE LIPS THIS MORNING

P.S. WHAT A PITY OUR GOALIE DIDN'T SAVE THIS LITTLE LOT

Celebrate Coronation year with more National Savings

ENGLAND 3 HUNGARY 6

WE COULD HAVE CELEBRATED THEN!

JACK DUNKLEY

AND AT THE END, HUNGARIAN WHOOPEE

1953: STANLEY MATTHEWS

They beat us 6-3. Oh, they played well! Where we lost the game, I always feel, was that no-one marked Hidegkuti. He played dropped back in the middle of the pitch. Now, any skilful player, you've got to mark him, but Hidegkuti had 15 yards of space all the time to work the ball in. I remember, as we were coming off at half-time, our centre-half Harry Johnston saying he didn't know whether he should follow him or not. Then Puskas started, too. We had no chance. Hidegkuti killed us and Puskas scored one of the greatest goals ever with his left foot.

I had an on and off game. They just hit us for six. Their defenders were good but, if you're winning 3-1 or 4-1, your defenders always play better. Our defenders were having a very rough time. It was one of those games and, you know, in those days, nobody ever blamed the manager. They always blamed the players and rightly so, I suppose. Crikey! We were terribly disappointed after the match: it was awful! But they were the best I'd ever seen. The next game against them we lost 7-1. I was away with Blackpool and I didn't play, thank goodness! We were playing in Strasbourg: better that than Budapest.

INTERVIEW, 1998

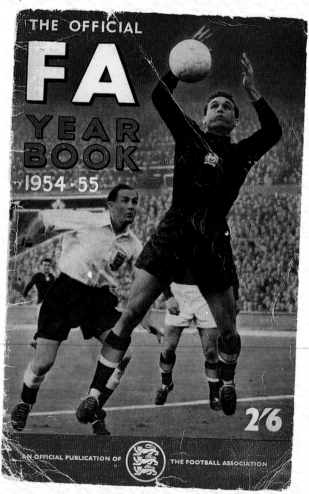

THE OFFICIAL FA YEAR BOOK 1954-55

2'6

AN OFFICIAL PUBLICATION OF THE FOOTBALL ASSOCIATION

1953: BILLY WRIGHT

If I take the liberty of describing one more of the six Hungarian goals – three of them by Puskas (2) and Hidegkuti in one superbly aggressive seven-minute spell – it is simply because I was directly involved.

Puskas, the incomparable Puskas, suddenly bobbed up in front of me with the ball. I moved into the tackle firmly, quickly and with my eyes on the ball. Nine times out of ten that tackle would have won possession. But this was the tenth time and my opponent was Puskas. He dragged the ball back with his studs and my striking leg met . . . just air. In the same incredibly quick movement the great Hungarian pivoted, his left foot flashed and there was the ball nestling cosily in the back of the net.

**ONE HUNDRED CAPS,
ROBERT HALE , 1962**

Merrick goes down too late to stop Hungary's third goal, scored by Puskas.

The three goals that broke England's heart

By BOB FERRIER

ENGLAND'S record, unbeaten at home in ninety years of football, was shattered yesterday.

It went to a glorious team from Hungary, a team of fire and fury and imagination and technical brilliance. The equal

| ENGLAND | 3 |
| HUNGARY | 6 |

gkuti took a pass from Bozsik right half tapped

the shot going in off Ecksley

Next Puskas beat Ramsey all ends up by simply trailing the ball back with his foot and shooting a goal from a ridiculous angle.

Then right half Bozsik

was 6—2 against England. The brilliance of the Hungarian passing had blinded and gagged this England team. Ramsey scored from a penalty after an hour's play but we could hardly hope for four more

1955: JACKIE MILBURN

When the subject of substitutes for League games is up for discussion I for one like to hear the views of other people, for there is much to be said for and against them. But no one has yet been able to put up a good argument against the allowing of a substitute during the FA Cup Final which is generally recognised as the 'Match of the Year'.

Let's face this all-important fact: no footballer in the Final is going to fake an injury. If a man is injured at Wembley he is injured. There's no question of anybody trying to pull a fast one. With this thought uppermost in mind, is it fair to the side which has fought like tigers to reach Wembley that, through no fault of their own, they should be penalised? Is it fair to football teams who are opposing sides one or more men short that they should not be allowed to give of their best? And just as important, why should the match of the year lose its label as an attraction because substitutes are not allowed?

GOLDEN GOALS, STANLEY PAUL, 1957

TRAUTMANN: NECK BROKEN

TEN-MAN BLACKBURN CRASH TO WOLVES

FOREST'S DWIGHT SCORES— THEN STRETCHERED OFF!

1957: PETER MCPARLAND

The game was a bit tense early on, a case of sticking in there and trying not to make a mistake. The incident: Jackie Sewell crossed from the right and I came running in from the left. I'd picked my spot to head it back across Ray Wood. It was really a good chance. I got a good header on it but Woody had come out and it went straight to him. I kept running and we were going to meet shoulder-to-shoulder. At the last minute, Woody sort of turned away and I hit him here, with my head on the side of his face.

I went down and, the next thing I knew, Wembley was spinning around me. I thought that was me finished. I just put my hand to my head to see if I was bleeding. I just waited for the trainer to come on, hoping that Wembley would stop spinning round. Five or ten minutes later I'd run it off. Big Duncan Edwards came after me and gave me a clout. I was jumping up to flick a ball on and Duncan come in behind me and punched me in the small of the back and then moved away off! Things were all right after that.

I did feel sorry for Ray Wood. Here, the lad had got to Wembley and been taken off after six minutes. It was playing on my mind. The crowd was booing me, too. When I came in at half-time, the trainer, Billy Moore, came after me: *They're on your back now, Peter. Only one thing you can do to shut them up: stick one in the back of the net.*

About twenty minutes into the second half that's what happened. I think Johnny Dixon got it over and I was in ahead of Duncan Edwards and hit it from around the penalty spot. I dived and caught it full flush: it bloody flew in, top corner! It wouldn't have mattered who'd been in goal. And as I fell forward after heading it, I found myself thinking: *You've scored a goal in a Cup Final.* The words actually came into my mind.

INTERVIEW, 1997

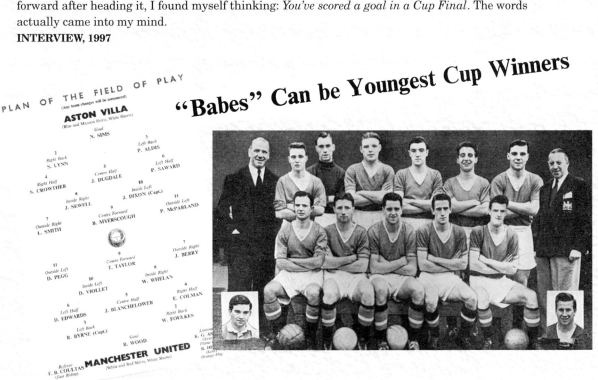

PLAN OF THE FIELD OF PLAY
(Any team changes will be announced)

ASTON VILLA
(Blue and Maroon Shirts, White Shorts)

Goal
N. SIMS

Right Back   Left Back
S. LYNN   P. ALDIS

Right Half   Centre Half   Left Half
S. CROWTHER   J. DUGDALE   P. SAWARD

Inside Right   Inside Left
J. SEWELL   J. DIXON (Capt.)

Centre Forward   Outside Left
B. MYERSCOUGH   P. McPARLAND

Outside Right
L. SMITH

Centre Forward
T. TAYLOR

Outside Left   Outside Right
D. PEGG   J. BERRY

Inside Left   Inside Right
D. VIOLLET   W. WHELAN

Centre Half   Right Half
J. BLANCHFLOWER E. COLMAN

Left Half   Right Back
D. EDWARDS   W. FOULKES

Left Back
R. BYRNE (Capt.)

Goal
R. WOOD

MANCHESTER UNITED
(White and Red Shirts, White Shorts)

Referee
F. B. COULTAS
(East Riding)

"Babes" Can be Youngest Cup Winners

SIR ARTHUR ELVIN

1899 – 1957

1958: NAT LOFTHOUSE

1953 was a great final to be a part of, though obviously I'm sorry we lost. Everyone in the world wanted Stan Matthews to get that winner's medal and it was a similar situation when we played Manchester United in the 1958 Cup Final, after Munich. If I hadn't been involved, I would have wanted Manchester United to win on that occasion. But my profession was playing football, my club was Bolton Wanderers, they paid my wages and the crowd gave their money to watch me play. I wanted Bolton to win and our fans to go home happy after a great win. Fortunately that happened but you had to show a certain amount of respect that day because I had lost some very good friends in the Munich tragedy: Duncan Edwards, Tommy Taylor, great players.

I scored the first goal in about the first two or three minutes. I remember Bryan Edwards had broken through the left-hand side and I just came in and side-footed it past Harry [Gregg]. It really was a hell of a ball by Edwards, he practically made the goal by beating the defence. To go one up so early really boosted us. I am glad that we won 2–0 and not 2–1 because then they could have always said that the result would have been different if it were not for that charge on Harry Gregg. We won 2–0, so it was a good night.

There was a great team spirit in that 1958 side and that is because we had a great coach by the name of George Taylor. Each one of those players that played at Wembley that day cost £10 to sign professional forms. We were all local players. And being hometown boys it meant so much to come all the way down to London and bring the cup home.
INTERVIEW, 1997

1958: MARTIN TYLER

In the fifties the amateur game was still pretty pure, in that money hadn't come in to start the process that turned amateur football into part of the non-League pyramid. It wasn't just winning, it was about a right way of winning and Woking certainly reflected that.

It was a very different time: fashion hadn't been invented. People still wore their dark overcoats, trilby hats, flat caps. I had a scarf, red and white, that had been made on a very modern gadget, the knitting machine. There were no replica kits, of course. I tried to get my mum to get me a red and white halved shirt. The sports shop got one – red and white quarters. I said: *That's no good to me. Those aren't our colours.* You could buy rosettes at the ground. There would be special editions, say, of the *Evening Standard* for big Amateur Cup games. There were souvenirs like that but there was nothing in the way of merchandising or marketing, other than a red and white halved metallic badge I had as a member of the Woking supporters' club. That membership was my guarantee of a ticket to watch them at Wembley in 1958. The Amateur Cup Final in those days was a real national occasion.
INTERVIEW, 1997

SKIPPER'S GIFT DAY

Ilford 0, Woking 3

TWO goals by Reg Stratton and John Hebdon in the last twelve minutes gave Woking skipper Charlie Mortimore a wonderful climax to his thirtieth birthday.

by
DENIS FOSTER

For Charlie's skilful thrust down the middle of their four-international attack had been Woking's inspiration.

But, though their first-ever Amateur Cup triumph was thoroughly deserved, the near-rout foreshadowed in Woking's opening blitz never materialised.

And for half an hour in the second half it looked fair odds on battling by-line Ilford grabbing an equaliser.

Praise Ilford for retaining their poise after a dreadful start. Three times keeper Gibbins mis-kicked the ball in goalmouth mêlées.

Full backs Simmonds and Chase also cleared off the line, and there were near-shaves galore before...

coolly picked a spot in the roof of the net from Stratton's corner. Littlejohn and ... equalised on ...

Charlie Mortimore and the Cup.

Cleator Cumberland

The comfort of a cap with the ease of a beret. Price 10/6, Beretcap-de-luxe 15/-

News from every man's angle

KANGOL BERETCAP

Time Table and Programme of Music

It isn't half time we had HOT BOVRIL

ANY time's a good time for hot Bovril. Best of all when you're feeling all in. Bovril cheers you, revives you, sustains you. Its goodness warms you through and through — puts you right back on top of your form. And helps you to stay there!

BOVRIL – *rich in the goodness of beef*

Published by WEMBLEY STADIUM LTD. (Copyright). Printed by McCORQUODALE, LONDON, S.E Concessionaires for Programme sales, DETTS, SON & MALVON, Wimbledon, S.W.19.

1961: DAVE MACKAY

Going into the Final we were really confident as a team but worried, too, because this was something special, trying to do something that hadn't been done before. The game itself, obviously Chalmers getting hurt was the thing. You know, throughout my career they called me 'swashbuckling': I was up and down the pitch, even sometimes to the extent of leaving the defence a bit exposed. When Chalmers was injured, though, I remember thinking to myself: *They're down to ten men, it's impossible for them to beat us*. There was nothing actually said between myself and Danny Blanchflower, but I decided then to just sit and play, in the old left-half position, not go forward; leave the boys up front to get the goals and make sure Leicester would get nothing.

Once they were down to ten – Chalmers stayed on but he was a cripple – there was no need for me to go crazy. The pressure had all been on us beforehand: winning the Cup, beating Leicester had nothing to do with it. It was all about doing the Double. So now it was just about scoring the goals. The ball was played up to Bobby Smith. He spun, turned the centre-half, whacked it from ten or fifteen yards. Then Terry Dyson, who'd missed a chance earlier, got a diving header and that was that. It wasn't a great game because doing the Double was so important. But it was a great side, lovely balance right through the team.

INTERVIEW, 1997

THE FOOTBALL ASSOCIATION CHALLENGE CUP COMPETITION

FINAL TIE
LEICESTER CITY
v
TOTTENHAM HOTSPUR

SATURDAY, MAY 6th, 1961   KICK-OFF 3 p.m.

EMPIRE STADIUM
WEMBLEY

OFFICIAL PROGRAMME   •   ONE SHILLING

Champions

1962-68

The world – football and everything else – took a revolutionary turn in the 1960s: Spurs did their bit, as far as the game was concerned, to speed that process along. Before Danny Blanchflower and company beat Leicester at Wembley in 1961 the Double had shimmered, a holy grail always just beyond the reach of even the greatest teams. Once Spurs had got their hands on both the domestic game's great prizes in a single season anything might be possible. In the ensuing years a modernised Wembley would witness a turning of the international tide as English clubs started winning European competitions and the national team gloriously beat the best in the world.

Whatever lay ahead, though, 1962 had a familiar ring: England were dumped out of a World Cup on the other side of the world and, at home, Spurs returned to Wembley successfully to defend the FA Cup. If anything, they were now an even better side than the one which had done the Double, having acquired in Jimmy Greaves the greatest goalscorer of his generation whose prolific career – embracing a profitable, if short-lived, adventure in Italy – and voluble personality marked him out as one of a new breed of football heroes.

For much of the 1961/62 season it had seemed that Spurs would continue to sweep all before them but Alf Ramsey's Ipswich beat them to the League title and Benfica squeezed past them in the European Cup semi-finals so that beating Burnley in the FA Cup Final was their sole reward at the end of an unforgettable season. At Wembley it took Greaves, who had scored a hat-trick in England's 9–3 humiliation of the Scots there the previous year, three and a half minutes to make his mark with the kind of finish that helped him stand comparison with the world's best. Running away from goal and pursued by Burnley defenders, Greaves, in the words of Brian Glanville, writing for the *Sunday Times*, 'stopped dead, as though he himself had realised the futility of the enterprise; then all at once, when everybody had rushed past him, he turned on the ball, left-footed and trickled a gentle, insidious shot along the ground, out of Blacklaw's reach'.

Burnley, their homespun image in stark contrast to that of worldly Spurs, fought back to equalise but a goal from Bobby Smith, a shot on the turn much like that which had opened the scoring against Leicester in 1961, and a Blanchflower penalty took Tottenham back into Europe. They went on to win the Cup Winners' Cup in 1963, achieving England's first success in European club competition by beating Atletico Madrid 5–1 in the final. That first giant step for English club football was taken in Rotterdam; the second, two years later, would be celebrated by a 100,000 crowd at Wembley.

'I remember the Old Man saying it would be five years before United would be able to recover. It was five years almost to the day in 1963 that we won the FA Cup.' Bobby Charlton was, of course, a Busby Babe in 1957 and a member of the team which had emerged from the wreckage of Munich to meet Bolton at Wembley in 1958. He faced Leicester, too, in 1963 in a Cup Final which proved the truth of Matt Busby's words. David Herd (twice) and Denis Law were the United scorers in a dashing 3–1 win.

Charlton and his team-mates went into the game as underdogs, having avoided relegation from the First Division only by beating Leyton Orient the previous Saturday. Expensive stars – Quixall, Setters, Herd, Cantwell, Crerand and Law – had misfired all season and faced a Leicester side whose strength lay in the cohesive teamwork which United had so conspicuously lacked. It was, though, a day which belonged to Manchester's talented individuals, particularly the costliest of them, Denis Law, for whom Busby had paid a record £115,000 to bring back from the Italian club Torino.

Never had a Final taken place so far into May, three weeks late on the 25th, after a backlog of fixtures piled up during an exceptional, snowbound winter. Nor had one ever been so dominated by an individual performance, according to the *Daily Mirror*'s Peter Wilson: 'Denis Law had one of those days of which most men can only dream. Never a foot wrong, never a moment when he wasn't the inspiration of Manchester and the lash for Leicester . . . this was more of a one-man Cup Final than even Stanley Matthews' . . .'

Law's outstanding contribution was one of the footballing highlights of an auspicious year for Wembley as the stadium started preparing for the greatest day in its history (a 2–1 victory for England against a Rest of the World team in a game held to mark the 100th anniversary of the founding of the FA was another). Improvements were all the more heralded for being long overdue. The prospect of a World Cup Final to be played there in 1966 – even if the new team manager Alf Ramsey was alone in believing England would be contesting it – was incentive enough and Wembley's owners spent some £500,000 to bring their forty-year-old property up to date.

Most of the money was spent on a roof which covered both ends as well as the stands to keep all 100,000 spectators dry. Fibreglass panels let light in through the thirty-six feet of roof nearest the pitch, though not enough to prevent Scotland leaving England in the shade during the first game played beneath it. Their 2–1 win was all the more stirring for the Scots being down to ten men after an early injury to their captain Eric Caldow. The 15,000 new seats meant 44,000 spectators could sit, not that Scots fans wanted to.

Given the imperious mastery of Rangers' Jim Baxter they would have stood and cheered all afternoon. Reporting and broadcasting on Scotland's famous victory, meanwhile, was done from a new 300-foot gantry suspended in the rafters high above fans' heads.

At long last, too, Wembley was given the opportunity to make proper use of the floodlights installed towards the end of Sir Arthur Elvin's tenure. Since their inauguration in the late 1950s the FA had been unwilling to sanction their use for anything but the closing stages of games played on gloomy afternoons. After a successful trial in April for a youth international between England and Northern Ireland, however, the two countries met again in November in the first full international scheduled for an evening kick-off under floodlights at the stadium.

The occasion proved a success both for Ramsey's team, who ran in eight goals, and for Wembley: the 55,000 crowd nearly doubled the usual attendance at games against Northern Ireland. With hindsight it made the football authorities' decision to play Wembley's first European Cup Final earlier that year in daylight on a Wednesday afternoon seem all the more absurd. Thanks to Matt Busby's determination to establish Manchester United's place on the world stage and to Spurs' achievement in reaching the semi-final of the competition the previous year, the meeting of Benfica and Inter Milan on 22 May 1963 enjoyed a prestige not lost on an English audience. The three o'clock kick-off on a working day, however, contributed to keeping the crowd down to a disappointing 45,000.

Benfica arrived at Wembley as defending champions. The absence of a capacity crowd did nothing to dampen the enthusiasm of those who were there, such as the great Eusebio who would return to delight Wembley full houses in 1966 and 1968: 'In the press-box hundreds of journalists from all over Europe were gathered to see the famous team that in the last two years had won the top European football trophy in inter-club competitions. Television cameras swallowed us up in the first shots of the broadcast. Photographers swarmed upon us and up in the rows of seats red flags and hopeful banners were waved. The chanting was clearly heard: "Ben-fi-ca! Ben-fi-ca! Ben-fi-ca!"'

Despite an opening goal by Eusebio, however, a debilitating tackle on the influential Coluna and two fine goals laid on for Jose Altafini by a young Gianni Rivera helped Inter to a 2–1 win. The attendance notwithstanding, the 1963 European Cup Final had been successfully staged and the final of the Cup Winners' Cup was awarded to Wembley two years later. May 19 1965, turned out to be quite a night and Wembley, this time, would be jammed to the rafters to enjoy it.

Walter Winterbottom's attempts to revolutionise coaching in England and his insistence that the domestic game had much to learn from continental models had begun to make their mark by the time he was replaced as national team manager by Alf Ramsey in 1963 after a fourth unsuccessful stab at the World Cup in Chile the previous year. Nowhere in the country did the new ideas and new methods flourish more productively than at West Ham United.

Malcolm Allison, just begining a coaching career, and the new manager Ron Greenwood were eager for change, as their West Ham contemporary John Lyall would later recall: 'We were students of the game. We sat for hours talking football, reviewing games, talking tactics, discussing training.' Reward for the hard work which went hand in hand with the willingness to learn came with West Ham's first appearance in an FA Cup Final since Wembley's first in 1923.

Although Preston, with the seventeen-year-old Howard Kendall becoming the youngest player to appear in a Final, were a Second Division side, West Ham were the more anxious. John Sissons, who scored the first of two equalisers on the way to a 3–2 victory, admitted afterwards: 'Honestly, I have never been so nervy during a match.' West Ham's winner, from Ronnie Boyce, arrived two minutes into injury-time. The adage about winning being not just the best but the only thing has seldom been more memorably justified. After stuttering to victory in 1964 West Ham returned to Wembley the following year and, stylish and assured, beat Munich 1860 2–0 in the European Cup Winners' Cup Final on the greatest night in the East London club's history.

As with many grounds, but to a degree perhaps unmatched elsewhere, Wembley's atmosphere changes dramatically when games are played at night under floodlights: the pitch, a dazzling green, stands out against the darkness of the grandstands and the stadium seems to close in on itself, focusing a theatrical intensity on the spectacle at its heart. Both clubs rose thrillingly to the occasion – the Germans were cheered off the pitch even as West Ham celebrated victory – to provide a game as high in technical quality as any in the stadium's history. Jim Standen in goal had made a series of outstanding saves as Munich 1860 threatened to break West Ham's territorial domination before two late goals from the winger Alan Sealey turned the game deservedly in favour of the English team.

The Londoners' pattern of play, as sophisticated as their opponents', was based on the 4-4-2 adopted with such success by Brazil among others. For the system to work properly, a team needed a central defender blessed with vision and passing ability as well as the more traditional defensive attributes. West Ham – and England – had Bobby Moore. Ron Greenwood thought his captain's best-ever game for the club was in the final against Munich.

In describing the essential role played by Moore in West Ham's system Greenwood identified the qualities which would make the United captain's contribution so crucial the following summer when an English team and a German team would meet once more at Wembley with an even greater prize at stake: 'He was the linchpin. At the back Bobby could read along the line and cover the whole area. Everyone was tight going forward and Bobby played loose, free, behind everyone else, and the team could go forward with the confidence Bobby was always behind them, reading anything coming through, mopping up. It was a joy to watch him play.'

Alf Ramsey was a man of many qualities, most of them undervalued outside the England dressing-room both at the time and since. His defining virtue was his single-mindedness. According to Roger Hunt, one of eleven Englishmen who, under Ramsey's guidance, would find out what it felt like to win a World Cup Final, 'he never stopped working towards that big objective – morning, noon and night'. When offered the England manager's job in 1963, after Walter Winterbottom's assistant Jimmy Adamson turned it down, Ramsey made clear he would accept only on the understanding that he was free to organise the national team's affairs without interference. He then promptly announced that England would win the World Cup in July 1966. Those who did not judge him presumptuous considered Ramsey foolhardy to leave himself so defenceless a hostage to fortune. In fact, the new manager was drawing a line in what had, for a decade, been the shifting sands of England's international rehabilitation.

The mark was set – for himself, his players and anyone else who cared to pay attention. By setting out the target of his ambitions, leaving no room for doubt or manoeuvre, he established from the outset that no distraction – from players, public, press or his employers, the FA – would be permitted to cast a shadow across England's predetermined path towards the 1966 World Cup and glory.

Ramsey's start was not auspicious. Although his contract – and, therefore, his sole responsibility for picking the team – did not start until May 1963, he oversaw both England's failure to qualify for the following year's European Cup of Nations after a 5–2 defeat in Paris and the Baxter-inspired victory of the Scots at Wembley five weeks later in the Home International Championship.

Although the World Cup would be played at home, the first eighteen months of Ramsey's preparations for the tournament were scheduled, for the most part, away from Wembley. His priority was to make England difficult to beat by establishing a settled defensive pattern and this was best achieved in games where his team was not charged with taking the game to visiting opposition. Banks, Cohen, Charlton, Moore and Wilson were able to develop as a unit, as the left-back Ray Wilson would later recall: 'The defence never changed for years: the goalkeeper Gordon and the back four – George, Big Jack, Bobby and me. All Alf did was tinker the system further upfield.'

Although there were some promising performances away from home during that first year and a half – 'We used to get goals on the break because we had the solidity to win the ball, then we had people who could use it,' according to Wilson – the Wembley crowd had seen little evidence of the England team being likely to fulfil Ramsey's rash promise. Indeed, in October 1965, when Austria won 3–2 to become only the third foreign side to defeat England at the stadium, press and public alike were ready to dismiss his team's chances of making home advantage count the following summer.

In the event it would be twenty games – and England would be world champions – before they lost again. Although his cool manner and unswerving sense of purpose were often mistaken for intransigence, Ramsey's team-building towards the World Cup at Wembley was as flexible as it was careful. The problem for England was that, while the settled defence was in place and included world-class talents in Banks, Wilson and Moore, further forward Ramsey was sure of the quality of only two players, Bobby Charlton and Jimmy Greaves.

Wembley's illusion of width promises wingers room to enjoy themselves. In fact, at seventy-five yards across, it is no bigger than average and before the World Cup excellent club players like Ian Callaghan, Terry Paine and John

Connelly (all of whom were included in the final squad for 1966, nonetheless) failed to convince at the highest international level. To Ramsey's credit, rather than persevere with his favoured system at the expense of the talent available to him, he modified the team pattern to exploit what his best players had to offer.

The England manager continued to experiment right up until the last game at Wembley before the World Cup began. Bobby Moore was England captain and, after a successful debut in a 1–0 home win over West Germany in February, Geoff Hurst had established a place in the squad. A third West Ham player won his first international cap against Yugoslavia in a 2–0 England victory little more than two months before the tournament's opening game. Martin Peters' tactical awareness and reading of the play around him were to prove crucial in the World Cup's later stages when Ramsey dispensed with conventional wingers in favour of the more adaptable and, as he saw it, reliable talents of Peters and Alan Ball. As Roger Hunt would remember: 'Alf did try with wingers for a while but once he tested 4-3-3 he always knew that was our strongest shape.'

The 1966 World Cup kicked off at Wembley on a Monday evening, 11 July. Whether England had enough great players to see them through to a final in less than three weeks' time no one, save perhaps Ramsey himself, seemed sure. What was certain, according to the right-back George Cohen, was the mood in the England camp: 'There was a great team spirit and it was well-balanced. It didn't matter what you did, whether you played cards or went for a walk, everyone joined in. Jack Charlton always said the spirit was greater than that of any club. Alf's changes were gradual and the camaraderie built up over time.'

That camaraderie, above and beyond the contribution of any individual player, was the quality Ramsey had identified as his team's greatest strength and the embodiment of his own ambitions. Sure enough, in the sapping extra half-hour against West Germany in the final, although people would point to Moore's calmness, Ball's running and Hurst's goals, team spirit would be paramount in taking England to the top of the football world.

The tournament's opening game, the host nation versus Uruguay in front of a 75,000 crowd, offered little promise of what was to come. The evening was embarrassing off the pitch and a crushing anti-climax on it. While the opening ceremony proceeded without a hitch, under the stands all was not well. 'There was enough electricity in the air of the England dressing-room on opening night to run a small power station,' according to Roger Hunt. Seven England players had arrived at Wembley without their official identity cards and the Hungarian referee was unwilling to let the game start until the team's trainer Harold Shepherdson had raced back to headquarters, at the Hendon Hall Hotel, to collect them.

Meanwhile the Queen welcomed the world to Wembley: 'I welcome all our visitors and feel sure we shall be seeing some fine football.' Her Majesty did not prove the best of judges: the ninety minutes which followed were a huge disappointment. Uruguay sat behind the ball for the duration and celebrated a 0–0 draw as if it had been a victory. Despite England creating fifteen chances the evening seemed to confirm English fans' worst fears, summed up in the *Daily Mail*: 'England played with endless heart as we knew they would. But this will never be quite enough.'

The next game at Wembley, on 13 July, was between the other two teams in England's qualifying group, France and Mexico, and an equally uninspiring affair. At least the crowd of 55,000 saw a goal by each team. Mexico then returned three days later to face England, who had put eight goals past them on their only previous visit to the stadium in 1961.

With another disappointing game meandering towards half-time England's frustration was blown away in an instant when Bobby Charlton, who had carried the ball towards a retreating defence from inside his own half, let fly from twenty-five yards. As the ball sped past the Mexican keeper Ignacio Calderon the Wembley crowd exploded as much in relief as in celebration. Though the press remained critical, even after Roger Hunt had tapped in a second goal, England had taken a giant step towards the quarter-finals.

Uruguay had beaten France 2–1 at White City before they returned to Wembley for a 0–0 draw with Mexico, for whom Antonio Carbajal, a veteran of the 1948 Olympics and four previous World Cups, took over from Calderon in goal. England then beat France 2–0 in front of a 92,500 crowd to win the qualifying group. Two goals from Roger Hunt ensured a routine, unspectacular victory. The game, though, was not without incident, at the centre of which stood a player whose technical shortcomings were often the stick used to beat the England team and their manager.

Certainly Nobby Stiles' qualities as a man-marker and defensive shield had not been employed thus far in games where the vision and passing ability he lacked had been identified as the virtues England most sorely missed. Worse, a crude, late tackle on France's influential Jacques Simon saw Stiles booked. Calls for him to be dropped from England's forthcoming quarter-final against Argentina came from the FA and some quarters of the press. For a couple of days the matter took on the quality of a moral crusade. Fortunately for Stiles, and the team, Ramsey remained loyal, as always, to his player: 'If Stiles goes, I go.' Neither of them did.

Instead it was the wingers who made way. Connelly, Paine and Callaghan had each played in one of the group games. Against Argentina Ball and Peters both started and Greaves, having cut his shin badly against France, was replaced by Hurst who, thirteen minutes from time, headed in Peters' cross to take England into the semi-finals. The game, though, will be remembered for scenes as unseemly as any in Wembley's history.

Of the eight teams left in the tournament Argentina were arguably the most technically gifted and, in Ermindo Onega and Luis Artime, had the most creative forward pairing. It was soon clear, however, that their manager Juan Carlos Lorenzo had sent his team out to kick England players as often as they kicked the ball as well as to harass, obstruct and provoke.

Herr Kreitlein, the German referee, was unprepared for the challenge to his authority and in the words of Brian Glanville, 'rushed hither and thither, inscribing names in his notebook with the zeal of a schoolboy collecting engine numbers'. Things came to a head nine minutes before half-time. Antonio Rattin, the Argentinian captain, protested too much over a colleague's booking and was sent off. Rattin, however, looming over the slight, balding figure of Herr Kreitlein, refused to budge.

A dozen confused minutes elapsed, with the game in danger of being abandoned, while the arguments raged. Policemen had come on to the pitch, such was the apparent threat to what order remained, before Ken Aston, in charge of the tournament referees, managed with a little Spanish and much gentle persuasion to prise Rattin from the proceedings and direct him towards the visitors' dressing-room. The game continued while the Argentinian captain trudged slowly away along the touch-line, looking back as if stunned by the injustice of it all and pausing, in a last defiant gesture, to wipe his hands on one of the little Union Jacks being used as corner flags.

Though Argentina's ten remaining players showed how talented a side they were in the fifty or so minutes which remained, the mood inside Wembley remained tense. After Hurst scored, the left-winger Oscar Mas was seen to cuff a small boy who had run on to the pitch to applaud his hero. At the final whistle the referee needed a police escort to protect him from the incensed Argentinian players and staff. Alf Ramsey, meanwhile, came out to prevent his players exchanging shirts with their opponents before, as Martin Peters would remember, 'they urinated in the corridor outside the England dressing-room and a chair came flying through the door; the Argentinians wanted a fight'.

In the aftermath Ramsey made his one mistake of the tournament, describing the Argentinian players as 'animals', a turn of phrase – if not a sentiment – he would regret and apologise for later but not before it had intensified the ill-feeling between the two nations. With Brazil and Uruguay also on their way home nursing grievances about refereeing standards, the 1966 World Cup would leave South American football wary and resentful in its future dealings with Europe.

After the poor entertainment during the group games England's quarter-final, if nothing else, had given the crowd something to get worked up about. Although the national team had not as yet covered itself in glory, Ramsey's men could, at least, be cast as the good guys, models of self-control in the face of Argentinian villainy: 'Why are we waiting?' sang England fans during the unsavoury hiatus before exchanging insults with Rattin as he finally beat his slow retreat.

Three days later an even bigger crowd was treated to a very different kind of spectacle. To the excitement of a place in the semi-final would be added the delight of watching the most open and attractive match of the summer. England versus Portugal was a contest still fondly remembered by all who witnessed and took part in it. After the cynicism and brutality of the Saturday afternoon the Tuesday evening brought 'a game which exceeded all possible expectations', according to Portugal's star of the tournament Eusebio. Martin Peters, too, would later remember the game both for the spirit in which it was contested and for the hero who emerged that night: 'I committed the first foul and that was for a push just before half-time. Nobby Stiles won that match for us because he marked their star player, Eusebio, out of the match.'

The Portuguese did not commit a foul until nearly an hour had passed, by which time England led by Bobby Charlton's first-half goal although, as Eusebio recalled, 'the crowd continued to suffer because the one-goal lead was in no way reassuring'. Relief was not long coming. Charlton cracked home a second, a shot on the run from the edge of the box, struck so sweetly that several Portuguese players shook his hand in congratulation as the teams made their way back to the centre circle.

Minutes later Eusebio dispatched a penalty after Jack Charlton had handled on the line and England supporters were back on the rack. But a last-gasp save by Gordon Banks, seconds from time, prevented the game needing an extra half-hour. Wembley rejoiced. England were in the final and had won through with a performance, at last, of which to be proud.

While the England players celebrated in the dressing-room, the manager was moved to remark: 'Gentlemen, I don't often talk about individuals but I think you will agree that Nobby has today turned in a very great professional performance.' The crowd stayed on meanwhile, as Eusebio would remember, and 'made a special call for the Portuguese team just as if, instead of having been beaten, we had been the winners'.

Portugal made do with third place, secured the following Thursday with a 2–1 victory over Russia in a match so dismally lethargic that many of the 70,000 spectators had headed for home by the time Jose Torres netted the late winner. England, meanwhile, prepared to meet West Germany on Saturday afternoon in the World Cup Final. These were anxious days for several members of the team. Bobby Moore went down with tonsillitis the morning after the semi-final; Roger Hunt and Geoff Hurst sweated, too, as they waited and wondered.

Though the team had settled, unchanged for the two previous games, Jimmy Greaves had recovered from the injury sustained against France and many assumed room would be found for him in Ramsey's plans for the final. Hunt was aware of the mood: 'I had a lot of criticism in the press. To the writers I was only a worker. They wanted a genius. They wanted Greaves.' Hurst did his best not to think about anything at all: 'I used to go to the shops in Hendon to buy toothpaste or shampoo; my room ended up looking like a salesman's sample bag, full of stuff I didn't want and would never use. But it used up time.' Ramsey, characteristically, stuck by the players who had brought success within reach and left an inconsolable Greaves out of the side to face Germany: Banks, Cohen, Wilson, Stiles, Charlton J, Moore, Ball, Hurst, Hunt, Charlton R and Peters would compose the most celebrated line-up in the history of English football.

The twenty days of England's World Cup summer seemed to unfold according to their own dream-like logic, allowing the nation to set aside the responsibilities and frustrations of ordinary life. On 11 July England had made their start so prosaically it was hard to believe that in less than three weeks Martin Peters and the rest would be waking on a dull Saturday morning with a whole nation willing them towards what had so recently seemed an improbable conclusion. 'It was real Boys' Own stuff,' said Peters. 'Travelling on the coach to Wembley was a fantastic sight. Everyone had flags. Just getting through the crowd up Wembley Way was a struggle.'

Inside the stadium, which had developed a reputation for a staid response from its home crowd to international football, anxiety, anticipation and excitement were at a pitch intense enough to astonish Hugh McIlvanney writing in the *Observer*: 'Wembley was charged with an atmosphere it had never known before. Long before the teams appeared the great crowd was chanting and singing.' Those fans were in for an afternoon as dramatic, emotional and exhausting as any among them had ever witnessed.

The game itself has become England's favourite sporting memory, as familiar, inspiring and spectacular as the greatest myths. It really happened, though. England won 4–2 after extra-time: a 93,000 crowd at Wembley and 600 million watching on television or listening to the radio around the world cheered, gasped, wept, leapt and stood or sat slack-jawed in amazement as a marvel of a football match took place on the afternoon of 30 July 1966.

Helmut Haller gave Germany the lead; Bobby Moore's quick free-kick was headed in by Hurst to equalise. Twelve minutes from time Peters swept England into what seemed a deserved and match-winning lead, only for the Germans to level in injury-time. This much was ordinary, if exciting enough. The first ninety minutes had passed.

Before the extra period the two teams rest on the Wembley pitch below the Royal Box. The Germans sit or lie, receiving massage, feeling the match may now be about to tip their way. England, meanwhile, stand huddled, Stiles insisting 'we can do this lot', Ramsey telling tired players to 'go out and win it again'. The crowd, struck dumb by Weber's late equaliser, begins to find its voice again before the daunting half-hour which remains.

Extra-time is extraordinary: heart-stopping, operatic, ablaze. Stiles prods the ball down the right wing, Ball outpaces Schnellinger (despite thinking at the time 'I'll never get that') and crosses into the penalty area where Hurst turns smartly and hits his shot against the underside of the bar. It bounces down and Roger Hunt turns away yelling, 'It's there', while defenders insist the ball has not crossed the line. Gotfried Dienst, the Swiss referee, instinctively signals a goal. In deference to German protests he consults his Russian linesman but Tofik Bakhramov is either unwilling or unable to contradict the man in charge. The ball, therefore, in accordance with the laws of dramatic structure and football history crosses the line without actually doing so. Cheers which have been stuck fast in English throats are released as the referee's finger points to the centre-circle. They break around the stadium, a deafening Mexican sound wave, as the crowd wakes from the endless minute-long spell. England lead 3–2.

Then, with seconds remaining, Bobby Moore plays a one-two with the tireless Alan Ball in his own penalty area, ignores Jack Charlton's considered advice – 'Whack it out!' – and moves between the two German forwards who are closing upon him. Looking up to judge his team-mate's run, Moore curls a long pass over the exhausted German defence into the path of an equally exhausted Geoff Hurst. England's centre-forward runs, half-staggering, goalwards before hitting the ball as hard as he can. Spectators, anticipating the final whistle, have already started to run on to the pitch as the shot whistles high past Tilkowski and into the net.

The game is over before it can restart. Hurst himself will be sure he has got his hat-trick only when he looks up later to check the stadium scoreboard. A roar echoes around Wembley: relief, delirium, pride and joy. In the press-box Hugh McIlvanney, a great Scot, is already finding words to describe England's finest hour: 'Then we were yelling and stamping and slapping one another. The sky had been overcast all afternoon but now the clouds split and the sun glared down on the stadium. Maybe those fellows were right when they said God was an Englishman . . . The scene that followed was unforgettable. Stiles and Cohen collapsed in a tearful embrace on the ground. Young Ball turned wild cartwheels and Bobby Charlton dropped to his knees, felled by emotion . . . Moore led his men up to the Royal Box to receive the gold Jules Rimet trophy from the Queen, and the slow, ecstatic lap of honour began. "Ee-aye-addio, we've won the cup," sang the crowd, as Moore threw it in a golden arc above his head and caught it again.'

It has been said that the single tactical decision most crucial to the outcome of the 1966 World Cup final was that which saw the German manager Helmut Schoen detail a young Franz Beckenbauer to track Bobby Charlton through the game. Indeed Charlton, whose powerful shooting and willingness to seize the initiative had done so much to bring England to Wembley on 30 July, had a relatively quiet game. Schoen, though, to achieve that end, stifled the talents of Germany's best means of overcoming England on the day.

The younger Charlton brother was already a renowned figure, at home and abroad, by the time the World Cup came to this country. In the same year he was voted the European Footballer of the Year. Born in Northumberland, he had been advised by his uncle, Jackie Milburn, then Newcastle United's centre-forward, not to start his career at St James' Park and he signed instead for Manchester United in 1953 as a fifteen-year-old.

Club and country would enjoy Charlton's services throughout the 1960s, not only his considerable talents as a player – two-footed, athletic, a devastating body swerve and a fierce shot – but also his remarkable dignity and sportsmanship. His contribution to England's success during the 1966 World Cup – his performance against Portugal in the semi-final was one of the most significant of the tournament – was the high point of a twelve-year international career.

He was back at Wembley two years later for a European Cup Final which would climax an extraordinary decade in the history of Manchester United and in the life of Charlton himself. Charlton was twenty at the time of the Munich Air Disaster in 1958 and one of a handful of survivors who, with Matt Busby, would go on to rebuild the club. He and United remain synonymous to this day.

Victory in 1963's FA Cup Final had been a start. League Championships would follow. For Matt Busby, though, the European Cup – pursuit of which had claimed the lives of so many United players – was the challenge towards which he now bent all his own and a new generation's ambitions. After the bravest of attempts in the 1966 competition, 1968 brought Busby and his players to the very threshold. On a warm Wednesday night, 29 May, United ran out at Wembley to face Benfica in the final of Europe's most prestigious club competition.

Thirty years on, football fans who do not support Manchester United stand up, so the song goes, to hate them. Things were very different back in 1968. The previous decade, since Munich, had told a story which had gripped the national imagination. Sixty thousand fans travelled from Manchester to be in the capacity crowd at Wembley. When United emerged from the players' tunnel the cheers of those die-hards were echoed by the best wishes of supporters all over the country: the game was a national event, unifying English football's partisans to a degree only the World Cup in 1966 had ever matched.

Benfica were giants, including Coluna, Augusto, Torres, Simoes and the impeccable Eusebio from the Portuguese team which had run England so close at the stadium less than two years previously. Charlton and Nobby Stiles, playing for United, had good reason to remember that game, having contributed the decisive performances on the night. Alongside them was George Best, brave and elusive, whose manner and, above all, smile had established him as a new kind of star for a modern generation. United, though, were without the injured Denis Law, a Wembley winner in the past with his club and with Scotland, whose place went to a youngster celebrating his 19th birthday that day, Brian Kidd.

Young though he was, Kidd, like his more experienced team-mates, was well aware of the significance of the game which lay ahead: 'It wasn't just that this was the final. I think everyone had this feeling that we had to win to finish the job for the Boss, after all this time. You didn't have to talk about it but, however old you were, you knew just what it meant to him. I don't think it really entered our heads that we were playing for ourselves.' Winning for the Boss, Matt Busby, meant winning for the club and in memory of those United had lost.

During a grudging, anxious first half it seemd as though the game would not sustain the weight of expectation. Cruz clumped Best, Stiles clumped Eusebio; Benfica hit the bar, David Sadler shot wide with only the keeper to beat. Prose became poetry ten minutes after half-time, however, when Charlton, with a rare header, put United in front. Sadler, who had provided the cross for the first goal, might have finished the game himself with a second, only for his shot to hit the goalkeeper's foot and loop over the bar. Rather than the final word, the moment was the cue for the real drama to begin. Benfica equalised ten minutes from time, Jaime Graca scoring from

Torres' knock-down, and would have won but for Eusebio's decision, just before the end of normal time, to blast rather than place his shot from the edge of the box when clean through. Alex Stepney, in goal, made a momentous save, diving to his left.

As the two teams prepared for extra-time, Matt Busby, though surely more aware than anyone in the stadium of what the next half-hour might mean, spoke calmly to his team, uncluttered concentration focused on the detail of what was now required: 'Try to keep possession. Play for width. Don't stand off, come and meet the ball and keep attacking.'

Before Benfica had time to catch their breath from the restart, a moment of rare grace tipped history United's way. Stepney's long clearance was touched on by Kidd to find George Best racing goalwards, swerving past the full-back Cruz and round the goalkeeper Henrique before sliding a shot into the net. Within ten minutes the game was won; an athletic, close-range header by Kidd and a second goal for Charlton secured the most famous of victories, enjoyed in tears by Charlton, Busby and the team's other Munich survivor Bill Foulkes, while the triumphant chants rang around Wembley. The final page had been turned, after ten long years, on one of football's most inspiring and emotive chapters: 'Champions of Europe! Champions of Europe!'

1963: HENRY COOPER

Cassius Clay he was in those days. He'd won an Olympic Gold medal; he'd been a pro for some time. The next fight after me he beat Sonny Liston for the world title. We'd seen film of him, he was a big guy but moving like a middleweight, and he had all the mouth, didn't he? He was a promoter's dream, really, with the poetry: *He gives me jive, I'll stop him in five.* And then he arrived in the ring wearing a crown. He was a showman but tongue-in-cheek with a twinkle in his eye. And I was on a percentage, too, so it was all right by me.

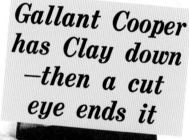

Cassius Clay

Henry Cooper

Most of my professional career I lived in Wembley, seven or eight minutes from the stadium. It was like my home ground. That night we had a 40,000 crowd and a marvellous atmosphere: I remember the chants – *En-e-ry!* Fair long walk from the dressing room, it was, out of the players' tunnel and we wore plastic bags over our boots in case they got wet on the way to the ring. Ali was never a dirty fighter and, at Wembley, he was still a bit amateurish: I messed him about inside, made his nose bleed in the first round. He kept appealing to the referee. I got a badly cut eye in the third round and my corner wasn't sure about continuing. I said: *I can catch him in the next round.* And while they were umming and aahing, the bell went. At the end of the fourth round, I caught him and he was on the deck but it was too late: the bell went when the count was at five.

I've talked to Angelo Dundee since and he admits he couldn't have got Ali right in the 50-odd seconds he had. Ali was out. So they had to make a commotion. He ripped the stitching in one of his gloves and called the referee over: they had to send back to the dressing-room for a second pair and it ended up a two and a half minute interval which was what they needed. Ali came out for the fifth, hit me on the eye again. It was pumping blood and the referee had to stop the fight.

INTERVIEW, 1998

Gallant Cooper has Clay down —then a cut eye ends it

1963: DENIS LAW

I don't know if it's the same now. There are so many different games at Wembley. But in those days to play there you either had to play in a Cup Final or play for your country in an international. You were just happy to have got there. You'd watched it on the telly down the years: this beautiful pitch, the bands, the man in the white coat: Cup Final day! It really was your dream, to play at Wembley.

Leicester were a good side. They'd been going for the Double, so they were favourites. We had a disaster of a season, we almost got relegated, but it's amazing what happens in Cup Finals. The underdog comes through. It just so happened we clicked. Everything went right. Everybody played well. You go 2-0 up and you're thinking: *This is our day!* There was a bit of a battle when they got a goal back but then David Herd got the third and that was that.

The game was a blur. I remember my goal: Crerand got the ball on the left, knocked it across the penalty area; the ball came behind me really and I just swivelled and whacked it and it went past Banksy's right hand. You know, then, it wasn't just you were playing in a Cup Final: to actually score a goal. I remember thinking after that: *I really don't care now if I never come back!*

INTERVIEW, 1998

1963: DAVE MACKAY

After the 9-3, to beat England with 10 men was the thing: we won 2-1. Beforehand we were terrified. We had to make sure 9-3 didn't happen again. We had a good team. Bill Brown was in goal. Eric Caldow got injured in a tackle with Bobby Smith and was carried off after 25 minutes. We all played well but Jim Baxter was brilliant, he scored the two goals.

Wee Willie Henderson was up against Ron Flowers, spun him around all afternoon. Twenty minutes from the end, Willie shouted out: *Don't give the ball to me, I've had enough. I can't do anymore.* I felt like strangling him because I was feeling the same way: we'd run our socks off. If they'd got a draw, I'd have committed suicide. And taken Willie with me. That was a great afternoon.

INTERVIEW, 1997

ON TOP THROUGHOUT THE GAME

Look! Above you is the famous new Wembley roof – 218,000 sq. feet of British Aluminium Rigidal* sheeting – forming part of the largest covered area in the world, and providing shelter for the whole Cup Final crowd for the first time in history.

Rust-free, long-lasting aluminium needs no painting or other surface treatment, and virtually no maintenance. More and more clubs are improving the spectators' lot with British Aluminium overhead – is yours?

Unilux transparent sheeting supplied by U.A.M. Plastics Ltd. is used for the remainder of.

ors – Bovis Ltd.

ctors –

Croydon

ers –

ow & Partners

BRITISH ALUMINIUM COMPANY LTD

Norfolk House   St. James's Square   London SW1

Published by WEMBLEY STADIUM LTD. (Copyright).   Printed by MCCORQUODALE, LONDON, S.E.
Concessionaires for Programme sales, BETTS, SON & MALTON, Wimbledon, S.W.19.

B.85

CALDOW INJURY MARS BIG MATCH

THE new-look Wembley Stadium had its first m... airing on Saturday when a capacity 100,000 cro... turned up for the England-Scotland international.

THE FOOTBALL ASSOCIATION CENTENARY YEAR

1863 – 1963

ENGLAND
v
SCOTLAND

SATURDAY, APRIL 6th 1963   KICK-OFF 3 pm

WEMBLEY
EMPIRE STADIUM

OFFICIAL PROGRAMME   ONE SHILLING

1965: KEN BROWN

In the '64 Cup Final we were disappointed about how we'd played and part of the thrill in 1965 was going back to Wembley to make up for that. It was against a German team, too. We always went to Germany for pre-season training and we'd had some great games against German sides. Although he never actually said so, I think Ron Greenwood was a great admirer of their approach to football. We always used to say at the time, if we played in the Bundesliga, we'd win it.

So playing against Munich 1860 was a bonus for us because we understood the way they played. We had a lot of confidence going into the game that we could do well against them. I remember JimmyArmfield always said about us: *Don't give them the lead, they'll never give you the ball back.* In '64 it hadn't been like that. The Preston game was a typical cup tie, I suppose, and we came out on top. The Cup Winners' Cup Final, though, was a joy to play in.

It was an evening game, too, wasn't it? The atmosphere was always different somehow: there was something about it that lifted you. Being at home – being at Wembley, so many West Ham fans in the crowd – was a big advantage. All we thought about beforehand was playing well. We played football for the love of it, really. The game wasn't all about money then. That night the satisfaction was that West Ham played well.

INTERVIEW, 1998

JULES RIMET CUP
WORLD CHAMPIONSHIP
ENGLAND 1966 JULY 11-30

WEMBLEY · EVERTON · SHEFFIELD · SUNDERLAND · ASTON VILLA · MANCHESTER · MIDDLESBROUGH · WHITE CITY

Nobby

Stiles

Never stops running

OFFICIAL SOUVENIR

2/6

1966: NOBBY STILES

When the season finished, 28 players came to Lilleshall from which a squad of 22 was going to be picked. Two weeks training: I'd played 65 games that season already; that training was the hardest I'd ever done. We were so fit it was unbelievable. Then we went on a tour of Scandinavia and finished up in Poland, where we won 1–0, and that was when we really started to believe in ourselves.

The first game we drew 0–0 with Uruguay. It was like Euro '96 and the Switzerland game. There was so much expectation and the team got canned afterwards. It was the same for us. Uruguay were a good side, actually. But they came to Wembley and just got everybody behind the ball and there was no score.

We were due to play Mexico at the weekend and, what Alf did the next day, he took us all down to Pinewood Studios. Now all the papers were saying England should be out working on the training pitch. But we went to Pinewood: Sean Connery was making a Bond movie, Yul Brynner, George Segal, Cliff Richard were there. They laid on a big open-air buffet and we all got pissed. It was the best thing Alf could have done. Instead of brooding we had a great day and it relaxed us.

So when it came to Mexico everybody was knocking us and they were difficult to break down too, but Bobby Charlton scored a fantastic goal and we all felt: *Now we've got it!* Again it was like Euro '96 and

FOOTBALL MONTHLY'S

WORLD CUP

SOUVENIR

ENGLAND 1966

FIVE SHILLINGS

WORLD C

Gro

GROUP 1

July 11 — England v Uru
July 13 — France v Mex
July 15 — Uruguay v Fra
July 16 — Mexico v Eng
July 19 — Mexico v Uru
July 20 — France v Eng

GROUP 2

July 12 — W. Germany
July 13 — Spain v Arge
July 15 — Switzerland
July 16 — Argentine v
July 19 — Argentine v
July 20 — Spain v W.

Saturday Matches Kick-off 3 pm
decided on League basis, viz. po
on July 2

Semi-Finals
July 25 (Everton)
Winner Match No. 1 v
Winner Match No. 3
July 26 (Wembley)
Winner Match No. 2 v
Winner Match No. 4

Gascoigne's goal against Scotland. That gives you the lift and the confidence.

The feeling of the people and the atmosphere at Wembley changed from game to game. It had been so tense against Uruguay but then, as the tournament went on, you could feel the crowd getting behind us: *Go on, lads.* I think it was Bobby's goal against Mexico – such a great goal – that changed it. For us, too: Alf had said we would win the World Cup; we didn't say anything but we started to believe we could.

Our next game against France we won comfortably, 2–0. I got booked for a challenge on Simon. He was a good player and they were starting to get back in the game; he was causing the trouble. Their goalie threw it out to him and I went in, meaning to take him and ball. Well, he let it run a moment and I caught him with a terrible tackle. It hadn't been intentional but it was the kind of tackle you'd be sent off for now. The press and TV crucified me – the only person who stuck up for me was Jimmy Hill – and a Fifa official reported me.

The following Saturday we were going to play Argentina in the quarter-final. We trained at Highbury on the Friday, working on set-pieces, and I was expecting to be out of the team. I saw Alf walking over to me and I thought I'd had it. All he said was: *Nobby, did you mean it?* knowing I would answer him honestly. I said: *No, Alf, I didn't.* He said: *You're playing tomorrow.* You can imagine how I felt. What I didn't know until years later was that he'd been called up to the boardroom at Highbury and the FA selectors had told him I shouldn't play in the quarter-final. Alf told them he'd resign if I didn't.

INTERVIEW, 1998

N ENGLAND 1966: JULY 11th-30th

atches, Dates, Grounds, Kick-off times

aguay, France, Mexico
embley, White City)

embley)
ley)
te City)
hbley)
mbley)
nbley)

GROUP 3 Brazil, Hungary, Portugal, Bulgaria (matches at Manchester United and Everton)

July 12 — Bulgaria v Brazil (Everton)
July 13 — Hungary v Portugal (Manchester United)
July 15 — Brazil v Hungary (Everton)
July 16 — Portugal v Bulgaria (Manchester United)
July 19 — Portugal v Brazil (Everton)
July 20 — Hungary v Bulgaria (Manchester United)

W. Germany, Spain,
d (Matches at Sheffield
, Aston Villa)

and (Sheffield Wed.)
ton Villa)
heffield Wednesday)
any (Aston Villa)
d (Sheffield Wed.)
Aston Villa)

GROUP 4 Chile, U.S.S.R., Italy, N. Korea (Matches at Middlesbrough and Sunderland)

July 12 — U.S.S.R. v N. Korea (Middlesbrough)
July 13 — Chile v Italy (Sunderland)
July 15 — N. Korea v Chile (Middlesbrough)
July 16 — Italy v U.S.S.R. (Sunderland)
July 19 — Italy v N. Korea (Middlesbrough)
July 20 — Chile v U.S.S.R. (Sunderland)

bley, July 16—7.30 pm). All others 7.30 pm except Wembley, July 19—Kick-off 4.30 pm. Groups will al average. Winners and runners-up in each group qualify for the quarter finals which will be played

embley (Winners Group 1 v Group 2 runners-up)
underland (Winners Group 2 v Group 1 runners-up)
verton (Winners Group 3 v Group 4 runners-up)
heffield Wednesday (Winners Group 4 v Group 3 nners-up)

y 28: Play-off for third and fourth places (Wembley)

FINAL WEMBLEY
July 30: Kick-off 3 pm

1966: NOBBY STILES

I took a lot of stick, even from the Wembley crowd, about the tackle on Simon. But on the morning of the Argentina game – typical of the British when you've got your back to the wall – outside the hotel people were calling out. *Go on, Nobby*. And when we got to Wembley, there were about 2,000 fans with a huge banner: *Nobby for Prime Minister*. That gave me such a lift.

Alf's instructions before the game were: *Keep your discipline. Don't get involved.* Which, to be fair, we did. Alf had gone to battle for me and I wasn't going to let him down. The game was a bit tasty and we knew it would be. The sad thing was that they were a great side, a great footballing side. They didn't have to do what they did. With cameras now, they'd never get away with it: nutting you after the ball's gone, spitting in your face. It was unbelievable.

Anyway they were rolling around after every tackle. One bloke, after we went down, grabbed my foot and pulled it into his chest. They were trying to get me sent off. Sad: if they'd have played it would have been a hard game. It was anyway, even when they were down to ten men: they were very well organised, lots of ability. But Alf had known what it would be like and he had us ready. Oh, we had a bit of a sing-song at the hotel that night.

INTERVIEW, 1998

1966: ANTONIO RATTIN

The 1966 World Cup was the last before blanket television coverage. If you look back, all World Cups before 1970, the host nation always did very well. Fifa wanted the local teams to do well for economic reasons because, back then, the main income was from ticket sales. Now, of course, there are other ways to make money from the World Cup.

It was a coincidence, wasn't it, that in the quarter-finals an Englishman refereed Germany v Uruguay and a German refereed our game? Uruguay had three players sent off and lost 4–0. At Wembley there were more than 70,000 fans cheering for England, which influenced the referee. I tried to point out to him several times that I was the captain. I even asked for an interpreter. I got sent off. I would say we were playing against 12 men.

The game had been held up for 20 minutes. I felt I was leaving my team at a disadvantage especially because, before substitutes were allowed, we weren't able to change things around tactically. I went off and sat on a little red carpet that was laid there. The Queen wasn't there but it turned out this carpet led up to her box. I watched the game for five or six minutes and then started walking towards the dressing-room. The crowd were throwing sweets at me. When I got to the corner flag, I twisted it round and insulted them. The crowd then started throwing beer cans, so I left quickly in case I got hurt.

We stayed in London for two days after that. The taxi-drivers wouldn't let me pay because they thought the sending-off had been unfair. In department stores people asked for my autograph and apologised for what had happened. This is why I admire the English so much. They are straight and understand right from wrong. I love London. If I could afford to, I would live there.

INTERVIEW, 1998

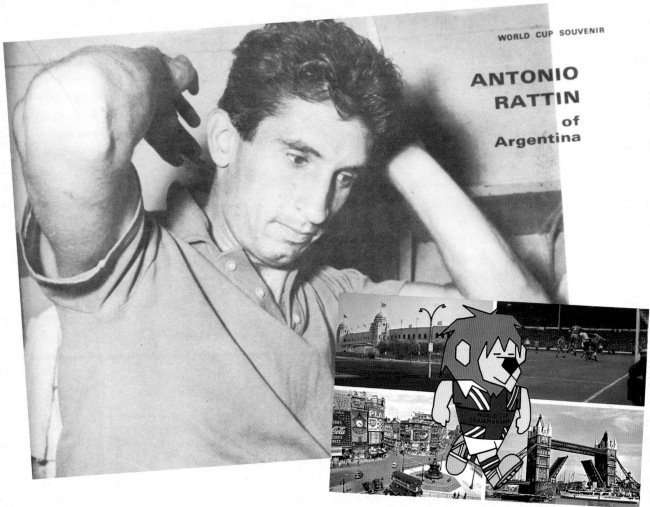

WORLD CUP SOUVENIR

ANTONIO
RATTIN
of
Argentina

1966: NOBBY STILES

At the team meeting before the semi-final we watched recordings of them playing. Alf got them from the TV people; no one else had them. We talked about who was dangerous: Torres? Coluna? Eusebio? And the consensus was that Eusebio was the one to watch. I'd only man-marked a player five or six times in my career: I marked Onega in the quarter-final and I'd marked Eusebio when United played Benfica in 1965. Alf asked all of us what we thought: *Should we man-mark Eusebio?* The answer was yes. And who should do it? *Nobby.*

The Portugal game was the best in the tournament. I think you have to say there were two great sides on the pitch. The passing was great by both teams; it was twenty minutes into the game before anyone committed a foul: Bobby Charlton, again, was superb on the night. Roger Hunt made run after run, making room for Geoff. Everybody in the England team knew what they had to do.

After the Argentina game we'd gone back to the Hendon Hall Hotel and, after about eight weeks locked away together, we were allowed to have some friends come over for the evening; no women, mind. On the Wednesday night, after the semi-final, we all gathered downstairs to celebrate. Alf stood there and said: *Gentlemen, you may have two drinks this evening. It will not be like Saturday when you were all rat-arsed. Just two drinks because in three days' time you are going to win the World Cup. Then I will make sure you are all permanently pissed.*

INTERVIEW, 1998

SALUTE THE MEN WHO MADE HISTORY

BANKS COHEN CHARLTON, J. MOORE WILSON STILES CHARLTON, R. PETERS BALL

WORLD CHAMPS!

WORLD CUP VERDICT

ENGLAND .. (1) 4
Hurst 19, 100, 120
Peters 78

W. GERMANY (1) 2
Haller 12
Weber 89

93,000
(After extra time)
Score at 90 min. 2—2

THE RATINGS

ENGLAND
BANKS (Leicester) ... 8
COHEN (Fulham) 7
J. CHARLTON (Leeds) 8
MOORE (W. Ham) ... 9*
WILSON (Everton) ... 7

STILES (Man. Utd.) ... 8
R. CHARLTON (Man. Utd.) 7
PETERS (W. Ham.) ... 7

BALL (Blackpool) ... 7
HUNT (Liverpool) ... 7
HURST (W. Ham.) ... 7

WEST GERMANY
TILKOWSKI (Dortmund) 7

HOTTGES (Bremen) .. 7
SCHULZ (Hamburg) .. 7
WEBER (Cologne) ... 7
SCHNELLINGER (Milan) 7

BECKENBAUER (Bayern) 8*
HALLER (Bologna) ... 7
OVERATH (Cologne) ... 7

HELD (Dortmund) ... 7
SEELER (Hamburg) ... 7
EMMERICH (Dortmund) 7

Ref: G. Dienst (Swit.) 6
★

MATCH FACTS

Goal attempts: England 47, Germany 38.
Goal attempts from outside penalty area: England 33, Germany 24.
Goal attempts from inside penalty area: England 14, Germany 14.
Shots on target: England 16, Germany 12.
Shots blocked: England 10, Germany 13.
Shots off-target: England 21, Germany 13.
Fouls: England 19, Germany 12.
Handling: England 2, Germany 12.
Offside: England 6, Germany 12.

England		Ger.
v. Uruguay	......	0-0
v. Mexico	......	2-0
v. France	......	2-0
v. Argentina	...	2-0
v. Portugal	......	2-1

WEST GERMANY
v. Switzerland 5-0
v. Argentina 0-0
v. Spain 2-1
v. Uruguay 4-0
v. Russia 2-1

Hurst hits first Final hat-trick

MAURICE SMITH REPORTS FROM WEMBLEY

THEY'VE WON! They've made it! After extra time—after their two finest hours.

So I owe Jimmy Greaves two bob. For England's bunch of no-hopers, the side I and thousands of others were saying a month ago didn't stand a chance, are now world champions.

Champions not only for ability, but for sheer guts and fighting spirit.

For the team took it all on the chin and still came back smiling.

And it was as good as over when three-goal Geoff Hurst beat the black-shirted acrobat in the German goal, Hans Tilkowski, for the second time.

His shot hit the bar, bounced down and was scrambled away.

But while England appealed and Swiss referee Gottfried Dienst hesitated, the Russian linesman Bakhramov waved his flag.

It wasn't a red flag—he held an orange one. But for England it was the green flag for go. Hurst's third goal in the last seconds of extra time was almost a formality.

Hurst's hat-trick was the first-ever in a World Cup final.

● Hurst leaps to head . . . 1—1 for England

Goalkeeper Tilkowski was injured in this clash with Hurst (No. 10).

Lone-wolf Alf sees it come true

So Ramsey's "wingless wonders" finally proved themselves Ramsey's "rousers," the team all the world's footballers and all the bad luck genius of yesterday, just couldn't beat.

I will never believe Germany justly earned the equaliser that sent them into extra time with only 30 seconds to go.

Held, so often the German danger-man, brought the ball down with his arm to set it up for Weber to equalise.

I saw it clearly.

Banks had no chance. All any England player in the strange red garb could do was to hold up his hands in protest. But the referee wouldn't listen.

England, we all swore, had been robbed.

Bobby Moore, the captain idiots of "turf" as they awaited extra time.

Nobby Stiles, Roger Hunt, Martin Peters rubbed tired muscles.

Wilson staggered dazedly around after a kick on the head, receiving trainer's attention.

The Germans had to be patched up, too.

For these teams in that 90 minutes had flung everything at one another. Heavyweight champions, each sparring for an opening, and leaving themselves open to counter-punches as they did so.

We told ourselves that the 30 minutes of extra time would be Soccer at a crawl.

But once more how wrong we were. It was action-packed stuff with a thrill every minute and it was England forcing the pace. They came out for that final titanic clash like men who had run a marathon and were still capable of raising a sprint finish.

Battered

Tired, battered—but still intent on proving the Germans couldn't last with them.

"Truly, heroes all. England had, in fact, given Germany a goal start and still a beating.

Haller had got the first goal after only 13 minutes with Banks unsighted.

Peters, his colleague at West Ham, had forced England to bring it back from the end, only for Weber to snatch that dramatic German equaliser.

A test of nerves? This

was ordeal in the acid bath.

And still England came through like sterling silver.

There wasn't a man among them who failed. There wasn't a man who had anything but legs of lead and lungs stretched to bursting-point at the finish.

Yet before they did their lap of honour the players to pat team manager Alf Ramsey on the back as he came out on to the field in response to the crowd's call: "We want Alf. We want Alf."

For this, as they all knew, was just as much Ramsey's triumph as their own. The triumph of a man who never lost faith.

The vindication of a lone wolf who taught his men to believe in him and in themselves.

It was a team triumph. And also, it was a triumph of brothers, symbolised by the weary embracing of the two Charlton boys as the crowd roared their heroes home.

Supreme

But above all, this match that no one among this 93,000 crowd will ever forget had turned out to be yet another star-studded performance from the England captain Bobby Moore.

It was Moore's cool head that kept England steady in defence when the Germans crammed on the pressure.

It was Moore's able prompting and passing which set England repeatedly on the attack, especially on the wings when their efforts through the middle looked in danger of breaking down.

It was Moore who encouraged them and kept them going to their supreme effort.

Frankly, I wasn't happy about Ramsey's decision to leave out Greaves. But Ramsey was right again.

How can anyone criticise him the way Hurst, Ball and Peters played?

Little Ball, with his flam-

ing red head flitted all over the field, chased and tackled for every ball and never gave the Germans a chance to settle down.

Peters wasn't quite so prominent as I have seen him, but Hurst took over the real Greaves poaching in the real Greaves manner.

Not the most attractive of players to watch, this 25-year-old West Ham boy has the knack of losing himself for periods in a game.

Then, wow, he's bouncing back full of menace.

Magnificent

A special pat on the back for Nobby Stiles, the little man from Manchester who has been subjected to so much irritation and has felt the flail of criticism.

He had his trials and troubles here with an over-pedantic referee. But Nobby just took it and walked away.

Don't let's forget him in this hour of England triumph, for Stiles had to turn over a new leaf after the preliminary rounds and, by golly, how magnificently he did it.

Gates: The £200,000 receipts at Wembley yesterday were a record for any match.
Attendances totalled 1,458,043—a World Cup record.
Average for 32 games: 45,576.

The Queen 'thrilled'

● SIR STANLEY ROUS, President of F.I.F.A.: "The Queen enjoyed it tremendously, and was thrilled during the final part of extra time. She kept asking: 'How much longer to go?'"

● ALF RAMSEY: "It's been a great satisfaction to me. I had no fears after 90 minutes or during the game.

"It was not generally appreciated the English players were

good players and they were underestimated. I said that it would take a great side to beat us because we are a great side."

● NICOLO CAROSIO, Italian TV commentator: "England's great victory was a triumph of skill, endurance and strength. The way they gritted their teeth after that shock German equaliser was fantastic. Without doubt the best team in the competition won the trophy."

● Haller (No. 8) has just scored the first goal of the Final. Emmerich

THE BIG FIGHT—BRIAN LONDON'S STORY IS ON PAGE 13

1966: NOBBY STILES

Walking out that day, representing our country in the World Cup Final: we felt so proud. Lining up for the national anthem, you got that feeling down your neck. I love that moment; you see athletes experience it at the Olympics. We couldn't wait to get playing. It was a funny thing, we had five world-class players in our squad: Banksy, Mooro, Bobby, Jimmy Greaves and the fifth was Ray Wilson. The first German goal was the only mistake I ever saw Ray make but, in a way, that settled us down, got us on with the job.

At the end of normal time, if you look at the film, you see all the Germans laid out, getting a rub. The only England player sitting down was Bobby Moore, who just sat with his knees bent up. Alf came over and said: *Look at them, they've gone*. The thing was, towards the end, we'd just been hitting the ball out anywhere into the stands.

Alf said: *For the last ten minutes you were playing not to lose*. Even though they'd equalised – they should have had the advantage – he told us to keep playing whatever happened: *Now go out and win*.

The other thing, then, I'll always remember was that Jimmy Greaves came over to me. Jimmy had been injured against France, a bad cut, and Geoff had come in and scored against Argentina. A lot of people thought Roger Hunt would be left out, although none of us did, but Jimmy hadn't got back in the team. I know how hurt he was – he still is – but he put his arm round my shoulder just before extra-time and said: *Keep 'em going, Nobby*. The third goal: that was the longest pass I ever played in my life. I had the ball and I heard this squeaky voice: *Nobby!* Alan Ball, best player on the park: I played it over Schnellinger's head and he was away. Crossed it in, Geoff hit it and, when I saw Rogert Hunt wheel away, I knew it was in. Strikers always follow the ball in, don't they, even when they can't get to it?

When I weighed myself after the game I was 10st 4lb, the lightest I'd ever been. In the second half of extra-time I got played in towards the byline and, as I turned to cross it, I just felt everything go: *whoosh!* Everything drained away. The ball bobbled off my foot and I heard the crowd groan. I just stood there. I never felt anything like it before or since. It just felt like I had nothing left. Bally came running past me: *Move, you bastard, move!* And I did. slowly, like it was all happening in slow motion.

The one who hadn't panicked at the end of normal time was Bobby Moore. He saw everything, Mooro, never shouted but he was always talking to you. And right at the end he brought the ball down on his chest, a little shimmy, and that long pass for Geoff. Afterwards I asked Alf about the fourth goal. This was how meticulous he was: he said he hadn't really seen it. He'd been watching Overath and was very impressed that, after 120 minutes, he was gaining on Geoff all the time.

INTERVIEW, 1998

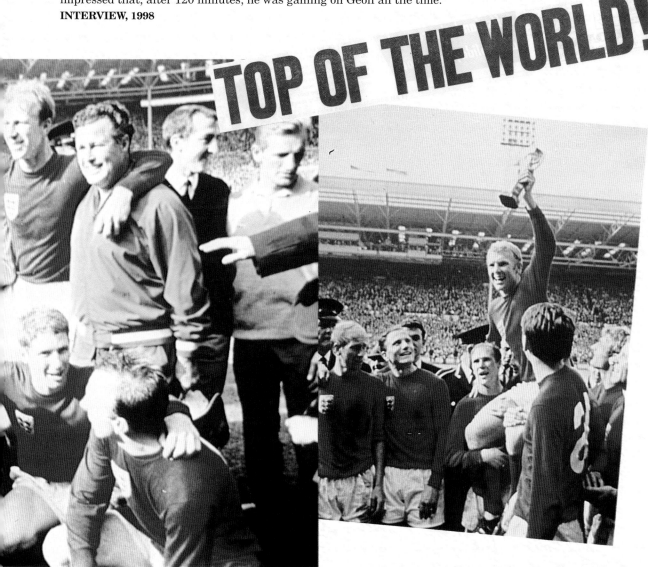

TOP OF THE WORLD!

BUSBY: I'm so proud

1968: SIR BOBBY CHARLTON

Benfica were really afraid. We had a psychological edge over them as any match they had against us in the past was a real struggle for them. England had beaten most of them at Wembley in 1966 and Manchester United had beaten them on their own ground, so they were up against it from the start.

I scored the first goal and I have to admit that there was a lot of luck involved. I made a run into the box and hoped to take a defender with me but the cross came over from Dave Sadler and I got a head on it, which was unusual for me. We were comfortable but from nowhere they scored and Alex Stepney had to make a couple of great saves to keep us in the game, one from Eusebio, and force it into extra-time.

Then the famous George Best goal virtually won it for us. In a one against one with the keeper, he was the best I have ever known and, once that went in, there was no way back for Benfica. They didn't have the stamina for it. Brian Kidd got another one for us and I got a second, which was when the emotion started to come through.

So many things had happened to Manchester United over the years with the accident and everything, so we just had to win that European Cup. With Matt Busby still there as manager, it had to be won and I felt sensational when we pulled it off. I was standing on that Wembley pitch feeling absolutely knackered but I thought, *Well, life is great*. I had never really thought about everything it meant in the build-up to the game. All I was bothered about was winning. But seeing the old man at the end and the tears in his eyes, it was wonderful. A great night for the people of Manchester and Manchester United.

SKY TV INTERVIEW, 1997

Kings of Europe

Lav
goa
Bus

By BRIAN JAMES : Manchester Utd. 4, Benfica 1

After extra time. Score at 90 mins. : 1—1.

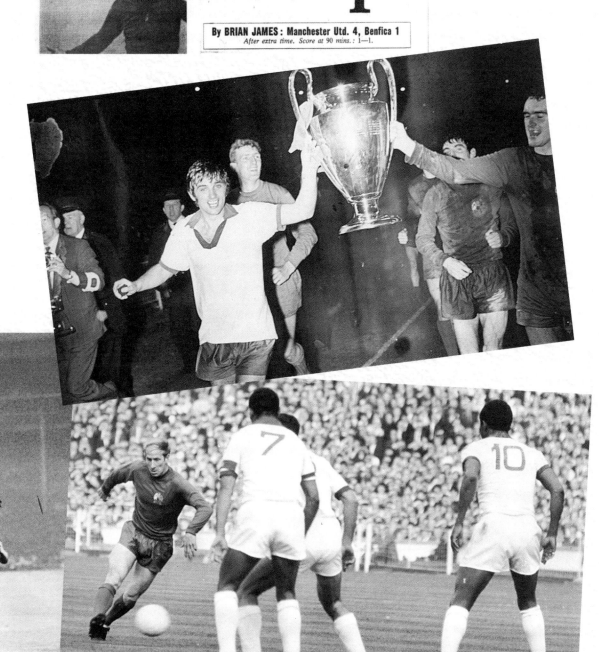

Losers Make Their Own Arrangements

1965-75

In 1961, the year Spurs did the Double, an intelligent and aggressive campaign by the Professional Footballer's Association brought the long overdue abolition of the maximum wage. The Fulham and England captain Johnny Haynes became the first English footballer to earn £100 a week. Two years later George Eastham took his case against his former employers Newcastle United to the High Court to overturn the archaic regulation by which clubs retained a player's registration, restricting his right to move elsewhere in search of better pay or conditions even at the end of a contract.

These two significant developments behind the football scenes meant that whatever rewards lay on the increasingly promising horizons of the English game would be enjoyed, for the first time, by the players themselves and not just the clubs for which they played. They were among a series of changes, from inside the game and without, which would sweep into football's every corner in the years which followed. For better or worse, by the time Arsenal had emulated their North London neighbours and won the League and Cup in 1971 – to the accompaniment at Wembley of a song called *Good Old Arsenal*, its lyrics composed by Jimmy Hill who had led the PFA's campaign ten years earlier – football was obviously and profoundly different as a sport, an industry and a spectacle.

The increasing – and increasingly unpredictable – cost of running a professional football club in the early 1960s coincided with a continuing drop in gate receipts, as alternative Saturday afternoon distractions saw attendances drift downward from their unsustainable post-war high. The pressure to succeed came now from the bank manager as well as from the terraces. A new culture, driven by apparent economic necessity, emerged: avoidance of defeat was becoming an end in itself. The fear of failure – and, with it, a more or less cynical pragmatism – soon threatened to dominate the English game.

One team above all defined the new mood. As recently as 1962 Leeds United had been struggling at the foot of the Second Division. The management of Don Revie, who had made his mark at Wembley in the 1950s as a player, focused on resilient defensive organisation, the combative midfield pairing of Billy Bremner and Bobby Collins and a steadfast unwillingness to take risks. It worked. Leeds were promoted in 1964 and lost out to Manchester United only on goal average in the race for the 1965 League title.

Leeds reached Wembley for the first time in the same 1964–65 season to face Liverpool who, under a similarly forceful, if more charismatic, manager Bill Shankly, had risen themselves in recent years from Second Division mediocrity to win the Championship in 1964. Shankly's team, like the boss himself, could be inspired and expansive on their day, but they too made avoiding defeat the key to their approach.

The 1965 Cup Final was predictably dour and sterile. It was long, too: not until three minutes into extra-time did Roger Hunt reward Liverpool's greater share of possession. At last Leeds were forced from their defensive shell and equalised through Billy Bremner. Ten minutes later, though, Ian St John's flying header won the match for Liverpool. Gerry Byrne, Liverpool's left-back who had played for 117 minutes with a broken collar-bone, took the honours, as Bill Shankly stressed afterwards: 'All the lads should give their medals to Gerry; he deserves the lot.'

The 1965 Final was the first of many to reflect football's new mood. In 1967 the first all-London Final had an almost parochial feel out of keeping with Wembley's usual sense of national occasion on Cup Final day, few outside the capital taking much interest in the match. Spurs won 2–1 against a Chelsea side who seemed distracted by wrangles over bonuses and ticket allocations before and after a dull game.

The following season, as Brian Glanville reflected in the *Sunday Times*, 'it was not the Final we had hoped for . . . tempers were bad and much of the football was worse'. Only a Jeff Astle goal separated the winners West Brom from their opponents Everton after extra-time. In 1969 a single goal – from Neil Young of Manchester City – was once more enough to win the Cup. The game's best player, Allan Clarke, finished on the losing side and Leicester were relegated from the First Division at the end of a season full of rows behind the scenes at Filbert Street. Manchester City, in the halcyon era of Bell, Lee and Summerbee, disappointed on the day, winning, according to Frank Butler in the *Manchester Evening News*, only because 'they were a more methodical side'.

The exception to the trend of tight, unspectacular Finals had proved the pragmatist's rule, ironically weeks before a utilitarian England side was to bring the national game its greatest reward. The 1966 fixture was a thriller but turned on the kind of defensive error most teams of the period bent all their efforts to avoid. After Sheffield Wednesday had surrendered a two-goal lead against Everton their centre-half Gerry Young gifted the winning goal: 'You go to trap it, like you would in hundreds of other games. Derek Temple, for some reason, had wandered in off the wing. I don't know what he was doing there. The ball went past me and he was through. He hit a great shot. I looked round for somebody to blame but there was nobody. It was my fault.'

The 1966 Cup Final made a hero of an Everton reserve, Mike Trebilcock, who came in for the injured Fred Pickering at late notice and scored two goals in five minutes either side of the hour to rescue the game. The equaliser was the signal for other Evertonians to make names for themselves, as Sam Leitch described in the *Sunday Mirror*: 'Trebilcock was thrown to the ground by two overjoyed Everton fans who had invaded the pitch. One London copper dashed on the field, dived at one fan, missed him. A second policeman then sprinted after the fan and crash-tackled him to allow six policemen to lift him struggling from the ground. All this in front of Princess Margaret and all soccer's VIPs.'

The invasion was no more malicious and considerably less dangerous than that which had marked Wembley's first Cup Final but it illustrated how life on the terraces, as elsewhere, had changed in the intervening decades. Most significantly, England's youth had discovered an autonomy freed from traditional models of behaviour established by ties to family, community and work. There was a new, brash and partisan mood in evidence, off the pitch as well as on it, an aggressive 'us' and 'them' attitude which reflected both teenage fans' intense identification with the teams they supported and those teams' success-at-all-costs culture.

Since the late 1950s violence attached to football – attacks on property, the police and opposing fans – had become increasingly common, another reason many traditional supporters were turning their backs on the game. The huge crowds, which included thousands of 'neutrals', and the sense of being part of a showpiece occasion largely militated against such problems at Wembley. Attacks on ticket touts had been reported in the 1920s and were understandable, if not justifiable. Scenes before the Liverpool versus Leeds final, however, were reported as being particularly 'bloodthirsty'. Clashes between opposing fans outside the stadium would become increasingly common during the 1970s.

For the most part, however, Wembley's atmosphere on match-day brought out the best in the modern fan inside the stadium. The 1965 Final, so forgettable as a game, was memorable for its first experience of the Kop. Liverpool's fans were a model every other team's supporters sought to emulate. Never mind the match; the banners, the serried ranks of scarves and the chants and anthems and booming, bottomless roars which echoed round the arena were like nothing Wembley had seen or heard. The nation watched and listened to TV's live coverage that May and supporters have made putting on a show themselves part of every Cup Final since. This was not just a question of dressing up and acting the fool a bit, as many had been doing for decades. What the Kop was up to – and others soon would be – was mass, ritualised and awe-inspiring. The confrontation on the pitch found its match in a confrontation between the terraces at either end of Wembley: 'Ee-aye-addio, we're going to win the Cup.'

England versus Scotland fixtures had been enlivened for decades by raucously patriotic visiting fans, the sedate majority of the home crowd refusing to be stirred by the partisan din from the Scots. For the game on 15 April 1967, tens of thousands streamed south for what they considered would be the real World Cup Final. Nine months on from England's glorious summer of 1966 here was the opportunity for the Scots, at a stroke, to establish themselves as world champions by turning over an old enemy unbeaten in nineteen matches.

Bobby Charlton was well aware of how perfect a stage it was for a Scottish upset: 'It meant more for the Scots to beat the English than it did for the English to beat the Scots, especially the year after we won the World Cup. If anybody had said to me who, out of all the teams in the world, will come to Wembley and beat you, I would have said the Scots.' And so it was, thanks in large part to another characteristically arrogant performance from Jim Baxter.

England had injury problems before and during the match; Jack

Charlton scored one of England's two goals while upfield as a makeshift centre-forward. Scotland, though, were fearsome, with Baxter the general and Law, Bremner and Gemmell his willing, gifted lieutenants. A 3–2 win, with goals from Denis Law, Bobby Lennox and Jim McCalliog, was barest evidence of the manner of Scotland's victory. Alan Ball was the prime victim of the mocking, casual keep-ball orchestrated by Baxter in midfield.

Scots fans were in heaven as they watched their team taunt England, the world champions. Thousands of them streamed on to the pitch to celebrate at the final whistle, treating Wembley with the same disdain the players had shown their hosts. Many dug up bits of turf as souvenirs; the centre spot turned up in Glasgow early the following week. Baxter's apparent contempt for his English opponents had been the icing on the cake for the supporters, as he was well aware: 'It was fantastic for the fans because it's their pilgrimage. Every two years they put down their half-quids or their pounds or whatever it may be and they go down there and to get a victory is great for the players but it's terrific for the fans if you can rub salt into the wounds.'

England's success in the World Cup briefly reversed the downward trend in the numbers watching football, offering proof, if it were needed, that the well-being of the national team could have a profoundly beneficial effect on the health of the game at club level. Indeed the late 1960s and early 1970s would also see a significant increase in the number of people playing football.

Showpiece games at Wembley had been largely immune from the malaise of falling gates. Nonetheless supporters' rekindled enthusiasm for football in the wake of 1966 was felt at the stadium, too. Scotland's famous victory in 1967 had been witnessed by the capacity crowd traditional for the fixture. Games in the same year against Spain, Northern Ireland and the

USSR drew nearly full houses. Eighty-five thousand watched England lose to Scotland in a Schoolboy International in April; 75,000 saw Enfield and Skelmersdale draw 0–0 in the Amateur Cup Final (Enfield winning the replay 3–0 before 55,000 at Maine Road). Even the Oxford versus Cambridge Varsity match, now moved to midweek, attracted nearly 20,000.

Wembley's appeal, of course, was by no means restricted to football. A women's hockey international between England and Ireland in March 1967 drew 60,000 spectators. The year's rugby league final, despite the unfashionable pairing of Barrow and Featherstone Rovers, was watched by the Queen, the Duke of Edinburgh and nearly 80,000 fans. Speedway and Gaelic Games played to huge crowds, too, at one-off events, while Wembley's grandstand restaurant buzzed every Friday when greyhound racing's glitterati turned out for the evening card.

Unsurprisingly the Football League jumped at the opportunity to invest its new knock-out competition, the League Cup, with the prestige and potential gate receipts which came with a Wembley Final. Conceived as a means to increase income for smaller League clubs by giving them an extra chance to meet First Division clubs, the competition's final had previously been played on a home-and-away basis at the grounds of the two clubs involved. In 1967 the final came to Wembley for the first time and the promise of a place in European competition for the winners was a further incentive to the big clubs' involvement.

The 100,000 crowd on 4 March ensured the day would become a firm fixture on the Wembley calendar thereafter. The game itself, between Queens Park Rangers and West Bromwich Albion, did much to establish the competition's distinctive appeal. A Third Division club had never reached an FA Cup Final, far less won one, so QPR's success gave the League Cup's Wembley career an attention-grabbing start.

First Division West Brom, who would return to the stadium in 1968 to beat Everton in the FA Cup Final, raced into an early lead with two goals from Clive Clark, until recently a QPR player. The Third Division side, however, stuck at their task to give a young Rodney Marsh the opportunity to orchestrate one of the great upsets in the stadium's history. Roger Morgan pulled a goal back, Marsh himself, after cutting in from the wing past two defenders, struck a splendid equaliser and the centre-forward Mark Lazarus bundled in a late winner.

The gloss was taken off the victory and, perhaps, the competition's credibility when, as a Third Division side, QPR were denied the opportunity to compete in the following season's European Fairs Cup. The League Cup Final's place in the calendar, in March, when the League and FA Cup competitions are still building towards their climaxes, means it has never shaken off entirely its status as an added, if often memorable, distraction in the midst of a season whose traditional big events have long been part of the game's landscape.

The League Cup's slightly parochial feel, however, has its benefits for supporters, with far more tickets available to the competing clubs for its Wembley showpiece than for the FA Cup Final. Two years after QPR's unlikely debut at the stadium tens of thousands of fans made their way to Wembley from Wiltshire in the hope of watching another Third Division side pull off the impossible in the League Cup Final.

Whereas QPR's First Division opponents West Brom had been struggling for form, in 1969 Swindon Town faced Arsenal, whose consistency in the League would see them finish fourth behind the champions Liverpool six weeks later. Again, though, the Third Division side rose unexpectedly to a Wembley occasion in front of a capacity crowd. Ten minutes before half-time Swindon took the lead through Roger Smart. In goal Peter Downsborough then produced a brave performance for the best part of an hour to keep Arsenal at bay before his mistake four minutes from time allowed Bobby Gould to equalise.

Extra-time set free the day's hero. The Swindon winger Don Rogers had been largely peripheral to the action in normal time but he turned the last half-hour into a one-man show, first poking a corner over the line to put his side ahead and then, a thrilling flourish, charging half the length of the pitch to crash home a third. Although Arsenal's League position earned them the place in Europe again denied to the Wembley winners, Swindon had given their fans a day they would never forget. For the losers, too, it had been an occasion to remember, one which Bob Wilson, the Arsenal goalkeeper, felt was crucial in spurring them on to greater things: 'I truly believe that the rise of the Double side stemmed from that afternoon at Wembley. We came home to headlines about the "Shame of Arsenal" and a lot of us were determined it would never happen again.'

One of Arsenal's excuses after the 1969 League Cup Final – the effects of a flu virus was the other – was the appalling condition of Wembley's famous pitch – 'a cabbage patch', according to the Manchester City manager Joe Mercer before the FA Cup Final two months later. It was not a case of the old one wearing out. A new pitch had only just been laid, using turf from the Solway Firth in Cumberland. Poor drainage saw it deteriorate badly and the situation was exacerbated by the arrival of four-legged competitors in the summer of 1968. At the 1948 Olympics, despite heavy rainfall during the second week of the Games, the equestrian events had left little or no impression on the playing surface. In 1968, however, show-jumping returned to the stadium and, in two years, gave Wembley's pitch a fiercer pounding than it had received in four decades of football.

Since the War the Royal International Horse Show had been held at White City. A move was precipitated after 1967 by the building of the Wood Lane flyover. The re-routing of traffic during construction severed the arena from its stabling facilities and, for six days from 23 July, the fences went up at Wembley instead. The following summer, a particularly wet one, the show-jumpers left the pitch a churned-up morass. It had already been decided, because the stadium was too large a setting for the event, to move the Royal International show next door to the Empire Pool, where the Horse of the Year Show had been staged successfully since 1958, but the transfer came too late to avoid the criticism heaped on the stadium by the condition of the surface for the 1970 FA Cup Final.

Leeds United, the team of the year, and Chelsea arrived on 11 April – the season's fixtures having been rescheduled to aid England's preparation for that summer's World Cup in Mexico – to find a pitch that was half mudflat, half beach, the latter thanks to sand rolled into the surface's most heavily worn areas. The conditions had much to do with the game being surprisingly open, prompting the Chelsea manager Dave Sexton to describe the occasion as a 'great day in the English way of life'. Brian Glanville writing in the *Sunday Times*, observed that 'the thickly sanded pitch must have made the players feel like travellers lost in the Sahara'.

Leeds betrayed their uncompromising reputation for giving nothing away by twice allowing Chelsea back into a game that ought to have been beyond them. A Jack Charlton goal was equalised when the hapless Gary Sprake allowed Peter Houseman's speculative shot to squirm under his body. After Mick Jones had restored Leeds' advantage Ian Hutchinson got in front of his marker to nod Chelsea level a second time. Best efforts gave way to tired legs in extra-time and the 2–2 draw was the first unresolved FA Cup Final in Wembley history.

Leeds felt hard done by, according to Eddie Gray: 'I mean, we totally outplayed them. We were hitting crossbars and missing chances. When we looked at it after the game we couldn't believe we'd come off the park and it had been a draw.' Revie's team had another shock in store. In the replay, on a half-decent pitch at Old Trafford, Chelsea came from behind again, this time to win 2–1.

The Wembley surface struggled through three more fixtures, a 3–1 win for England over Northern Ireland in the team's last home game before the 1970 World Cup, a Challenge Cup Final in which Castleford squeezed past Wigan 7–2 in front of a capacity crowd, and the final of the FA Trophy, a new knock-out cup competition for football's semi-professional clubs, at which 28,000 fans watched Macclesfield beat Telford 2–0. Experts from the Sports Turf Research Institute were given £30,000 to restore the playing surface to its former glory. As Wembley's first pitch had been cut from a nearby golf course, it was fitting that the new one should have a similar provenance. The turf was grown at Ganton golf course in north Yorkshire; the pitch was in perfect shape, ready to take a long stud, by the following May.

Although Merseyside and Manchester clubs had hoarded most of the silverware and Don Revie's Leeds best typified the pragmatic, modern approach, Arsenal's winning of the League and Cup double in 1971 offered the most succinct definition of how football had changed in the ten years since Spurs had become the first side to pull off the feat in the twentieth century.

Arsenal's success stuck in the craw of most outside Highbury. Spurs' Double team had been starry, cavalier and creative. What business had this functional, hardworking team, assembled mainly from Arsenal's youth system by Bertie Mee and Don Howe, emulating Bill Nicholson's brilliant 1961 side? The criticism, though, from press and fans alike was about as constructive as bemoaning gravity. Football had changed. Arsenal, no less than their predecessors, had the qualities their place in time demanded of them.

In one important respect the rigours of the era make the achievement of Mee's team all the more remarkable. Spurs before them, Manchester United and Arsène Wenger's Arsenal team since, all enjoyed the luxury of coasting through the closing stages of their League campaigns, their Cup runs or both. In 1971 not only did the eventual Double winners catch Leeds to clinch the title by winning their final League game, at Tottenham of all places, five days before the Cup Final; Arsenal had also come back from 2–0 down against Stoke before winning the semi-final replay which took them to Wembley.

Only Liverpool, in 1986, were ever run so close for their Double.

Like their peers Arsenal made it their business to avoid defeat. What eventually set them apart, though, over the course of a punishingly long season, was an irresistible will to win, personified by the club captain Frank McLintock, who had been on the losing side in four previous appearances at Wembley, with Leicester in 1961 and 1963 and then with Arsenal in the League Cup Finals of 1968 and 1969. The Arsenal team he led out on 8 May 1971 was brave, resilient and superbly well-organised.

The game, against a Liverpool side rebuilding for a new decade they would soon dominate, was played in sunshine rather more brilliant than the football on show. Liverpool opened the scoring in extra-time when Steve Heighway surprised Bob Wilson with a shot which flew in off the near post. A pass into Liverpool's area by Eddie Kelly was turned into an equaliser when George Graham ran across Ray Clemence, perhaps getting the faintest of touches to the ball as he passed. Then, with minutes to go, the Islington-born Charlie George, a local hero if ever there was one, took John Radford's pass in his stride and struck the winner from twenty yards. As Kenneth Wolstenholme, commentating for the BBC, exclaimed: 'George has done it!', the scorer lay flat on his back, lank hair across the once-more perfect turf, while his team-mates descended upon him. Though the sports pages damned his and his team-mates' victory with faint praise George remains unconcerned to this day: 'Winners celebrate. Losers make their own arrangements.'

A year later Arsenal were back at Wembley to face Leeds. Having already fallen off the pace in defence of their League title, they surrendered the FA Cup to an Allan Clarke header eight minutes into the second half. The Final was a brutal affair on and off the pitch. There was fighting outside Wembley before the game and the Leeds team bus had its tyres slashed. Inside the arena barely a minute of play had passed before the first scything late tackle flew in. Four players were booked – an unprecedented state of affairs for a Cup Final – while Arsenal's Alan Ball, according to the *People*'s Mike Langley, was lucky not to be sent off: 'Referee David Smith didn't even book him. Perhaps by then his pencil was worn to a stub.'

After their hard-fought victory at Wembley Leeds were expected to complete the Double by taking the one point they needed from a game at Wolves on the Monday night to win the League. 'Double Up Tomorrow' read the *People*'s headline on Sunday, only for Leeds to lose 2–1 at Molineux and leave Derby County champions. Leeds' Cup Final win had been the first in the club's history. Jack Charlton, Billy Bremner, Johnny Giles and Norman Hunter had all been on the losing sides in 1965 against Liverpool and 1970 against Chelsea. Don Revie's team, however, had earned a reputation for falling at the final hurdle all too often and 1972, despite success in the Cup, ultimately proved a disappointment. It was less keenly felt, though, than that inflicted the following May when Sunderland pulled off one of the most celebrated of all Wembley's FA Cup Final surprises.

Leeds' 1973 side comprised eleven full internationals, representing a club which had been ensconced for half a decade in the top three of the First Division. High technical quality, matched with a sometimes brutal professional attitude, made them the era's most difficult team to beat. Alan Hoby in the *Sunday Express* could be forgiven the hyperbole in describing that season's Cup Final as 'the Sunderland miracle'.

Just after the half-hour a Billy Hughes corner dropped to the midfielder Ian Porterfield, who volleyed the ball past the Leeds keeper David Harvey. Thereafter the struggling Second Division side held fast. The centre-half Dave Watson mastered Allan Clarke and it fell to the goalkeeper Jim Montgomery to produce the moment for which the game is best remembered, an extraordinary double save – 'it defied every law of human anatomy,' according to Hoby – from Trevor Cherry's header and Peter Lorimer's follow-up in the second half. Sunderland, managed by Bob

Stokoe whose warmth and openness were in such stark contrast to his opposite number from Leeds, became the first side from outside the First Division to win the FA Cup in forty-two years.

Leeds, though, were not the only team to suffer disappointment tinged with ignominy at Wembley in 1973. The stadium saw the England team, too, complete a fall from grace which, ironically, helped to pave the way for Don Revie's brief and notorious reign as manager of the national team later in the decade.

Scotland's 3–2 win at Wembley in 1967 provided only the briefest of interruptions to the progress of the England team under the control of Sir Alf Ramsey, who was knighted earlier in the year. They finished third in the 1968 European Championship, a campaign best remembered for a 1–0 victory over Spain in the first leg of the quarter-final, played on a balmy May evening with 100,000 jammed into Wembley to celebrate the continuing success of the class of '66.

As holders, England did not have to qualify for the 1970 World Cup but friendlies at Wembley and elsewhere gave supporters every reason to be confident that the team going to Mexico could emulate that of 1966. The last six games at the stadium before England left saw five wins, including a 4–1 hammering of Scotland, and a draw. All, it seemed, was well in the world.

In fact, although England's quality would be recognised by the eventual winners Brazil among others, a quarter-final against West Germany was to prove their undoing, a 2–0 lead being squandered by poor goalkeeping and ill-timed substitutions. At the time it was a crushing disappointment. In retrospect the defeat marked the beginning of the end for the most successful England set-up of the modern era. Although the team embarked on another unbeaten run until the end of 1971, the following years would see Sir Alf's best, but increasingly hesitant, intentions lead England back down the path towards football hell.

On 29 April 1972 West Germany came to Wembley for the first time since the 1966 World Cup Final. If any of the 100,000 crowd imagined they were to see England avenge their elimination in Mexico, they were in for a shock. The Germans, with Franz Beckenbauer in commanding form in the libero role and Gunter Netzer running England's midfield ragged, dominated throughout to win 3–1. The defeat all but extinguished hopes of qualifying for that year's European Championship and proved to be Wembley's last sight of two heroes of 1966: Geoff Hurst was substituted towards the end of play; Gordon Banks was to have his international career finished by injuries sustained in a car crash later in the year.

Three weeks later a crowd of only 64,000 watched a dispirited England succumb to a Terry Neill goal for Northern Ireland and the following year saw bad turn into a great deal worse. By the autumn of 1973 the Charlton brothers had ended their international careers in a game at Wembley to mark Britain's entry into the Common Market – Bobby Moore's last game for his country would follow in November – while a stuttering qualifying campaign for the 1974 World Cup left them needing to beat Poland to secure a place in Germany the following summer.

Alan Ball had been sent off during a 2–0 defeat in Katowice the previous June and on 17 October only Martin Peters remained from the team that had so famously won the World Cup at the stadium. Buoyed, though, by the 7–0 defeat of Austria in Wembley's previous international and trusting Brian Clough's offhand assessment of the Polish goalkeeper as 'a clown', the 100,000 crowd had every reason to feel optimistic. Jan Tomaszewski, in fact, put on the performance of his career to keep England's strikers, Clarke, Chivers and Channon at bay. That many of his saves owed as much to luck as to judgement made his resistance all the more galling. Worse, twelve minutes into the second half Poland broke away to score when Norman Hunter was dispossessed on the halfway line and Lato's shot eluded the normally reliable Peter Shilton. Allan Clarke equalised from the penalty spot soon afterwards but the goalless half-hour which followed was as tormenting as any passage of play in the international team's history. A 1–1 draw meant World Cup elimination.

The hapless Hunter would bemoan England's luck afterwards ('I have never played in a more one-sided game in my life') but the following day's papers were in no mood for excuses. Nor, it transpired, were the blazered gentlemen of the FA's International Committee. Sir Alf was relieved of his duties in May 1974. His employers, it seemed, had been in accord with the headline writers the morning after the Poland game who succinctly described failure to qualify for the 1974 World Cup as 'The End of the World'.

All, though, was not lost for English football. As the fortunes of the national team fell, so those of England's club sides rose on the European stage. Leading a charge which included Derby, Nottingham Forest, Spurs, Arsenal, Newcastle, Leeds and Aston Villa were a Liverpool team who dominated the 1970s and much of the 1980s with an authority which emulated, then surpassed that imposed on the game by Arsenal in the 1930s.

The 1970s had opened with Wembley playing host to Ajax and the incomparable Johann Cruyff for the stadium's second European Cup Final. The Dutch masters were midway through a run of three consecutive victories in the competition and 90,000 spectators turned up on 2 June 1971 to see 'total football' in action for themselves. Panathanaikos, a Greek side managed by a Wembley hero of times past, Ferenc Puskas, were swept aside, losing 2–0. Most of the crowd that night would have been surprised to discover that an English team, Liverpool, stood ready to pick up the baton when Cruyff and company let it drop.

Bill Shankly had rebuilt Liverpool's successful side of the 1960s and in 1972–3 they had won the League title and the Uefa Cup. The following season brought them to Wembley and an FA Cup Final against Newcastle United, who were appearing at the stadium for the first time since a hat-trick of Milburn-inspired victories in the 1950s. Although much of the pre-match attention focused on the latest Geordie hero in a No. 9 shirt, Malcolm Macdonald, and his quotable plans for dismantling Liverpool's defence, the game itself resulted in an embarrassing 3–0 defeat for United.

For Newcastle (who, as the saying goes, were lucky to get nil), only two players impressed: Terry McDermott and Alan Kennedy. Both would line up in Liverpool's next Cup Final team. Meanwhile 1974's hero had been Kevin Keegan, bought for £50,000 from Scunthorpe in the wake of Liverpool's defeat at Wembley by Arsenal three years previously. Brian James described his achievement in the *Sunday Times*: 'Yesterday's man was Kevin Keegan. He scored two goals, and what more could we ask of a man in a final? We might hope that he would take those goals with a nerve that made nothing of the burden of the occasion. Keegan did. We might hope that he provide, too, touches of fantasy to liven the end of a game that had mostly been about the realities. Keegan did.'

Bill Shankly was characteristically ebullient, predicting that Liverpool would do the Double the following season. His belief in his team endeared him to his players even as his respect for the club's supporters endeared him to them: 'Shanks is the only boss in the English league whom the fans think more of than they do the players,' observed Keegan after the game. The general truth of the manager's predictions as to what Liverpool would go on to achieve was borne out, even if the Double lay some time in the future. The surprise was that the 1974 Cup Final turned out to be his last game in charge of the club.

Bill Shankly retired in July, leaving the pursuit of even greater glory in the hands of his undemonstrative, though no less purposeful, assistant Bob Paisley. The new man's first serious responsibility was the Charity Shield against the champions Leeds, played at Wembley for the first time on 10 August. The game finished 1–1, Liverpool winning the stadium's first-ever penalty shoot-out. The main incident, though, of a desultory afternoon was the sending-off of Billy Bremner and Kevin Keegan after the two had come spectacularly to blows.

There is no such thing as bad publicity, they say, and the punch-up at least ensured the occasion did not pass unnoticed. The following March Ted Croker, the secretary of the FA, wrote to Wembley's managing director James Harvie-Watt: 'Now that the unfortunate incident ... has receded into the background, the match itself was considered a great success and we would like to think it could become an annual event at Wembley.' And so it did, as often as not involving Liverpool and thus lending credibility to their fans' re-christening of the stadium as 'Anfield South'.

Liverpool were very much the present and the future. In 1975 the FA Cup Final was an opportunity to celebrate the past. Now playing for Second Division Fulham, Bobby Moore bade farewell to Wembley. But the perfect sentimental finale for one of English football's great careers failed to keep to the script. Moore's old club, West Ham, beat his new one with two Alan Taylor goals in five minutes early in the second half.

Moore, though, was happy just to have had the opportunity to play a last game – one he could not have foreseen after leaving Upton Park – at the stadium he had graced with club and country for nearly fifteen years. Walking off after the match, his team-mate Alan Mullery, also making his last Wembley appearance, expressed disappointment at the result. Moore, apparently, took a longer view, looking back across an historic era at whose heart he had stood, a calm centre while so much changed around him: 'At our age we shouldn't be playing in a Cup Final. Enjoy it while you can.'

1965 IAN ST. JOHN

It was a very strong team. We'd no weak links. There was nobody who was brittle, nobody with a character defect. They'd always give their all. You wouldn't come off and say: *I don't think he was trying*.

When we got on the bus, I'll never forget, it was Shanks's *Desert Island Discs* on the radio and the Boss was: *Must listen to this, lads*. So on it comes. And he's standing in the middle of the bus in the passageway: *This is a good song*. They were *Danny Boy* and Scottish songs, and the lads are all laughing. He was all chuffed that we were listening to this. Then we got up near the ground and you start seeing the fans. Liverpool were one of the instigators of banners. Before that people had rattles, scarves and that was it.

When Bobby Collins injured Gerry [Byrne], we all thought Gerry had broken his leg at first. It turned out to be his collarbone. It was a different time for football – no substitutes – so Gerry played on and only he could have done it. They put a strapping on and off he went. In fact he set up the first goal. He was such a brave man. That probably won us the game.

After I scored the [winning] goal, there was nine minutes to go and it was a lifetime. We're thinking: *Let's just hang on*. I don't even remember going up the steps. I [just] remember us going round the ground with the Cup, and in the dressing-room afterwards.

THREE SIDES OF THE MERSEY, ROBSON BOOKS, 1993

1969 DON ROGERS

We got hammered for much of the game, to be honest – took a battering and came out winners. Swindon had never achieved anything, so you can imagine what it was like down here, the club looking forward to a final at Wembley. We were invited everywhere. And that season there was a great team spirit; everybody went together. I've always said we didn't need a manager. I was getting all the headlines but none of the lads were jealous of that, even though it was unfair to the rest of the team. We were a family. We'd had a great year and we were an experienced side. We really thought we had a chance at Wembley, even though none of us had played there.

I always think supporters have the better time at Wembley in that they can take in the occasion. As players you're just concentrating on the game. The best feeling was coming out of the tunnel – we were wearing these funny skin-tight red tracksuits, made us look like ballerinas – and the noise hit you. I thought: *Crickey, me! What's this?* 100,000 people in one place can be quite frightening, you know. But once the whistle goes, you take no notice.

We knew they had a better team than us, that they'd win 19 times if we played them 20. We had one chance. We were fit as fiddles, knew we'd last 90 or 120 minutes, so a heavy pitch suited us. As I remember the game, it seemed like we'd have an attack and then, for the next three or four minutes, they'd be down our end banging in shots and crosses. We defended really well and got more and more confident as the game went on. Roger Smart scored that fluky goal and Bobby Gould equalised with four or five minutes to go.

I've always said it was fate really. If they hadn't equalised, I wouldn't have scored my two goals in extra-time. I was pleased with my first one but the second, that long run, people like that kind of goal. They remember them. They still remember that one. I knew all along how I was going to beat the keeper. When it hit the net, the feeling was unbelievable. That was it. Finished. I turned around and all that came out of my mouth was: *Now we've won the Cup!*

INTERVIEW, 1997

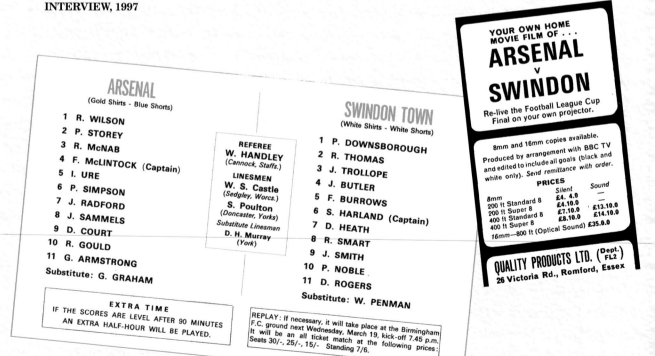

1971: BOB WILSON

We went to Wembley on the Friday and it was chucking it down. It was decided that we would wear long studs, but I was worried about damaging this famed Wembley turf. Bill Shankly was there and he just said to me as we walked off to head back to our hotel: *This will be a nightmare pitch for keepers, Bob, a real nightmare for you, son.*

We knew the routine at Wembley, but Shanks had a young side who may not have known the drill. What happens is that an FA official knocks on your door and then you are expected to go out and stand in the tunnel while you wait for the dignitaries to get into place out on the pitch. That wait can be the biggest nightmare of the day. So when they knocked this time, Bertie Mee just said: *I'm finishing my team-talk.* Then they banged again three minutes later and they were frantic. Frank McLintock said: *I've got a broken stud.* Liverpool must have been in that tunnel for about three or four minutes before us and I'd bet that Shankly was cursing under his breath. He was a great psychologist, but I think he knew he had been done on that occasion.

On the Heighway goal he cut inside and I adjusted my position thinking that he was going to cross it. But when I look back at it now, I can't believe how far out I was. I always remember falling back and hearing it ping off the bottom of the post. It didn't deflect the ball but it flew in and Frank McLintock gave me this awful look. It was a terrible moment and I instantly thought: *I've cost us the Double*.

Then a few minutes later we equalised with what was one of the weirdest goals you will ever see. George Graham's run actually fooled everyone and I still believe he got a touch on that ball as his response to the goal suggested that he knew he'd just touched it. When you look back now, it was one of the softest goals ever, but it brought us back into it.

When Charlie scored I thought to myself: *God, we're ahead and we've just got to hang on for eight minutes now.* I was a long way away from the celebrations but I remember Charlie lying on the turf and everyone jumping on top of him. You then believe that someone is looking down on you and wanting you to make history. The legs were on automatic pilot once Charlie scored and after I caught a corner in the last minute there was a great roar and I knew that it must have been their last chance. I took my time on the goal-kick and then the final whistle went.

INTERVIEW, 1997

1973: PETER SHILTON

Playing at Wembley for your club, winning is everything. With England, on the other hand, apart from 1966 and Euro '96, most Wembley games are friendlies or qualifiers. The games with most at stake tend to be in big tournaments elsewhere. I can only remember two matches that had that real intensity at Wembley: against Poland in 1973 and Hungary in 1981 in World Cup qualifiers.

The build-up to the Poland game was incredible. England had won the World Cup in '66, then gone out in the quarter-final in '70. We thought we had a decent side and were desperate to get through to the '74 tournament. Our group came down to the last game, needing to beat Poland to qualify. That was one of the best Polish sides ever: they went on to finish third in the World Cup.

There was quite a bit of apprehension in the dressing-room before the game. As England goalkeeper at Wembley, the opposition comes not wanting to give anything away and so you have to deal with just the occasional breakaway: the hardest games for keepers. You have to keep warm, concentrating, in the game. It looks like you're having an easy time but a goal like the one Poland scored that night can happen at any time.

INTERVIEW, 1998

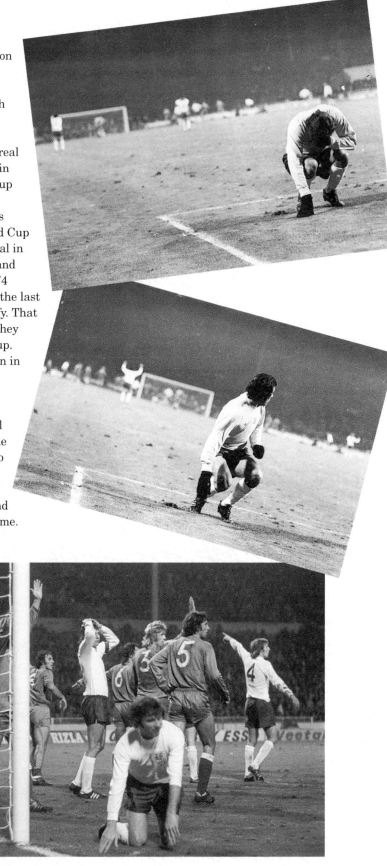

1973: BRIAN MOORE

My favourite FA Cup Final by a considerable distance would be the Sunderland v Leeds game of 1973. Working in television, there is nothing more you can wish for than a classic game between underdog and giant. Sunderland were in the old Second Division and not really looking like they were going anywhere. Surely they had no chance against Leeds who, under the management of Don Revie, were undisputedly the best side in the land: a very powerful outfit and seemingly unbeatable. The odds on them to beat Sunderland and win the Cup must have been shorter than in any Cup Final before or since.

The game was just remarkable. Ian Porterfield's goal opened things up but you could envisage nothing but a Leeds equaliser for the rest of the game. Wave after wave of attack from the side who

were quite clearly the better from a technical point of view, yet Sunderland made up for all that with incredible desire. Then came Montgomery's double save and, the moment it happened, you knew it was history in the making; a wonderful moment. I think the reality then struck home that the unthinkable was about to happen. Leeds were going to lose.

The scenes after the final whistle live long in the memory. Bob Stokoe throwing his arms around Montgomery and the dawning amongst the shell-shocked Leeds players that they were beaten. You really would struggle to produce a Cup Final to rival 1973. I have been to FA Cup Finals both before and since that Leeds v Sunderland game and you cannot beat it for drama and tension.

INTERVIEW, 1998

1974: TERRY McDERMOTT

Kevin Keegan, Tommy Smith, Emlyn Hughes: I was playing against my idols! You don't like to get beat in a Cup Final, but if you're going to lose to anyone, you'd choose that Liverpool team. There'd been a little bit of talk beforehand about me going to Liverpool; quotes from Shanks, saying he'd been interested in me when I was at Bury before I signed for Newcastle in '72. I swapped shirts with Phil Thompson after the game. I'm sure he said something like: *You'll be playing for us, shortly.* Three months later I was.

I honestly thought at the time we had a good chance of winning the Cup. We were playing quite well and we had a decent team: Jimmy Smith, Bobby Moncur, Terry Hibbitt, Malcolm Macdonald. In the end, though, me and Al Kennedy were probably our best players, the two least experienced: Alan had come up through the ranks, I'd joined from Bury. Maybe that meant we just went out thinking of it as another game of football. We didn't have the nerves. I remember we came in at half time, thinking: *There's no way we can lose this.* It was 0–0, we'd played so badly and we thought we couldn't play as badly second half. We were worse. It was frightening. I've got a tape of it at home. We weren't even at the races.

INTERVIEW, 1998

KEEGAN'S KNOCKOUT PUNCH!

Two minutes from the end of the 1974 F.A. Cup Final and Kevin Keegan *(extreme right)* is about to hammer home Liverpool's third goal. In the 57th minute Keegan had opened the scoring. A sad day for Newcastle United indeed.

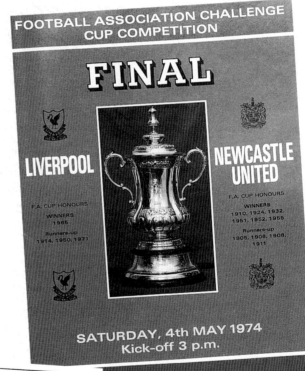

FOOTBALL ASSOCIATION CHALLENGE CUP COMPETITION

FINAL

LIVERPOOL

NEWCASTLE UNITED

F.A. CUP HONOURS
WINNERS
1965
Runners-up
1914, 1950, 1971

F.A. CUP HONOURS
WINNERS
1910, 1924, 1932,
1951, 1952, 1955
Runners-up
1905, 1906, 1908,
1911

SATURDAY, 4th MAY 1974
Kick-off 3 p.m.

WEMBLEY STADIUM

FIFTEEN PENCE

1975: ALAN MULLERY

It was a massive occasion for Fulham. They had been to a semi-final twice before but to get to a Cup Final meant so much to what was a relatively small club. We didn't have a great side but Bobby Moore pulled people along with him. A player like John Lacy turned into a half-decent centre-back playing alongside him every week and Les Strong was being talked of as a potential call-up for the England Under-23 side. Bobby had a great effect on people around him and in a team where there were no great stars, there was Bobby Moore and everyone in the world knew who he was.

The build-up to the Cup Final was hilarious. I had been through it all with Spurs in the 1967 FA Cup Final and you were locked away for days and didn't see anyone to make sure you were mentally right for the big day, extremely professional. But Fulham could not have been more different. The squad went for a walk down the High Road in Fulham on the Thursday before the Cup Final, meeting the locals who were all so excited about the fact that we had got there. Banners out in the streets and all that. It was just such a relaxed atmosphere.

I felt we were the better side on the day but, unfortunately, our keeper Peter Mellor made a couple of bloomers and that won it for West Ham. Sad for him, especially because he had played so well all the way up to the Final. Losing was a major disappointment for me but it was different for Bobby. I didn't enjoy the day at all but he had been there before, won a couple of trophies with West Ham and, obviously, the World Cup. But I had to win, there was no point in me being there unless I was a winner.

Despite the defeat our party after the game was the best I've been at. Better than the Spurs parties when we won at Wembley in Cup Finals and I seem to remember the West Ham players turning up to join us towards the end of the night. We were in the Savoy and their party wasn't too good, so they all piled into ours, but it was that sort of occasion.

For Bobby to have been playing West Ham must have been special. And it was fitting that his last game at Wembley was an FA Cup Final. Wembley is a stadium that has graced football and Bobby Moore graced Wembley. He was a world-class player made for that stage. I know he loved the place.

INTERVIEW, 1998

A Tribal Occasion

1976-89

When Scottish fans invaded the Wembley pitch after a 2–1 victory over the World Cup holders in 1967, Englishmen shook their heads and smiled indulgently. It was not the first time it had happened, after all. No real harm had been done, beyond the loss of a few hundred fistfuls of turf as souvenirs. London was used to a mad Scots weekend every other year. Why not let them have their fun?

Ten years later, when another 2–1 win for Scotland precipitated another pitch invasion, condescension made way for righteous indignation on the part of the hosts. Ostensibly the invaders were just in high spirits. As one fan explained to Bow Street magistrates a couple of days later: 'The turf was from the spot where Kenny Dalglish scored the winning goal. I was going to take it home and put it in a jar on my mantelpiece and just watch it grow and remember the match.'

The scenes at Wembley on 4 June, though, and generally over the weekend, were darker and scarier than anything seen before during the rowdy celebrations which had, for the Scots, long been half the fun of a win over the old enemy in London. In 1977 nearly 300 arrests were made around the capital and at the stadium. More would have been apprehended during the pitch invasion, according to a police spokesman, but 'the 2,000 officers on duty could not stem the tartan torrent'.

The stadium itself took a rare battering, most symbolically in the tearing down of the Wembley goals. Gates had been stormed by ticketless fans before the game and bottles were thrown during it on to the track around the pitch. The Sports Minister Denis Howell called for an inquiry into events surrounding what he described as 'a tribal occasion rather than a sporting fixture'. Ted Croker, secretary of the FA, insisted 'we dare not allow this sort of thing to happen again'.

Football-related violence had been a threatening cloud over the game since the early 1960s. The fact that the problem had reached Wembley, to mar one of football's oldest fixtures, meant another line had been crossed in the increasingly malevolent stand-off between football supporters and the forces of law and order. Magistrates had seen fit to label fans 'mindless' and 'animals' for years; some fans continued to try to live up to the descriptions. The damage done to the game in the coming years would threaten to be irreparable.

The Sports Minister had set up a working party in the mid-1970s to look into soccer hooliganism. One of its recommendations was the installation of fencing as a crowd control measure. After the Scotland game questions' were asked as to why Wembley had not put up a barrier between spectators and the pitch. The fact that it had never seemed necessary – and perhaps still was not, the exception proving the rule – was no longer acceptable as an argument. Anti-riot fencing was ordered for Wembley the Monday after the Scots' invasion and was in place by November. Little more than a decade later the FA Cup Final would bring together a city – and the football world – at Wembley to lament the dreadful harvest thus sown.

Putting up with things – bad views, bad weather, bad teams – has always been part of the football fans' lot. The majority of supporters still watching regularly and hoping for a decent game rather than the chance of trouble had, by the mid-1970s, come to accept violence, or the threat of it, as part of the contemporary football scene. Ignoring the problem seemed easier than confronting it.

The scenes of mayhem in and around Wembley in June 1977, therefore, seemed less cause for concern among England fans than the dreadful state of the national team. After Sir Alf Ramsey's sacking in May 1974 and a brief interregnum under the good-humoured stewardship of Joe Mercer, the Leeds manager Don Revie had been appointed England manager in July. 'I made the first move; they did not contact me,' he said. 'I fancied being England manager.' Revie's apparent eagerness offered little clue to the shabby circumstances in which his reign would end.

The new man was no stranger to Wembley, an FA Cup winner as a player with Manchester City in 1956 and as a manager with Leeds in 1972. Revie had achieved a remarkable level of consistency in more than ten years at Elland Road, the warmth of the spirit he fostered within the club in marked contrast to the cold, steely pragmatism of the sides he produced. After England's failure to qualify for the 1974 World Cup the country needed a winner in charge. Revie came to the job on the back of a twenty-nine-match unbeaten run at Leeds. England then won six and drew three of his first nine games as manager, the sequence including a 5–1 thumping of Scotland at Wembley in May 1975.

Within months, however, it was clear that all was not well. Revie seemed unable to establish a settled side – he would use fifty-two players in the twenty-nine England teams he picked – or to foster the club spirit and sense of solidarity that had been his trademark at Leeds. England soon fell into a pattern which some observers had recognised as a weakness in Revie's management at club level: the tendency to fall short on a big occasion. However hard to beat, however thoroughly prepared, however convincing and stylish in unpressured situations, Leeds (and now England) too often lost the games that mattered.

No one cared that Malcolm Macdonald broke records running in five goals at Wembley against Cyprus when points dropped against Portugal and

Czechoslovakia meant England failed to qualify for the 1976 European Championships, and defeat in Italy a year later all but ensured that the 1978 World Cup would go ahead without us. The defeat by the Scots at Wembley, a particular embarrassment in security terms, was just one of many Revie's England team suffered. The stadium was no longer a stronghold. A superb Dutch side and a very ordinary Welsh one also recorded wins at Wembley within a couple of months of each other during 1977.

The manager jumped before he was pushed. While still in the England job, Revie negotiated a lucrative contract to take charge of the United Arab Emirates team. Rather than confide in his players, his employers or dispirited English fans, he announced his decision in the *Daily Mail* on 12 July 1977. The same journalists who had damned the Scots fans little more than a month previously now turned their outrage on Revie. The press coverage – and, indeed, the feeling among supporters – was almost as unseemly as Revie's behaviour appeared to be.

Little more than ten years on, 1966 already seemed a lifetime ago. The bitterness and resentment directed towards Revie were deepened by a sense of that heritage having been betrayed. Football had changed so much and this man personified, for many, all the ways in which change had been so much for the worse. The FA would eventually sue for breach of contract. Revie won the case but not before Mr Justice Cantley had added his voice to the crowd's, describing the affair as 'a sensational, outrageous example of disloyalty, breach of duty, dishonesty and selfishness'.

Football's age of innocence was long past, as the story of Don Revie's England made plain. In 1975 the Amateur Cup Final made way for a new competition, the FA Vase. Money had been changing hands, undermining the idea and the fact of 'amateur' football since the fifties. The introduction of the FA Trophy and now the Vase recognised the changing times. No longer were the professional and amateur games separate and hermetic. Realistic modern attitudes and practices rid football of the last vestiges of the 'gentlemen versus players' dichotomy. Non-League, part-time football became the lower rungs of a ladder which led up to the full-time professional divisions of the Football League.

The FA Vase was a competition for those who still played for fun rather than reward; the big guns of the old amateur game now competed in the FA Trophy. Neither Wembley final enjoyed anything like the prestige or allure of the Amateur Cup, which had attracted 50,000-plus gates to the stadium well into the sixties. Crowds fell away: in 1975 the first Vase Final, in which Hoddesdon Town beat Epsom and Ewell 2–1, was watched by 9,500 while, in the Trophy match, 21,000 saw Matlock Town beat Scarborough 4–0.

The Amateur Cup Final had enjoyed the status of a national event. The new fixtures, while thrilling and auspicious occasions for the participants and their fans, were more like private parties, essentially parochial in their appeal. Later additions like knock-out cups in various sponsors' guises for the League's lower divisions and the play-off finals would move the process along until each level of football's pyramid structure had a day out at Wembley of its own to enjoy.

The FA Cup, of course, remained the competition which bound the game together at all levels, its Wembley showpiece a more or less impossible ambition for thousands of players at the start of every season. The late seventies, following Sunderland's defeat of Leeds in 1973, saw Wembley enjoy a sequence of Final victories for underdogs which underlined the Cup's appeal for football's dreamers.

In 1976 the Manchester United manager Tommy Docherty joked that his team's semi-final with Derby represented the contest Wembley deserved, the implication being that neither of the other semi-finalists would stand much chance in May's big game. The United winger Gordon

Hill rubbed it in after the finalists had been decided: 'Who are Southampton?'

The team from the South Coast had been beaten in the 1900 and 1902 FA Cup Finals and achieved little in the seventy-odd years since. Manchester United were a young and dynamic side, full of rising stars. Southampton, meanwhile, relied on old heads – Peter Osgood, Mick Channon, Peter Rodrigues – to keep a journeyman team on course. There were few who fancied the chances of aging legs keeping up with young opponents.

Lou Macari was perhaps the first to realise that the favourites might be in for a fall. He would later remember feeling anxious in the tunnel before the game: 'We had a reputation as an up-and-coming side but we were stood alongside the Southampton team and compared to us they looked like men.' Young United froze and less than two hours later, thanks to a single Bobby Stokes goal, another Second Division side had won the FA Cup.

United, though, returned to Wembley the following May, this time as underdogs themselves, to face a Liverpool team which had already won the Championship and, the following Wednesday, would be in Rome to play Borussia Mönchengladbach in the European Cup Final. Docherty's young team had the chance to make up for the previous season's disappointment and to deny their arch-rivals a unique place in history.

The game itself was less than satisfying, as Peter Corrigan reported in the *Observer*: 'Like the inhabitants of the control room of a rocket launching site, Cup Final crowds are all too familiar with that moment when, after the button has been pressed and the first flames flicker, there is that awful feeling that the thing is not going to take off.' Sparks, though, flew for five minutes in the second half, long enough for goals by Stuart Pearson and Jimmy Greenhoff either side of a Jimmy Case equaliser to win the match for United.

In 1979 another very ordinary Final was brought to life for five minutes, this time to illuminate a climax to the game which only the 1953 fixture had ever matched for drama. Manchester United were again involved. With eighty-six minutes gone Arsenal seemed to be heading for a routine 2–0 victory with goals set up for Brian Talbot and Frank Stapleton by one of the era's outstanding talents, the Irish midfielder Liam Brady.

Arsenal might already have been planning their celebrations when Gordon McQueen and Sammy McIlroy scored goals in the space of two minutes to equalise. Brady later recalled his feelings as the initiative was snatched by United: 'When they pulled level I was dreading extra-time. I was knackered and we already had our substitute on.'

Arsenal's greatest post-war player set about sparing himself another half-hour. With a minute to go Brady picked up the ball in his own half and advanced forty yards before stabbing a pass wide to Graham Rix. In an instant the cross from the left had eluded the goalkeeper Gary Bailey, and Alan Sunderland beat Arthur Albiston at the far post to bundle in the winner. For United, according to Sammy McIlroy, those five heart-stopping minutes at the game's conclusion were 'like winning the pools only to find you hadn't posted your coupon'. Bobby Charlton, watching from the stands, said: 'It shouldn't happen to a dog.'

Arsenal's last-gasp victory in 1979 was their only success in three consecutive Cup Final appearances. In 1978 and 1980 Brady and company were the giants killed. The first defeat was by a goal for Ipswich by Roger Osborne, after which the scorer later remembered having to be immediately substituted: 'The shock of scoring, the tiredness, the elation, people jumping up and down on me: I was a bit dazed, really. We had a sub and I thought we'd be better off if he came on.'

Two years later Arsenal were again toppled as West Ham became the third Second Division side in less than a decade to win the Cup, with their midfielder, Paul Allen, at seventeen years 265 days, the youngest-ever Wembley Cup finalist. Trevor Brooking scored a rare headed goal after thirteen minutes and for the remainder of the game Allen's marking of

Brady was effective enough to stifle any hope of an Arsenal fight-back. Only a crude foul by Willie Young, indeed, prevented the youngster adding a second goal just before full-time. It was the start of a disastrous week for Arsenal, who lost on penalties to Valencia in the European Cup Winners' Cup Final in Brussels four days later.

The season was Liam Brady's last in England before embarking on a successful career in Serie A and, without their talisman, Arsenal subsided into mediocrity. Across North London, however, Tottenham's star was rising. An exciting, attacking side reached Wembley to face Manchester City in the 1981 Cup Final, the hundredth in the history of the competition. Glenn Hoddle was to White Hart Lane what Brady had been to Highbury: gifted and inspirational. Alongside the England international were two Argentinians, Osvaldo Ardiles and Ricardo Villa: the latter would eventually leave an indelible mark on Wembley.

Manchester City, under a new manager John Bond, had rescued a season which had looked likely, until Christmas, to end in relegation. Workmanlike in comparison to Spurs, they took the lead just before the half-hour with a flying near-post header from Tommy Hutchison who then, ten minutes from time, deflected a Hoddle free-kick into his own net for the equaliser. It stayed level through extra-time and Wembley prepared to stage its first Cup Final replay.

After little more than an hour of the first game Spurs' manager Keith Burkinshaw had substituted Ricky Villa. The Argentinian made no attempt to conceal how keenly he felt the blow to his pride as he trudged off towards the dressing-room, apparently inconsolable. Burkinshaw told later how Villa, when reassured that he would be in the team for the replay, 'opened up like a flower . . . all beams and smiles'. Villa's inclusion come the Thursday night was to prove well justified.

The Tottenham midfielder opened the scoring with a tap-in after seven minutes. Three goals followed in the next hour: two for Manchester City, a twenty-yarder by Steve MacKenzie and a Kevin Reeves penalty, followed by a Garth Crooks equaliser for Spurs. Time remained for one of Wembley's greatest ever individual goals to secure a Tottenham win. Picking up a pass from Tony Galvin outside the Manchester City area, Villa was confronted by a line of defenders but started forward and simply kept going. He swayed right, then left, past three challenges, his broad frame carried delicately towards the six-yard box, before sliding the ball under the advancing goalkeeper Joe Corrigan. Villa would later describe the moment for himself: 'Then I introduce the ball in the goal.' After his disappointment the previous Saturday, it was a climax to gladden the heart not just of the night's hero but of anyone watching the game. Tommy Hutchison would later admit: 'Even when I watch it now, I don't say, "Oh, I hate him for scoring." If you like football, if you've been brought up on the game, anybody would hold their hands up and say that's fitting to win a Cup Final.'

The 1981 FA Cup Final served notice that all was still well with football's oldest competition, Wembley's oldest fixture. The stadium itself, however, after nearly sixty years of wear and tear on a structure little altered since its construction, was beginning to show its age. An increasingly busy event programme paid for Wembley's upkeep but could not foot the bill for thoroughgoing and expensive modernisation.

In the early 1920s Wembley's contract with football's governing body had been crucial in establishing the stadium's long-term prospects. Now, in the early 1980s, the FA, while aware of the need to overhaul the venue which staged the game's prestige fixtures, was again ready to commit to a future there.

A new contract, signed in 1982, renewed the agreement between the stadium and its most important tenant for a further twenty years. Familiar terms – a split of gate and television receipts with Wembley keeping car-park, ground-advertising, match programme and catering revenue – helped ensure that the cost of running repairs could be met. Then, three years later in 1985, a new consortium led by Brian Wolfson took control of the stadium company. Significant investment, it seemed, was at last going to be made available to upgrade Wembley's facilities for the modern era.

Ron Greenwood had taken over as England manager; relaxed, adventurous and thoroughly honourable, he promised an approach very different from that of his predecessor, Revie. However, despite Greenwood's efforts and those of young, world-class talents like Bryan Robson, the team continued to lack conviction and inspiration.

While the international team struggled, however, qualifying for the 1982 World Cup thanks finally to a 1–0 home win over Hungary, English club football, on the pitch at least, enjoyed something of a golden age with Liverpool, at home and in Europe, setting the highest of standards.

In 1978 Wembley staged its third European Cup Final, the first to have been contested there by an English side. The previous season Liverpool had beaten Borussia Mönchengladbach in Rome. At Wembley, as holders, they faced the Belgian champions FC Brugge. Although the Uefa ticket allocation was designed to balance support, Ray Clemence recalled: 'I think the whole stadium was red and white that evening.'

The game proved a disappointment. Liverpool struggled to make headway against stubbornly unambitious opponents until a perfect Kenny Dalglish chip put the holders ahead. Dalglish hurdled the Wembley advertising boards, the celebrations – one man and nearly 90,000 devoted admirers – as memorable as any of the evening's football. Liverpool coasted the rest of the second half, although it took a goal-line clearance from Phil Thompson – 'the only shot they had', he pointed out afterwards – to prevent the final going into extra-time.

During the seventies and eighties Liverpool collected trophies like their young fans collected Panini stickers: eleven League Championships in twenty years a clear indication of the club's domination of the domestic game. Personnel changed, with Bill Shankly followed as manager by Bob Paisley, Joe Fagan and Kenny Dalglish. The team, too, evolved, one generation of great players smoothly making way for the next. The style of play, however, honed in the five-a-side games which were the hub of the Anfield training regime, remained the same: fluent and athletic, every player comfortable with the ball and the whole team resolutely unwilling to surrender possession. Never before had one club led the way so confidently for so long.

Wembley enjoyed its opportunities to witness Liverpool's dominance: FA Cup Finals, Charity Shields, four successive League Cup Finals in the early eighties and the defeat of Brugge in 1978. In a period, however, during which Nottingham Forest and Aston Villa also won the European Cup, English clubs were looking beyond the horizons of the domestic game. For Liverpool Wembley was just one stop on a triumphant tour of Europe's capitals. It would take the most parochial of rivalries to rekindle Merseyside's fascination with the stadium's unique tradition.

Having languished in Liverpool's shadow for too long, Everton under Howard Kendall were revitalised during the 1983/84 season and the League Cup – now the Milk Cup in deference to the tournament's sponsors – brought them to Wembley for the first final to be contested by the closest of neighbours from either side of Stanley Park.

The rain poured down and 120 minutes of football failed to produce a goal. None of that, though, tempered the enthusiasm around Wembley for the occasion of an all-Merseyside final. Everton's John Bailey would later remember: 'To run around the stadium and to see everybody together, everybody in different colours, my family in different colours, strangers from all over the country, different supporters' groups, together, smiling, having a go. You come off and think, "This is what every game should be like. Why be segregated? Why not mix?"'

Liverpool won the replay 1–0 at Maine Road and went on to win the League. Everton, meanwhile, recovered from their disappointment to return to Wembley for three successive FA Cup Finals, the first of them two months later. 'We went back to Wembley then and we never had an ounce of nerves in us,' recalled John Bailey. 'We knew we were going to win that Cup.'

Their opponents Watford were just glad to be there, the occasion crowning a previously unremarkable club's rise to eminence under the future England manager Graham Taylor. The club's chairman Elton John, whose money had allowed Watford to take full advantage of Taylor's commitment and ingenuity, was all but overcome and cried through the singing of *Abide With Me* before kick-off. Everton's attitude to proceedings was rather different, according to their centre-forward Andy Gray: 'Everything that was coming from Goodison Park was, we're going to win it.' And they did, thanks to goals from Gray himself and Graeme Sharp.

The following season was one of the finest in Everton's history as the club became League champions and won the European Cup Winners' Cup. A Wembley Cup Final against Manchester United was the campaign's only real disappointment: both the result – a 1–0 defeat – and the performance fell short of expectations.

The game might have been remembered only for Norman Whiteside's fine, curling twenty-yard winner in extra-time had not the day's real drama already happened. With less than a quarter of an hour to go in normal time, Everton's Peter Reid eluded Paul McGrath just inside the United half. Across came Kevin Moran with a lunging, ill-timed tackle which sent Reid flying. The referee, Peter Willis, would later remember: 'From a stadium that was very noisy, it went very quiet. It really did go quiet and I thought, "Oh, my gosh!" In a split second your life flashes before you and, quite frankly, I thought: "What do I do next?" I only had one choice and that was to send Kevin from the field of play.'

Moran – and most of the football world thereafter – felt the decision was harsh: 'I was trying to find out why he was sending me off. He just wouldn't talk to me. As far as I was concerned I wasn't even at fault for the tackle.' But there was no turning back by the referee. Only five players had ever been sent off at Wembley – Yugoslavia's Boris Stankovic the first, during the 1948 Olympics – and none in an FA Cup Final there. For Moran, United's eventual victory was scant consolation.

The 1985 Final was Manchester United's second in three years. In !983 they had beaten Brighton 4–0 in a replay after the underdogs had passed up the chance to win the first game, drawn 2–2, in its closing stages. The commentator's words 'And Smith must score' and the fact that, ten yards out with only the goalkeeper to beat, the Brighton forward Gordon Smith did not, have passed into Wembley folklore.

At the time United and Everton seemed the teams best equipped to challenge Liverpool at home and emulate their achievements abroad. Both, however, were to be denied their European adventures. Before the 1985 Final supporters of the two clubs donated £30,000 to a fund set up for victims of the recent Bradford disaster (fifty-five people had died in a fire which engulfed the main stand at the decrepit Valley Parade ground). Eleven days later appalling scenes at another hopelessly outdated stadium, the Heysel in Brussels, saw thirty-nine fans die when a wall collapsed as they tried to escape fighting between Liverpool and Juventus fans before the European Cup Final. The game itself, a 1–0 win for the Italians, was irrelevant after what had happened. Not so the ban on English clubs entering European competition imposed that summer as a result of Liverpool fans' active involvement in the violence. The 1985 European Cup Final was a dark episode in the history of a club whose grace and professionalism had illuminated two decades. Worse was to come.

Wembley's new owners, the consortium led by Brian Wolfson, spent the late 1980s expanding the stadium company's activities. Much of their attention was devoted to the exploitation of the surrounding facilities: the conference centre, exhibition halls and Empire Pool, by now renamed the Wembley Arena. Efforts were also made, however, to increase the activities of the stadium itself.

Wembley's contract signed in 1982 with the Football Association had ensured its exclusive right to stage England and showpiece domestic games for the next twenty years. A core business was assured but football also contrived new competitions – the likes of the Simod, Full Members and Makita tournaments – apparently on the assumption that money could be made by affording even the obscurest of tournaments the prestige of a Wembley final. The profusion, of course, did the stadium's own balance sheet no harm at all.

From time to time, furthermore, the law of diminishing returns would be turned on its head by particular circumstances. Two great clubs from Wembley history, Wolves and Burnley, for example, both reduced to life in the Fourth Division, met in the 1988 final of the Sherpa Van Trophy. Nearly 81,000 turned up determined to relive past glories despite the cravenly ersatz nature of the modern echo.

Wolves' 2–0 win was all but beside the point. The occasion and the setting were everything, as the Wolves manager Graham Turner observed: 'It didn't matter whether we were playing for the Sherpa Van Trophy, the FA Cup or the World Cup. It could not have been better. For lads from the Fourth Division to have that amount of support, to experience the colour and the noise, is unforgettable.'

Efforts were made, too, to broaden the base of Wembley's business. In 1986, for the first time since Henry Cooper's brave defeat by the world champion-elect Cassius Clay in 1963, boxing returned to the stadium. While Frank Bruno was never as convincing a fighter as Cooper had been he was, at last, another heavyweight English fans could take to their hearts. Nearly 50,000 turned up to watch him challenge the American Tim

Witherspoon for the world title. Ahead on points, the Englishman's weak jaw let him down in the eleventh round to deny Wembley the chance to stage a new world champion's first defence. Bruno's time would come: in 1995 a 23,000 crowd witnessed his last hurrah, a points victory over Oliver McCall which earned him the WBC title.

American football had first been played at Wembley in 1952; the USA Forces Championship raised funds for the RAF Benevolent Fund and the National Playing Fields Association. In 1983 a series of exhibition games featuring successful NFL teams began. In 1986, with interest in the sport buoyed by regular television coverage, more than 80,000 watched the charismatic Chicago Bears defeat the Dallas Cowboys 17–6 in the American Bowl.

Four more years of big crowds at the sport's Wembley showpiece helped convince the NFL that a toehold had been established for gridiron in the European market. The London Monarchs were England's team in the new World Football League and played home fixtures at Wembley in their first two seasons. But the novelty soon wore off, leaving the sport to find its own, more realistic level. The London Monarchs departed in 1992, the American Bowl the year after. What was left behind was a fresh approach to the stage management of stadium sports events. For better or worse, cheerleaders, masters of ceremonies and all-singing, all-dancing efforts to create a wholesomely hysterical atmosphere were here to stay.

Any atmosphere at all would have been welcome at England's games at Wembley in the eighties. Bobby Robson succeeded Ron Greenwood as manager of the national team after their elimination at the second-round stage in the 1982 World Cup in Spain. His first task was to qualify for the 1984 European Championships in France. Robson's England career kicked off with a 2–1 Wembley defeat in a friendly against West Germany. It was an inauspicious start and, in the coming months, the manager's enthusiasm stood in ever starker contrast to the lack of any shown by the home crowd.

Only 35,000 watched England beat Luxembourg 9–0 in the first of their European Championship qualifiers at the stadium. Even fewer, 23,600, showed up two months later for a friendly against Wales. On Saturday 26 March 100,000 fans saw Liverpool beat Manchester United 2–1 in the 1983 Milk Cup Final. Four days later Wembley was less than half-full as England stumbled to a 0–0 draw with Greece. In September the home team failed again, losing 1–0 to Denmark to make qualification for France all but impossible. It is to Robson's great credit that the next seven years, during which England would not again be beaten in a qualifying game for a major tournament, saw a steady rebuilding of the national side's fortunes in spite of a constant, and more or less vitriolic, campaign in the press to remove him from his job.

The emergence of world-class stars such as Gary Lineker and Peter Beardsley, the fitful brilliance of great talents such as Glenn Hoddle and John Barnes, the evident patriotism of stalwarts like Terry Butcher and Bryan Robson all hinted at better times to come. Before Italia '90 revitalised public interest, however, Wembley attendances for England games slumped to new lows. Even the Scotland fixture failed to sell out; other matches struggled to half-fill the ground.

Unsurprisingly the atmosphere changed, too. These were joyless times at Wembley, the crowd an uncomfortable mix of corporate hospitality packages, schoolchildren and a sullen rump of committed fans, some of whom would take advantage of events like the 1988 European Championships in Germany to sidestep the post-Heysel ban on English clubs and head off to the continent in search of trouble.

In April 1990, with less than 22,000 in the crowd (fewer than had watched a schoolboy international, a women's hockey match or the final of the Zenith Data Systems Cup the previous month), new hope for England emerged in the shape of a match-winning performance from a young Paul Gascoigne. Gascoigne had made his debut against Denmark at Wembley in 1988 but he came of age during the 4–2 defeat of Czechoslovakia – scoring once and setting up England's other three goals – as Robson gave him his head in the run-up to the 1990 World Cup.

The tournament – and Gascoigne's tears during a semi-final defeat by West Germany – did much to renew interest in the England team and, thereby, in football as a whole. Like the career of its most charismatic star, each step forward by the national team was followed by two in the opposite direction. When Wembley finally came back to life in time for Euro '96, however, the figure of Gascoigne would still be centre stage. His obvious flaws as a person would continue to cast his equally evident talents as a footballer into sharp relief. Gascoigne could light up Wembley and English football like no other player of his generation.

'Having clinched the League, while we were waiting for the Heysel game to be played, all our talk was of "We hope Liverpool win the European Cup and we can play them in the European Cup Final next year". That was what we were looking for, and the opportunity was denied us.' Everton's Andy Gray was expressing the disappointment of dozens of players and thousands of fans who lost the chance to experience European club competition in the wake of the disaster in Brussels in 1985.

Instead attention was forced back on to the domestic game and Wembley once more stood at the heart of things. The twentieth League Cup Final there celebrated with splendid symmetry that competition's particular appeal. Since becoming the trophy's first Wembley winners QPR had taken a place at football's top table, returning to the stadium twice in 1982 only to lose their FA Cup Final replay to Spurs by a single goal, scored from the penalty spot by Glenn Hoddle.

By 1986 they were an established First Division side and were expected to beat Oxford United, newly promoted and at Wembley for the first time. In the tradition established by Rangers themselves back in 1967, however, the favourites faltered and the newcomers took their chance. Oxford United's team included two players who would be back at the stadium in very different circumstances – and Liverpool shirts – before the decade was out: John Aldridge and Ray Houghton. Houghton, indeed, scored Oxford's second goal in a 3–0 win. The League Cup Final, as so often, had given a little club its very big day.

Denied the opportunity to face each other in the European Cup, Liverpool and Everton instead monopolised both major domestic competitions. Liverpool's player-manager Kenny Dalglish scored at Chelsea to win them the League title ahead of Everton just days before the first all-Merseyside FA Cup Final on 10 May.

Just as the League Cup Final two years previously, Reds and Blues mixed together at Wembley to invest a national occasion, watched on TV by millions around the world, with a sense of the rest of us being privileged to share in a single city's celebration of its own identity. Families, friends, work mates, divided by their allegiances at home, shared cars, buses and train carriages on the way to London where they stood and sat shoulder to shoulder at Wembley.

The game proved considerably more watchable than the 0–0 draw of 1984. Everton started brightly, driven on by Paul Bracewell and Peter Reid in midfield, the latter threading the through-ball on to which Gary Lineker, at the height of his powers, fastened to score the opening goal. In the League campaign, however, Everton's style and Lineker's forty goals had eventually been overhauled by Liverpool's dogged will to win.

The second half at Wembley summed up the course of the season. Ian Rush has pointed out since that, 'when you're a boy at school, your dream isn't to win the League, it's to score the winning goal in the FA Cup Final'. Here he scored twice, on his way to becoming the most prolific of all Cup

Final goalscorers. Craig Johnston got another and, for the first time, Liverpool had achieved the League and Cup double.

The friendliness around Wembley on the day in no way tempered the intensity of the rivalry on Merseyside. (Peter Reid, for one, cried off the open-top bus ride round Liverpool by the two teams the following day, unable, as a staunch Evertonian, to stomach the other lot's delight.) Just what the victory at Wembley meant to the red half of the city Ian Rush saw clearly after the game: 'I remember a supporter managed to get in the dressing-room. He came up to me and said: "You've made my life now. You've beaten Everton in the Cup Final. We've done the Double." And then he jumped in the bath with all his clothes on.'

Beyond the result, the goalscorers and the dry details each FA Cup Final has its own flavour, a cast, plot and set of circumstances which ensure it is distinct in character from any other. The fixture's traditional allure guarantees a high degree of intensity whatever the quality of the day's football. To the sense of heritage lent by Wembley and the competition, however, the two teams bring their own histories. It is a splendid chemistry, the disparate elements combining to produce, each year, an occasion more or less thrilling, the familiar ritual building to a climax which is always and atmospherically unique.

In 1987 Coventry City reached Wembley for the first time in their 104-year history. The management team of John Sillett, portly and all smiles, and George Curtis, hard-working and bluff, epitomised the club's appeal. Their opponents, Spurs, had won the Cup five times on five visits to Wembley. David Pleat's side, sophisticated and charismatic, employed a five-man midfield, which included Glenn Hoddle, Chris Waddle and Ossie Ardiles, to create chances for a lone striker, Clive Allen, whose forty-eight goals during the season had seen him voted Footballer of the Year.

Within two minutes Waddle's cross gave Allen the chance to score his forty-ninth and put Tottenham ahead. Dave Bennett soon equalised, only for Gary Mabbutt to scramble a second and put Spurs in front at half-time. Coventry, though, were not finished. Keith Houchen's equaliser just after the hour was a splendid diving header; the winner, early in extra-time, was a Lloyd McGrath cross deflected past his own keeper by Mabbutt: 'It just looped off the top of my knee up and over Ray Clemence and probably went into the only spot it could have gone.'

As Coventry collected the Cup, Sillett and Curtis made fools of themselves on the pitch as any delirious City fan might have done. Everywhere you looked in the winning team was a man with his own particular cause for satisfaction. Houchen, for example, would later reflect: 'Less than a year before, I'd been playing at Scunthorpe United in the Fourth Division and there I was, sitting with my team, singing "Here we go" with the FA Cup in our hands and 100,000 people in at Wembley. That's what you're in the game for.'

A year later everybody involved in any way with Wimbledon Football Club would have been happy to echo Houchen's sentiments. When their opponents Liverpool had won the Cup for the first time in 1965, Wimbledon had been scuffling along as part-timers in the old Southern League. In the past twelve seasons, since earning Football League membership, they had scrapped, schemed and sometimes battered their way into the top division and now faced the League champions in an FA Cup Final.

Rough-edged they may have been but their manager Bobby Gould's enthusiasm and their coach Don Howe's tactical insight had invested a side which played to its own strengths with the acumen to take full advantage of opponents' weaknesses. Just after the half-hour Wimbledon profited from a simple refereeing error: after Peter Beardsley had run through to score, Brian Hill disallowed the goal to give Liverpool a free-kick for a foul by Terry Phelan instead of playing the obvious advantage. Two minutes later

Lawrie Sanchez rose at the far post to head in Dennis Wise's cross.

Wimbledon, improbably, had the lead and, as Dave Hill described it in his biography of John Barnes, *Out Of His Skin*: 'Kenny's massive army fell into an eloquent silence as the time slipped away. In goal Beasant surpassed himself, rising to the occasion the few times Liverpool breached Wimbledon's stout resistance. When Aldridge was awarded a debatable penalty kick it seemed that the tide must turn. But the man who had seemed infallible from the spot failed to convert. "Lurch" lunged to his left, saved the kick and lifted the Cup.' Commentating for the BBC, John Motson delivered a line he can scarcely have imagined he would get the chance to use: 'The Crazy Gang have beaten the Culture Club.'

The 1987 and 1988 FA Cup Finals both enjoyed fairy-tale conclusions even if the latter was best forgotten as a spectacle. The 1989 Final, which again saw Liverpool and Everton face each other on a sunny Saturday in May, came at the end of a season which will always be remembered for the awful events at Hillsborough, Sheffield Wednesday's ground, on 15 April. Ninety-seven Liverpool supporters lost their lives after a crush at the Leppings Lane End minutes into their team's Cup semi-final against Nottingham Forest. The football world was stopped in its tracks, left to count the cost of decades of complacency, greed, ignorance and fear which had allowed crowd control to become a higher priority than crowd safety.

Wembley, ahead of its time, was already about to become an all-seater stadium, the decision having been hastened by crowd trouble during an England v Scotland game in 1988. (The same violent scenes led to the indefinite suspension of Wembley's oldest international fixture.) For now, though, the terraces and fences, like those which had contributed to the carnage at Hillsborough, were still in place.

There was talk in the disaster's aftermath of suspending the season's FA

Cup competition. Eventually, though, when football resumed, Liverpool won the replayed semi-final to set up a third all-Merseyside clash at Wembley. Everton's Pat Nevin would later reflect: 'Maybe it would have been a mark of respect for no Cup Final to be played that year but you have to respect what the friends and family of the people who died said and most of them felt it should go ahead.'

The Wembley fences came down and, on 20 May, Reds and Blues mingled at the stadium once again; with the outside world looking on, Merseyside fans joined to honour those who had been lost and to celebrate life going on. The city – and the staff and players of Liverpool Football Club in particular – had behaved with great dignity during the weeks of mourning. As the Everton manager Colin Harvey would later remember: 'By the time the Final came around, we'd settled a bit and they'd settled. The game was very competitive. What we both wanted was a game played in the right spirit and the crowd to watch it in the right spirit, which they did.'

It was a marvellous contest. John Aldridge gave Liverpool an early lead. Stuart McCall equalised just before the final whistle. Ian Rush, on as a substitute, put Liverpool ahead six minutes into extra-time, only for McCall to pull Everton level once more before Rush (who else?) guided his header from a John Barnes cross past Neville Southall for the winner.

The afternoon's most poignant moments had been before the game when Gerry Marsden led the crowd in singing Liverpool's adopted anthem *You'll Never Walk Alone* and then a hauntingly appropriate *Abide With Me*. Altogether more unseemly was the drowning out of the National Anthem in petty retaliation for a perceived slight on the part of the Royal Family. Worse still, handfuls of supporters took advantage of Wembley's fenceless perimeter to come on to the pitch six times during the game. So many came on after it that the players were unable to perform the lap of honour which might have set a fitting seal on an emotionally charged afternoon.

Perhaps the fact that a selfish and disrespectful minority marred an otherwise dignified and uplifting occasion was appropriate. For nearly twenty years the few had been ruining the football experience for the many. Hillsborough, in some respects, was the ultimate and tragic consequence of their efforts. Nearly a hundred deaths, apparently, were not sufficient to give them pause for thought. The 1989 FA Cup Final, though, will be remembered not for the stupidity of those pitch invaders but as the afternoon football took first faltering steps towards a saner future. As Pat Nevin said, recalling the aftermath of the game's darkest hour: 'Quite simply, that city couldn't have acted better, in a more noble way, in a more honourable way, a more thoughtful way than they did.'

1976: LAWRIE McMENEMY

Come the Final, everybody thought it would be Osgood or Channon who'd get the goal if we scored. Bobby Stokes had been missing chances in the League for weeks and, at Wembley, he got one in. Ian Turner kicked it out. It went wide on the right to Channon who passed towards Jim McCalliog. Jimmy helped the ball on, over the defence: Bobby was already running and just hit it, not a screamer, but right in the corner. I tried not to go too barmy but, for the next seven minutes, the bloody clock wouldn't move.

Bobby was a lovely man, no longer with us, sadly. He was delighted to get the goal, of course, and very proud. But like one or two others who became stars overnight at Wembley – Mike Trebilcock of Everton, Roger Osborne of Ipswich – he was a quiet man and would rather not have had all the fuss that came with it. We weren't a big club and Southampton winning at Wembley changed a lot of people's lives: players, supporters; it certainly changed mine. They had street parties down here for weeks after. The atmosphere was like I remember as a kid in the days after the War.

INTERVIEW, 1997

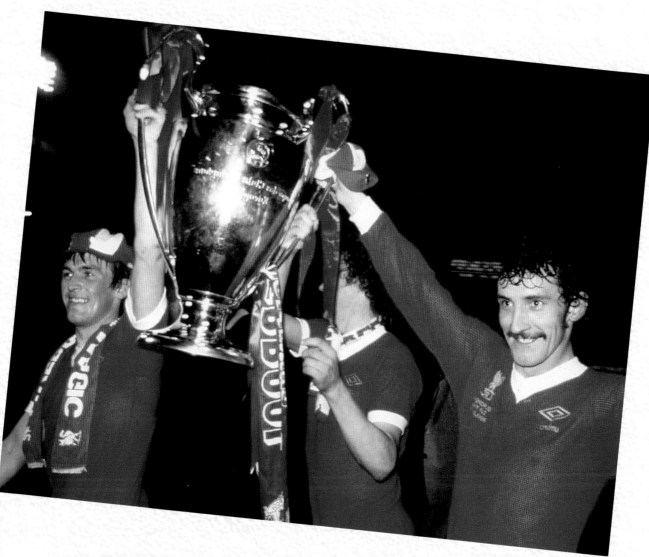

1978: TERRY McDERMOTT

You know, playing at an FA Cup Final at Wembley, the build-up is fantastic. From the semi-final onwards, it's on your mind every day. You go down the week before to London, soak up the atmosphere, you're waiting to go out in front of 100,000 people as it was then. The European Cup Final against Brugge didn't feel like that, didn't feel like the Cup Final. It was a very important game, of course, but it was just another game. Perhaps the Champions League is a more high profile competition now, but that game was missing something.

Of course, it wasn't a great game. We won: Graeme Souness played Kenny Dalglish through and he nicked it over the keeper. But in a Cup Final you think both teams would go out to win. I think Brugge went out looking for penalties: it would have gone to penalties that night. They just sat back and made it a nothing game. It's funny isn't it? The European Cup Final is probably more important but it didn't have the prestige of the FA Cup Final.

INTERVIEW, 1998

1978: VIV ANDERSON

I got my first England cap at Wembley against Czechoslovakia. It was a poor game on a freezing cold night but in many ways a momentous occasion, with me being the first black player to play for England. I remember getting telegrams from people like Elton John before the game but what I will always remember about the game itself is that one side of the pitch was solid, frozen hard, while the other side was relatively soft. So it was a case of wearing studs first half and rubbers in the second.

The media blew the whole occasion up but I never really got caught up in all that. The people around me at the time just told me to go out and play, reminding me that I was not just there because of the colour of my skin, though I knew that already. I was just a skinny kid from Nottingham who had a bit of talent.

It was a big thing at the time and you maybe don't appreciate it until a few years later. It was certainly the highlight of my career and whether you are white, brown, purple or blue it's the same. When you are fortunate enough to make an England debut at Wembley it is the greatest feeling in the world.

INTERVIEW, 1997

VIV ANDERSON, the first black footballer to play for England, takes the field ahead of Nottingham Forest team-mate Tony Woodcock.

It wasn't long (left) before he was showing Wembley last night what Forest fans already know—that he is a very cool customer. The occasion did not ruffle him, nor did world-class Czech winger Zdenek Nehoda. It was not an easy debut for Viv, but he coped in a way that suggests this could be the first of many caps.

He began the move that led to England's winner, and drew this praise from manager Ron Greenwood: "With such speed of recovery he was saving and diverting many dangerous situations. He was delightful, and to be involved in the goal was a bonus."

But Viv's mother, Mrs. Myrtle Anderson, was not at the game. Instead—out of a sense of duty—she went to work as usual at Highbury Hospital, Nottingham.

Viv didn't lack family support, though. His father Audley, a security officer, and his 18-year-old brother Donald were there to cheer him on.

1981: KEITH HACKETT

For me, it's always been about players. If the referee can just drift into the background and let the players perform, fine. You just hope that there'll be nothing controversial about the game which you'll have to live with afterwards. In the dressing-room you change, do your warm-up, take on liquid and just watch the minutes count down until there's a knock on the door: *Are you ready, Mr Hackett?*

Everybody's together in the cool at the bottom of the tunnel. You can hear the music. Players acknowledge one another. The managers are there, looking very smart. Then the FA guy pulls you all into line. I'm last out, so I watch everybody: one or two players go *Oh, no! Not him*, a couple smile, there's the odd *All the best.*

You walk up the tunnel and, as the front of the line hits the daylight, you hear the noise of the crowd which gets louder as you get nearer the end of the tunnel and the pitch. As you come out, it's incredible. You're blinded by the brightness of the sunshine, the colour: you're trying to focus and your throat really has gone dry. You hope no one's going to talk to you for a bit because you've lost it, really, with the tension and the adrenalin coming through.

THE EMPIRE STADIUM, WEMBLEY

No ticket genuine unless it carries a Lion's Head watermark below

FINAL TIE
SATURDAY, MAY, 9 1981
KICK-OFF 3.00 p.m.
YOU ARE ADVISED TO TAKE UP
YOUR POSITION BY 2.30 p.m.
1. This ticket is not transferable.
2. This counterfoil must be retained for at least 6 months.

TURNSTILES
F
ENTRANCE
79
ROW
31
SEAT
26

J.S. Lill CHAIRMAN
WEMBLEY STADIUM LTD
NORTH STAND SEAT
TO BE RETAINED
£13.00

SEE PLAN AND CONDITIONS ON BACK

In Celebration of The One-Hundredth
Football Association Challenge Cup Competition

FINAL TIE

Manchester City V Tottenham Hotspur

Saturday
9th May 1981
Kick-off 3.00pm

Wembley Stadium

Official Souvenir Programme
80p

There are two flags on the touchline which the teams have to head for, to line up and wait for the dignitaries to pass by. You're just thinking: *Come on, let's get on with the game.* You're buzzing but you've got to wait. It's all part of the history of the thing. The national anthem's played and then you get the nod. You take a slow walk to the centre of the field: call the two captains over, get through the formalities and then just wait for the time to creep up to three o'clock. You blow the whistle which, after all the waiting, seems like a real exertion, start your watch, check it three times and that's it: you're into the game.

F.A. CUP FINAL
WEMBLEY 1981

The replay was completely different from the first game: under floodlights, of course, and I think the players were more relaxed. The game was a bit hectic to start with, though. I had to talk to Gerry Gow, who seemed to have decided he'd kick Ardiles off the park, and caution several players. But then we had the goals.

MacKenzie's for City, if it hadn't been for what followed it, would have been talked about as the best goal at Wembley for years. But then, at 2–2, Villa scored the winner. It was incredible. I thought we were going to have another draw but he went off on this run. I was in a great position to watch, behind him and slightly to the left. I used to have a habit of waving advantage before anything had actually happened. I was expecting someone to crash in and take Villa out, so I was concentrating and waving play on: but nobody tackled him. He just went round the keeper and scored and then went off on a run to celebrate.

For me, it's what the game's about. Here's a guy who, a few days before, had walked off the pitch, substituted and – in his own eyes – disgraced. Now, when the final whistle goes, Ricky's the hero. And he's scored a goal, I'd say, as good as has ever been scored at Wembley.

INTERVIEW, 1997

Mirror Sport

Tears of joy for Spurs

Friday, May 15, 1981
No. 24,027
Telephone: (STD code 01)—353 0246

TRICKY RICKY!

RICKY VILLA, the big, bearded Argentinian who won the 100th FA Cup final for Tottenham, had made up his mind to go home before last night's super two-goal show.

Villa was the man who broke down and cried after being substituted in Saturday's 1-1 draw.

But in a thrilling replay he scored in the eight and 77th minutes, Garth Crooks got another after 70 minutes, and Tottenham took the Cup back to White Hart Lane. Coming back from behind to beat Manchester City 3-2.

So Wembley belonged to Villa and ten other white-shirted and sweat-stained Spurs players.

Villa, all smiles this time, said: "Tonight may have changed the future.

"Before the replay, and after Saturday, I wanted to leave Tottenham.

"I was starting to think I was a bad player. Everybody was always talking about my friend Ossie Ardiles and how brilliant he is. But Ricky? They did not say same about me.

"The club have offered me a new two-year contract. I am happy with the two years, but not with the offer. We will continue to talk.

Lucky

"After tonight anything and everything is possible."

Villa said of his memorable winning goal: "I have never scored a goal as good as this. I think I beat two men when I cut outside, and another when I came inside.

"Perhaps I was lucky with the shot. Another time it might have been blocked."

Keith Burkinshaw, the quiet manager behind Tottenham's return to Europe, recalled the great Spurs double side of twenty years ago when he said:

"They did it their way.

By HARRY MILLER

But I think we can say we did it our way. I don't think any side has ever won the Cup in a better way."

He added: "It was a marvellous winning goal by Ricky, I've got a lot of belief in him as a player.

"The nice thing is that in both the semi-final replay win over Wolves and then this one we have produced the best football since I came to the club."

Tottenham's victory could have a major effect on the shape of their side next season.

Glenn Hoddle, another of their stars whose contract has expired, said: "No decision has yet been made about my future. But I hope this was not my last game for Spurs."

Skipper Steve Perryman, who has been a major influence throughout Tottenham's Cup run, said: "Ricky's goal was a fitting way to end the 100th final that we won a typical Spurs style."

Crooks, scorer of the other Tottenham goal, said: "If I had not come to Tottenham I would be on a beach in Majorca now with Stoke on their annual club holiday.

City manager John Bond's told his club's fans: "Don't worry. We'll be back.

"We have nothing to cry over. It was a mighty battle."

What a difference five days make! Ricky Villa and Cup.

Celebrating the year of the cockerel! Triumphant S...

Frank McGhee's Final Verdict—Pages 30, 31

BULL WITH NO BELLOW

From RON WILLS in Bilbao

BRITAIN'S Tony Sibson is still the middleweight champion of Europe—but he turned in a performance unworthy of the title.

The 24-year-old Leicester lad earned a unanimous verdict from the referee and two judges to outpoint Spain's Andoni Amana over 12 rounds in the Bull Ring here last night.

But Sibson's manager Sam Burns said: "I think it's the worst I've ever seen Tony box. I can only think he was overawed by the occasion.

Below par or not, Sibson was too good for the Spaniard, who looked impressive but lacked any power in his punches. He was floored twice, once from a left hook in the second and again from a left jab in the seventh.

Printed and Published by THE DAILY MIRROR NEWSPAPERS Ltd. (01-353 0246) at and for Mirror Group Newspapers Ltd., Holborn Circus, London, EC...

MA QU SCO Rea P. MACKEN

1981

Thursday 14th May 1981 Kick off 7.30pm

One-Hundredth Football Association Challenge Cup Competition

FINAL TIE

Manchester City v Tottenham Hotspur

Wembley Stadium

Official programme 60p

REPLAY

1986: STEVE STONE

We went down to the game on a trip from Cleveland Hall Boys Club up on Tyneside and I remember getting on our little bus and heading down early in the morning and it took hours to get there. Then, when you see the place, the first thing that hits you is its size. Wembley is stupidly big, an absolutely amazing sight for a fifteen-year-old. I was never the biggest of lads, so the whole thing dwarfed me totally; it is an awesome sight.

What did surprise me about the night was standing around so many Londoners, which was a new experience, seeing them all cheer their own players. Arsenal fans wanting Kenny Sansom to do well, Spurs fans cheering for Glenn Hoddle. We felt like the only ones in the ground cheering for the Newcastle lads, Chris Waddle and Peter Beardsley. Seeing them play at Wembley for England was a massive buzz for me. It felt like they had come down with us in a way and I felt pleased that we were there to support them.

INTERVIEW, 1997

1988: BOBBY GOULD

Did we think we were going to win? We always did. On the Friday we changed over from morning training to an afternoon session: same time, same conditions as the game itself. Things just felt right. There was something in the atmosphere that afternoon. On the day, we got to Wembley from our hotel and when we got to the dressing-room – there's a booklet you get telling you where you've got to be and at what time – Don Howe got us all to put our watches back three minutes and from then on we always kept people waiting. It got on Liverpool's nerves, I've no doubt about that.

We were three minutes late coming out into the tunnel, and they'd got a bit impatient waiting for us. I went down the line of Liverpool players, shaking each one's hand and wishing him luck. And then our boys started a chant, from the front of the line to the back, like a war cry, which just echoed and rebounded around in the tunnel. Liverpool went white. The ref, Brian Hill, couldn't believe what was happening.

And then the first tackle of the game: Steve McMahon and Vinnie Jones. It was thunderous. I can see it now. That set the pattern: *You're Steve McMahon, the hardest man in the game. I'm Vinnie Jones and I'm here to challenge you.* Our plan was to shut them down as quickly as possible, to stop them passing. We knew we could do something at set pieces – they feared us in the air –and that's what happened for the goal. One blue shirt beat six or seven red shirts to the ball.

When they got the penalty, I think it was a case of the referee trying to balance up an earlier mistake when he'd blown up with Peter Beardsley clean through instead of playing advantage. The day before, Alan Cork and Dennis Wise had given Dave Beasant practice with penalties. They'd done them like Aldridge, you know, the shuffle then the kick placed to the left. I told you the Friday was important.

Don Howe and I just hugged each other after the game. We'd achieved what no one thought we could. In a way, being selfish, I hope no one does something like it again. But for the good of football, for the dream of it, it would be better if someone did. Every August, when the non-League clubs kick off in the FA Cup, you want players to be thinking; *I wonder if we can do it, I wonder if we can do a Wimbledon.*

INTERVIEW, 1998

1989: JOHN ALDRIDGE

For a couple of weeks after Hillsborough we didn't know whether we were coming or going. You just tried to do your best, rallying round, counselling the families, attending funerals. Football seemed a bit irrelevant really. I wasn't particularly interested in playing, to be honest, but Kenny Dalglish sat us all down, we talked about it and realised we had to. What helped me, helped all of us, was the friends and families of the victims who said we should.

The opposition couldn't have been better: the respect from the Everton players and staff and fans was fantastic. I can hardly remember the build-up. It wasn't like 1986 when everyone was excited in the city. It was muzzy and it all happened very quickly. In a way, because people remembered what had happened a few weeks before, the Cup Final was irrelevant. We had to give it relevance for the people who'd died. That was the reason for going to play it.

The game was a little low-key but it came to life in extra-time. I scored with my first touch – same end of the pitch as my last touch the year before. I even put the ball into the same spot as I'd meant to put the penalty against Wimbledon. Frightening. I thought I'd played quite well and I was surprised when Kenny subbed me late on. I thought, though, we were going to win 1–0 and I'd scored the winner. When Everton equalised right on full-time, I couldn't believe it. But it caught fire in extra-time, as we've said. Everton played well, Rushie and John Barnes combined for the two goals for us to win it. We wanted to win; it was a very competitive game. I wanted to win but it wasn't for me or for Liverpool Football Club. It was for all those people, not like any other Cup Final. It felt like a testimonial to the people who died.

INTERVIEW, 1998

Part Of Something Special

Music At Wembley

'It's 12 o'clock in London, 7am in Philadelphia and, around the world, it's time for Live Aid, 16 hours of live music in aid of famine relief in Africa.'

The words of Richard Skinner, the most famous in the history of music at Wembley, kicked off the world's greatest ever rock and pop extravaganza on 13 July 1985. Driven by the energy and commitment of Bob Geldof, Live Aid was thrown together in the space of a few short weeks that summer; its impact, at Wembley and around the world, ensured it is unlikely ever to be forgotten. For once music rather than sport took centre stage and, without question, Live Aid was a single event as significant and celebrated as any to take place at the stadium during the past seventy-five years.

The story of Live Aid is a remarkable one. During 1984 Michael Buerk's BBC news reports chronicling the appalling suffering of Ethiopian famine victims touched millions. Bob Geldof, lead singer of the Boomtown Rats, was himself shocked and inspired enough to respond to the cry for help in a way only he, perhaps, might have been capable of: he brought together the notoriously fickle world of pop music to create Band Aid whose *Do They Know It's Christmas/Feed The World* single, recorded to raise funds and public awareness, was number one by Christmas.

The next step was to stage a live event which would build on that success and take the message further afield. Again Geldof's energy made that possible and he would later remember that the choice of venue was essential to the success of the project's ambitions: 'I knew we needed to have a show that went beyond just England and encapsulated the world. Wembley had to be the centrepiece: for the thing to have any authority it had to be staged at Wembley.'

Geldof called upon the expertise of Harvey Goldsmith, an experienced music promoter with his own Wembley pedigree, to 'let everyone know that this thing was real'. Arrangements were made to link the London event to one which would be staged simultaneously at the John F. Kennedy stadium in Philadelphia. The touch paper, though, was lit by the involvement of BBC television, whose live coverage guaranteed the widest possible audience: Live Aid would eventually be broadcast to 155 countries.

With the framework for the event in place, Geldof now had to persuade the world's busiest and most temperamental stars to appear on a live bill with a radically new format at a venue which had never staged anything like it before. The stories, more or less true, of how bands were persuaded to take part are legion. On the same day, apparently, that Geldof was telling Queen, 'Dire Straits are doing it, so you have to', he was assuring Dire Straits that Queen had already agreed and that they would look bad if they did not follow suit.

Unsurprisingly, given the scale of the undertaking and the fact that goodwill rather than hard cash was making it happen, there was considerable apprehension as to how the day would unfold. Richard Skinner introduced Live Aid at midday on 13 July and also presented the BBC's coverage of the show: 'There was no such thing as a running order. That opening announcement was written, literally, a minute before the show started. Something else had been prepared but my producer just threw this sheet at me and we went with what I suppose has become something of a famous speech.'

Geldof himself showed Charles and Diana, the Prince and Princess of Wales, to their seats. Concorde marked the occasion with a fly-past. Status Quo got the day underway with *Rocking All Over The World*, Geldof – abrasive as always – having won the argument with those around him who doubted Quo's suitability or credibility as an opening act. Then, three-quarters of an hour in, the man behind the entire event took the stage himself with his band, the Boomtown

Rats. Geldof would later recall: 'I had never done Wembley before. The noise that day was just incredible, totally overwhelming. Halfway through *I Don't Like Mondays* I just stopped dead, looked around and took it all in, the magnitude of the event.'

While a benign air of organised chaos settled on Wembley during the course of that steamy Saturday afternoon, arrangements offstage unfolded like the stuff of village hall farce. Noel Edmonds' helicopter company was bringing stars to the London Transport cricket ground, from where they could be transferred to Wembley by police car: 'The problem was that London Transport had a big cricket match on that day and couldn't cancel it; so the umpire was given a whistle every time a chopper was about to land and all the players would have to shuffle off the field.'

Edmonds was also one of the MCs at Wembley for the day and it fell to him to introduce Phil Collins, who planned to appear at both the London and Philadelphia events with a transatlantic Concorde flight in between: 'I went on stage and gave the big introduction – "Here he is, the man who is about to create history by playing the two biggest gigs of all time on the same day ... Phil Collins!" A roar went up and out walked Sting. In the time I had gone out on stage and spoken for about a minute they had changed the running order. Sting gave me a bit of a funny look but it was that sort of day.'

Thanks to the atmosphere inside the arena and the unprecedented sequence of big-name performers, Live Aid was a musical – and fund-raising – success beyond even Geldof's wildest dreams. Paul Young and Alison Moyet preceded a stunning show from U2, remembered by many for the moment when the lead singer Bono plucked a star-struck young fan, Melanie Hills, from the audience for an impromptu hug in front of the watching millions. The Queen set which followed is generally regarded as having been the day's musical highlight.

Into the evening, performances from Elton John, David Bowie, The Who – reformed for the occasion – and Dire Straits rang round the world before the night's final act: Paul McCartney. Eleanor Levy covered Live Aid for *Record*

Mirror magazine and later remembered: 'The rumour was that the remaining members of The Beatles were going to appear together again. That never materialised but to get McCartney there at all was an achievement. He hadn't done anything live in years and then his microphone went down. It was amazing, really. There was Paul McCartney singing *Let It Be* and no one could hear him. A lot of the crowd started whistling but he was none the wiser and just carried on.'

Although it was not until 1985 and Live Aid that Wembley became as famous as a rock venue as it had been as a sports arena for over sixty years, music had been woven into the stadium's history, one way or the other, since its opening day. In 1923 the bands of the Irish and Grenadier Guards had been swept up, along with the Bolton and West Ham players, in the crowd that invaded the pitch before kick-off at Wembley's first Cup Final.

Massed bands and an Imperial Choir played central roles in one-off events at the stadium during the course of the Empire Exhibition. Edward Elgar conducted on one such occasion in 1924. The great composer – and committed Wolves fan – might have hoped to combine his two passions at Wembley at some happy date thereafter. Unfortunately Elgar, who went so far as to compose a chant *He Banged The Leather For Goal* in Wolves' honour, died in 1934, some five years before his beloved Wanderers made their first appearance in a Wembley Cup Final.

Almost as old a tradition as marching bands on Cup Final day was community singing – conducted by a 'Man In White' on a podium in front of the Royal Box and introduced at Wembley in 1927. Bruce Forsyth was the last in a long line to wield the baton. After the scheduled songs were drowned out by terrace chants in 1975, the routine was dropped although in 1989, before the all-Merseyside 'Hillsborough' Final, Gerry Marsden led the crowd in singing *You'll Never Walk Alone*. *Abide With Me* remains an emotional part of the build-up to kick-off at Cup Finals even today.

Music was part of the Wembley setting for rugby league and speedway fixtures during the thirties but full-scale musical events at the stadium did not resume until the Second World War. Military pageants, tattoos and displays (with musical interludes) by Civil Defence and youth organisations were as regular a part of Wembley's programme, aimed very deliberately at boosting public morale, as were wartime Cup Finals and international matches. The military shows, in particular, remained popular into the days of peace. The large crowds, though, began to decline in the late sixties and seventies. The tattoos moved to smaller indoor arenas like Earls Court. Their place on the Wembley calendar was soon filled by the pop concerts which for the past two decades have done much to keep the stadium economically viable while, at the same time, broadening and redefining its prestige worldwide.

The first pop event in 1972 was a rock-and-roll legends affair, as memorable perhaps for the tantrums behind the scenes as for the history – and music – made onstage inside the stadium. Screaming Lord Sutch, a great and eccentric English tradition in his own right, recalls the in fighting which took place between the Americans topping a bill on which he and his band, the Savages, were just pleased to be included:

'We had three of the biggest stars in the world all on the same show and the argument was who should top the bill. At one point neither Chuck Berry, Jerry Lee Lewis nor Little Richard would go on unless he was top billing. There was a bit of a scene and they ended up flipping a coin to see who went out last. Then, a few days before the show, they added Bill Haley and the Comets to the bill, who were bigger than any of the other three at the time. They should have closed out the show but Chuck Berry was adamant and he got his way in the end.'

The concert, nonetheless, was hailed as a success. The stadium, though, took some time to become established as a major music venue. Crosby Stills

Nash & Young became the first solo act to play at Wembley in 1974, while Elton John was part of a bill that also included the Beach Boys and The Eagles three years later. The Who's and AC/DC's concert in 1979 was the fourth and last of the decade and the first promoted by Harvey Goldsmith, who would emerge as a key figure in transforming Wembley's reputation for music during the following decade.

Goldsmith staged three shows at the stadium in 1982, with two nights by the Rolling Stones a major success. Mel Bush staged Elton John's gig in 1984 just a few days after Watford, the football club John was chairman of, had lost an FA Cup Final to Everton. Three Bruce Springsteen concerts in 1985 are rated as being among the finest ever put on at Wembley, though everything that year was overshadowed by Live Aid, which had a profound effect on the lives of those for whom money was raised and for those spectators and performers who participated in the event. The day also changed the way the music world regarded the stadium. Charlie Shun, currently the sales manager at Wembley, remembers Live Aid as 'the event which established Wembley as a major rock venue. We had only staged ten different music shows at the stadium before Live Aid but after that it all took off. 1988, '89 and '90 were the most successful years ever for both the stadium and the Arena in terms of music and that was primarily down to Live Aid'.

Queen's final two concerts at Wembley in 1986 took on extra significance after the death of lead singer Freddie Mercury; a performer made for the biggest stage of all. It was fitting that in 1992 the rock world gathered to celebrate his career in an event which came close to recapturing some of Live Aid's atmosphere. 'I don't think I have ever known anyone who commanded as much affection as Freddie,' reflects Paul Young, who performed at the concert backed by the remaining members of Queen: 'Everyone just loved the guy and I am sure he would have loved the event. I did Live Aid and the Nelson Mandela concerts at Wembley but the Freddie gig was probably the one I enjoyed more than any other.'

The stadium staged two concerts dedicated to Nelson Mandela, the first in

June 1988 prior to his release from prison and the second two years later when he was present. Both captured a moment in history but may not be remembered with as much affection from a musical point of view as the Live Aid and Freddie Mercury events. Those one-off occasions apart, individual performers have also left their mark: Michael Jackson's seven-night run in 1988 was a record that may never be broken at the stadium while the 83,000 who packed in to watch Rod Stewart in 1995 – with the stage positioned where the centre spot would be on a football occasion – set an attendance record for a music event at Wembley.

Nothing, however, in Wembley's music history touches the drama and emotional charge of Live Aid. Perhaps the most poignant moment of that day came as the Cars anthem *Drive* was accompanied by footage of famine victims in Ethiopia on the stadium's giant screens. According to Richard Skinner, it was the moment that defined Live Aid and the idea and fact of Geldof's extraordinary achievement in making it happen: 'None of us realised how emotional the day was going to be. As the whole thing progressed you began to realise that it was a truly global event, linking up with Philadelphia and everything that went with that. And then this astounding, astonishing moment when the Cars track *Drive* was played alongside the images of the starving in Ethiopia. Tears ran down the faces of almost everyone inside the stadium. To this day I cannot hear that song without thinking of Live Aid. It was a remarkable mix of emotions, of celebration and the realisation of why we were there.'

MILITARY MUSICAL PAGEANT

WEMBLEY STADIUM
SATURDAY 7th JULY 1973
Sponsored by the Evening News
in aid of
THE ARMY BENEVOLENT FUND

OFFICIAL PROGRAMME 15p

1985: BOB GELDOF

I knew that Live Aid had to be at Wembley; there was never any question about that. One because it was in London, the capital, and two because it is instantly recognisable around the world thanks to its incredible history. There isn't an equivalent stadium anywhere in the world. Its status as a legendary building is unrivalled and I think it is as much to do with rock as it is sport. Live Aid would not have had the authority if it was not at Wembley.

Hyde Park was an alternative and we could have had far more people at the event if it was staged there but the authorities probably wouldn't have let us do it and you have the problem of selling tickets for an event in a park. It was clear from the start that the real action was going to centre around the television audience; that is where the big finance could come from. And the television people were happy with us staging it at Wembley.

I had actually walked out into the middle of the pitch on the Friday and just standing there it seems huge, bigger than any stadium in the world. Those twin towers, the whole aura of the place is very unique and I hope that, whatever they do to it in terms of redevelopment, they retain that. It has become far more than just a North London thing, an English thing. It may not be the biggest stadium but it contains all the drama of decades of emotion and you feel that.

Wembley is such a strange name, but say it to anyone in the world and they will instantly know what you are talking about. The place seems to expand to fit the enormity of the event, to reach your expectations. It is an incredible structure and you always feel you are a part of something special at Wembley. All the karma of everything that has gone, the victories and defeats go into every event there.

When they knock the stadium down I will certainly ask for a little chip of it. And Wembley will come again, I have no doubts about that. It will still be Wembley, that site; it will still mean a lot to go there. You can never take away the emotions of all these years. They will just be putting a new wall around those memories. There will always be a feeling, *If it's not Wembley, what's the point?*

On Live Aid day Wembley encompassed the planet. The entire world seemed to be plonked inside it. When you have the stadium packed as it was that day it becomes something very personal. You feel like you can make eye contact with 80,000 people. You want to take it all in, not let it pass you by.

That was the noise I felt, of all the people watching around the world. And to hear some people say that Live Aid is the greatest event in Wembley's history is an amazing thing. They remember the 1966 World Cup Final and the commentary *They think it's all over'*. But equally, they remember the announcement *It's 12 o'clock in London, 7am in Philadelphia and this is Live Aid*. I am proud of that.

USP RADIO INTERVIEW, 1998

1996: BRYAN ADAMS

My first gig there was memorable because of the number of complaints we drew from the locals. We had the stage facing the Royal Box which was a different position from normal and no one realised that the sound was going to travel straight down Wembley Way and into the town itself. The local residents let the organisers know what they thought about the whole thing and it was ironic that the tour was given the title *Waking Up The Neighbours*.

When I went back in 1996 it was probably my best gig ever. That had the proper Wembley vibe, something you don't get at any other stadium in the world. To stand in front of 70,000 of your own fans is just incredible. You cannot describe what it means and at Wembley it means that bit more. To a Canadian, Wembley is the mecca and not many people are lucky enough to experience that. You go wobbly at the knees, for sure, and that happens at Wembley more than anywhere in my experience. The difference with Wembley is that any event staged there is a big deal, whereas other venues are just a part of a tour. I always say that you haven't done a proper tour of England unless you have played Wembley Stadium. For major acts it is the place to be, without doubt. If I never got the chance to do Wembley again, at least I could say that I had done my best gig there.

INTERVIEW, 1997

WEMBLEY STADIUM

MCP presents

BRYAN
ADAMS

SATURDAY 27th JULY 1996
(Subject to Licence)
GATES OPEN 2.00 pm
FIRST BAND 4.00 pm

ENTER BY TURNSTILE E

BLOCK — ROW — SEAT

309 — A — 26

CLUB SUITE 30

Coming Home

1990-97

Lord Justice Taylor, Paul Gascoigne and Rupert Murdoch would seem to make odd company at the national game's top table. In 1990 the three harboured profoundly different ambitions. Lord Taylor was the man charged by the government with responsibility for ensuring a Hillsborough disaster would never happen again. Gascoigne, his place in the England team controversial but assured, was preparing to take on the best at Italia '90. Murdoch, the world's most powerful media entrepreneur but struggling to establish his satellite television interest in the UK, was casting a beady eye over the world's most popular spectator sport.

The fulfilment of this unlikely triumvirate's aspirations changed radically the idea and substance of football during the early nineties, creating a new environment (the whole new ball game breathlessly promised by Sky TV) which would make the end of one chapter of the Wembley story inevitable and the beginning of a new one, come the Millennium, possible for the first time.

The Taylor Report, a thorough and considered document, charted a way forward for a game scarred by the consequences of neglect, ignorance and lack of leadership. The parties the Report addressed and those affected by it – club administrators, fans, government, press, police and local authorities – fastened on to a single proposal, practical, tangible and, for some, potentially profitable, which could be implemented amid considerable fanfare. The fuss that accompanied the advent of the all-seater stadium meant Taylor's work would be remembered chiefly for that single recommendation.

Wembley had envisaged a future without the standing terraces before implementation of the Taylor Report made the change imperative, and it had also put in place facilities to accommodate the new kind of football audience which all-seater stadia would attract. In 1989 executive suites and 4,000 new seats high under the Wembley roof – the Olympic gallery – were installed. The stadium was able to stage its first all-seated events the following year.

Forced to work within the limitations of the stadium's original architecture, piecemeal modernisation inevitably served notice on a stadium becoming increasingly outdated. For example, despite Wembley's efforts to improve sightlines by increasing elevation, the backless seats at the front of the terracing offered a disappointing view in comparison with other parts of the stadium. The grand design of 1923 had been for a different game in very different times. The need to rebuild, indeed to re-imagine, Wembley was becoming increasingly apparent.

The first all-seated FA Cup Final, in 1990, proved auspicious on the pitch as well as off it. Manchester United, under their previous manager Ron Atkinson, had won at Wembley in 1983 and 1985. After three years (and £13 million worth of player acquisitions) with Alex Ferguson in charge 12 May 1990 was an opportunity for them to emulate those previous successes, even if they looked a pale shadow of the sides that had thrilled Britain in the fifties and sixties.

Though folklore has it that the 1990 Cup campaign kept Ferguson in a job, long-term planning had been the key to the new manager's appointment and had informed Ferguson's approach to the task of taking United back to the top of the English game. Success in the Cup Final was, in fact, early reward for the vision and application behind the Old Trafford scenes which, soon enough, would make team and club the most powerful and influential forces in the land.

Their opponents Crystal Palace, however, ran them close in front of a capacity crowd now reduced to 80,000. Though newly promoted Palace finished the League season behind United only on goal difference, they went into the game as underdogs in their first FA Cup Final. They took the lead through a Gary O'Reilly header, only for United's captain Bryan Robson, who had led Ron Atkinson's Wembley sides too, to equalise ten minutes before half-time.

The best was still to come. Just after the hour Mark Hughes put United ahead. Ian Wright, barely fit after recuperating from a broken leg, came off the substitutes' bench and, within minutes, had eluded Mike Phelan and Gary Pallister to equalise. In extra-time Wright took advantage of Jim Leighton's goalkeeping error to score Palace's third before, seven minutes from time, Hughes scored his second to take the game to a replay.

Steve Bruce would later describe the 3–3 draw as 'a pleasure to be part of, one hell of a game'. The second meeting proved altogether more prosaic, a 1–0 win for United in an attritional, physical contest which only the partisan could enjoy. (Bryan Robson certainly did: 'I preferred the replay; we won the Cup. That made it a great game.') A forgettable spectacle was settled by a volley from Lee Martin, a young full-back whose career, unlike many of his team-mates', would never reach such heights again. Indeed that summer Martin was packed off to Germany as part of the United reserve team's close-season tour.

For the goalscorer's club, however, the narrowest of victories was of enormous significance. Martin himself later observed: 'When you score a goal like that – it was only the second I'd ever scored for United and it was my last for them, too – you know it is history in the making.' His captain, Robson, would still be around in seasons to come to be part of the success which that Wembley winner helped to make possible: 'Once you win one trophy, the confidence is there to achieve even more and that proved to be the case for that United team.'

England's Wembley preparations for Italia '90 were part of an unprecedentedly busy spring at the stadium. As well as the Cup Final the football schedule included two schoolboy internationals, Forest's 1–0 win over Oldham in a successful defence of the League Cup, the Zenith Data Systems Cup, FA Vase, Leyland Daf Cup and FA Trophy finals and, for the first time, the deciding matches of the League's divisional play-offs.

Cambridge United, Notts County and Swindon Town won promotion from their respective divisions after victories at Wembley over the May Bank Holiday weekend. The crowds at the three games – the best of them, 72,873, watching Swindon beat Sunderland in the Second Division final on the Monday – and the added edge the play-off system gave to the latter stages of the League season meant the fixtures proved popular enough and profitable enough to find a regular place on the calendar.

Bobby Robson's national side, meanwhile, recorded 1–0 wins over Brazil and Denmark, a 4–2 victory over Czechoslovakia and a 2–1 defeat by Uruguay in the last game at Wembley before the World Cup kicked off that summer. Much speculation at Wembley and in the press was centred on the inclusion of two promising talents, David Platt and Paul Gascoigne. A stirring run to the semi-finals in Italy, in which England's games were the most exciting of the tournament, would see both men emerge as heroes in the eyes of a new audience for a rejuvenated national game.

Platt moved out of the domestic limelight at once, beginning a successful career in Italy with Bari before lucrative transfers to Juventus, Sampdoria and, on his return to England in 1995, Arsenal. An undemonstrative, honest and disciplined professional, he would go on to captain England in the early nineties, his goals – a remarkable twenty-seven in sixty-two games – saving further embarrassment during Graham Taylor's ignominious reign as England manager.

Gascoigne, meanwhile, met post-Italia '90 stardom head on. His talents would illuminate much of 1990/91 before, ultimately, scarring both himself and the occasion in the course of the season's Wembley showpiece. While

Platt's phlegmatic sophistication earned him the respect of his peers and England fans, Gascoigne's personality – shamelessly emotional, unpredictable and alternately charming and boorish – singled him out for attention in the gossip columns as well as the sports pages.

England's World Cup performances against Belgium and Cameroon and the almost unbearable tension of the semi-final and subsequent penalty shoot-out against the Germans captured the imagination of a country glued to the TV coverage. No one did more than Gascoigne, heart on his sleeve in endless close-ups, to move the national game from the margins to which it had been consigned by crowd violence, mediocre product and shabby customer relations back into the mainstream of the national culture.

Tottenham Hotspur, for their part, began the new decade in all sorts of trouble: inconsistent on the pitch and facing bankruptcy off it. The problems behind the scenes at White Hart Lane, with a cast including Irving Scholar, Terry Venables and Alan Sugar playing out their soap opera in books, TV programmes, the popular press and the High Court, would rumble on. The immediate present, meanwhile, was rescued by the club's two bankable stars, Gascoigne and Gary Lineker, whose FA Cup exploits brought silverware to Spurs for the first time in nearly a decade and whose subsequent sales kept the ship afloat in the roughest of economic waters.

The season was dominated by their North London rivals Arsenal who won the League comfortably, losing only one game. A second Double seemed within reach before they were drawn against Spurs in the FA Cup semi-final. Interest in the game was sufficiently intense, this being the first time they had met at this stage of the competition, for the FA to decide that Wembley was the most practical venue. On 14 April 1991 the stadium staged its first domestic semi-final.

Whatever the arguments as to the appropriateness of playing the fixture at the venue which had for so long been reserved for the Final (with semi-finals played at Wembley in 1993 and 1994, too, the point remained moot for several years), Arsenal and Spurs produced a spectacle worthy of Wembley.

Within five minutes Gascoigne conjured a goal enshrined in the catalogue of Wembley's most memorable, bending a fiercely struck free-kick high beyond David Seaman from thirty yards. Spurs' star-turn dominated proceedings thereafter and was instrumental in the build-up to a second goal scored by Lineker from Paul Allen's cross. Although Alan Smith halved their lead just before half-time and Gascoigne was taken off after an hour to protect a groin injury, Spurs withstood Arsenal's second-half siege and a second Lineker goal ensured Terry Venables's side would be back at Wembley to face Nottingham Forest in the Final.

Although Brian Clough had guided Forest to four League Cup appearances at Wembley in a managerial career which encompassed success at the highest level in domestic and European club football, he had never before brought a team to an FA Cup Final. Under ordinary circumstances the build-up to Spurs v Nottingham Forest would have focused on one of the era's most successful, most charismatic and most controversial managers realising a long-cherished ambition. But 1991 would be Gazza's final even though he was on the pitch for less than twenty minutes of it.

As the teams took the field Clough took the hand of his counterpart Terry Venables, who in the preceding weeks had been putting together a consortium to take over beleaguered Spurs. Neither could have imagined how proceedings were about to unfold. After only a minute Gascoigne lunged, his foot chest-high, at Forest's Garry Parker. The victim went down in a heap, the perpetrator, wide-eyed and hyperventilated, shrugged and fidgeted. Sadly the referee Roger Milford smiled indulgently and did nothing.

Less than a quarter of an hour later Gascoigne threw himself into another reckless challenge, scything down Gary Charles just outside the Spurs penalty area. Thousands in the stadium waited while both players received treatment. The millions watching on TV winced at the wildness of the tackle as it was replayed in slow motion. Roger Milford had time to consider a course of action: 'Words were said, I knew Gazza was not going to continue.

Whether my heart ruled my head, or vice versa, I didn't take any action. To be really truthful, it was a sending-off offence ... but the sense of the occasion and everything that went on – Peter Willis got a terrible hammering a couple of years before that for sending off Kevin Moran ... doubt comes into your mind and I didn't do what perhaps I should have done.'

When Stuart Pearce drove the free-kick past Erik Thorstvedt to open the scoring it seemed justice had been served. Gascoigne left the field soon afterwards on a stretcher. He had ruptured cruciate ligaments in his assault on Charles, an injury from which his career would never wholly recover. His team-mates, however, rose to the challenge and, despite Lineker missing a penalty just before half-time, a shot by Paul Stewart and an own-goal by Des Walker four minutes into extra-time were enough to win the Cup for Spurs.

By then Gascoigne lay in hospital waiting to hear the worst about his knee. Brian Clough's disappointment understandably left room for little sympathy: 'When you're born with an exquisite talent you have a responsibility to use it, not abuse it. Gascoigne has abused his own gifts ... He received not one scrap of sympathy from me.'

Liverpool's victory over Second Division Sunderland in the 1992 Cup Final marked the end of the club's two decades at the very top of the domestic game. An unremarkable game was illuminated only by the opening goal in a 2–0 win, a volley hit on the turn from fifteen yards by Michael Thomas whose shot for Arsenal in the closing seconds of the most dramatic League game in history had denied Liverpool the Double in the Hillsborough year of 1989.

Football's balance of power was shifting from Anfield towards Old Trafford and Highbury. Rugby league, on the other hand, and its showpiece Wembley game, the Challenge Cup Final, continued to be dominated by the most successful team in the sport's history. For eight seasons in the late eighties and early nineties the stadium was a second home and impregnable fortress for the game's all-conquering superpower Wigan.

The Central Park club had returned to Wembley in 1984 for the first time since losing to Castleford in 1970. In the intervening years their fans had been to hell and back, watching one of the game's great names suffer the indignity of relegation before a renaissance engineered behind the scenes by a new board which included Maurice Lindsay, arguably the most influential figure in the sport's history, and on the pitch by a new coach, Alex Murphy, and fresh talent like Shaun Edwards who, at just over seventeen-and-a-half years old, became the youngest player ever to appear in a challenge Cup Final when he lined up against Widnes in 1984.

On the day Wigan were no match for a Widnes side captained by Eric Hughes who, along with Mick Adams and the hooker Keith Elwell, picked up a winners' medal for the fourth time after a 19–6 win. The game, though, marked a turning point, as Maurice Lindsay would later recall: 'Looking back it wasn't a particularly distinguished Wigan team and we made so many mistakes. After I had been in the dressing-room to commiserate with the players I had to come out into the tunnel which led to the pitch to control my emotions … Eric Hughes came across to speak to me. I shall never forget his words. He said: "I know you're upset but don't worry, your star is on the way up and Wigan will be back."'

The following year they were, to face Hull in Wembley's fiftieth Challenge Cup Final which would see Wigan's first success in the competition since 1965. The game is remembered as a marvellous spectacle – Hull's twenty-four points against Wigan's twenty-eight the most any losing side had scored at the stadium – enlivened by the contributions of ten southern hemisphere stars, including Wigan's New Zealand captain Graeme West and the Australian man-of-the-match Brett Kenny. As the rugby league historian John Huxley later observed: 'Television took the match to an audience of millions and did more to enhance rugby league's cause as a serious sport than almost anything it had achieved in its history up to that point.'

Wigan served notice then that they were back and, although the club did not return to Wembley for three years, an era of unparalleled success was on the horizon. The 32–12 defeat of Halifax in front of a capacity crowd in 1988 was the first of eight consecutive victories in the Challenge Cup Final. Shaun Edwards, a promising youngster in 1984 and 1985, not only played in all eight finals but in every cup tie on the way to Wembley between 1988 and 1995.

The 27–0 win over St. Helens in 1989 provided, perhaps, the sweetest of Wembley memories for the Wigan faithful, though the game was one of the most one-sided in the tournament's history. Wigan v St. Helens has the keen edge of the fiercest local rivalries, as the coach Graham Lowe had learned on his first day at Central Park: 'I was just crossing the car park when a Wigan fan came up to me and said: "I don't care what else you do with this club, just make sure you beat St. Helens every time."'

The 1989 final was Lowe's last in charge of Wigan and the ruthless demolition of St. Helens – to avenge, at last, Wembley defeats in 1961 and 1966 – was the most crowd-pleasing way imaginable for the New Zealander to take his leave. Kevin Iro touched down twice, Andy Gregory, Steve Hampson and the uniquely gifted captain Ellery Hanley once each. If the Wigan contingent in a capacity crowd thought life could not get more satisfying, they reckoned without a team which rewrote rugby league's record books in the early 1990s.

The Wembley finals – and TV coverage of them – enabled Wigan to reach a new audience for themselves and the sport. Beyond rugby league's traditional heartland punters who had never given the game a second thought had their interest kindled by the club's extraordinary success and the charismatic talents of its star players. One did not need to understand the finer details to be inspired by Shaun Edwards' courage – injured in a tenth-minute collision and playing the rest of the 1990 Wembley final with a fractured cheekbone – or thrilled by Martin Offiah's athleticism – picking up the ball a few feet from his own goal-line and charging the length of the field, a trail of opponents in his wake, to score against Leeds in 1994.

Edwards, Offiah, Hanley, Gregory, Betts were names that made the nation sit up and pay attention to rugby league. Wigan players were crucial, too, in a golden age for the international team. At Wembley Hanley captained a Great Britain Test side to its first home victory against Australia in over a decade. In 1994 he coached the side which repeated the achievement, winning 8–4, despite Edwards' sending-off. Success was reflected by the size of the crowds: in 1973 less than 10,000 had turned up at Wembley to see Great Britain beat Australia 21–12. In 1990 over 54,000 witnessed the 19–12 victory there and the 1992 and 1995 World Cup Finals, both won by Australia, attracted near capacity attendances to the stadium.

Wigan's eventual and spectacular fall from grace came about as a direct result of their unprecedented domination. On the one hand, the income generated from Wembley finals had become so regular a fixture on the balance sheet, underwriting transfer fees and top players' wages, that defeat at Salford in a Challenge Cup tie in February 1996 sparked a financial crisis; directors were soon facing legal proceedings. On the other, the injection of £87 million into the game – reward for agreeing a contract with Rupert Murdoch's satellite TV interests to create a European equivalent of Australasia's Super League – gave established clubs such as Bradford, St. Helens and Leeds and newcomers like London and Sheffield the chance to compete commercially with Wigan. Rugby league's most powerful club found itself having to come to terms with the sport's own version of the 'whole new ball game' almost overnight.

English clubs – Liverpool apart, whose ban stayed in place for a further year – were readmitted to European competition in 1990. Manchester United, although losing 1–0 in 1991's League Cup Final at Wembley to a Sheffield Wednesday team under their former manager Ron Atkinson, took a further step into what would become a hugely successful decade for them with victory in the European Cup Winners' Cup, beating Barcelona in the final in Rotterdam thanks to Mark Hughes' goal.

The lifting of the post-Heysel ban also put Wembley back on the European map. In 1992 the stadium staged its first European Cup Final since Liverpool's defeat of FC Brugge in 1978. The game meant a welcome return for the former Ajax and Holland star Johan Cruyff, now managing Barcelona. 'I have very good memories about Wembley,' he said beforehand. 'The stadium is beautiful, a cathedral to football. The English fans are very honest with me, they enjoyed the way the team [Ajax] played and the way I played. There was a lot of mutual respect. I think the English supporters will support Barcelona because we will be doing the attacking.'

Cruyff was right; his side eventually beat a cautious Sampdoria 1–0 in extra-time with a thundering free-kick from the Dutch sweeper Ronald Koeman. The crowd was a near-capacity 70,000, more than half of whom had travelled from Spain and Italy to experience Wembley first-hand. Off the pitch more than on it the occasion marked a colourful, good-natured and passionate return to the European arena, pre-empting the spirit which would, four years later, make the summer of Euro '96 so memorable at Wembley and elsewhere.

In 1993 the stadium staged the European Cup Winners' Cup Final. Parma beat Antwerp 3–1 in a one-sided game, a crowd of less than 40,000 reflecting the second-string nature of the competition. National cup competitions elsewhere in Europe enjoy nothing like the prestige or the allure of the FA Cup, which explains in part why English clubs have enjoyed success in recent years in the Cup Winners' Cup while continuing to struggle in the Champions League and Uefa Cup.

Parma's defence of the trophy in 1994 would falter in a final in Copenhagen twelve months later against Arsenal. George Graham's team, having won the League Cup in 1987, beating Liverpool 2–1 in the Wembley final, and then lost it 3–2 to the underdogs Luton in the following year's final, briefly threatened to take English football by storm when winning League titles in 1989 and 1991. By 1993, however, despite the acquisition of the most prolific goalscorer in the club's history Ian Wright, Arsenal had fallen behind a handful of northern peers, in terms of consistency at least. The consolation for their fans was the emergence of one of the domestic game's greatest-ever cup sides which completed a unique Wembley double in 1992/93, winning the League and FA Cups during a year which saw them play five games at the stadium.

A week after Cremonese had beaten Derby County 3–1 in the latest obscure competition awarded a Wembley final – the Anglo-Italian Cup – April's FA Cup semi-finals were played over a weekend at the stadium, the draw having thrown up two local derbies. Arsenal again met Spurs while fans of the Sheffield clubs, United and Wednesday, lobbied successfully for their semi-final too to be moved to Wembley.

On the Saturday over 75,000 made their way down the M1 to witness a match-winning display and marvellous free-kick goal from the Footballer of the Year, Chris Waddle, as Wednesday won 2–1. The following day's atmosphere was altogether less leavened by a sense of civic pride and communal celebration. In a meaner-spirited affair Arsenal had Lee Dixon sent off but won by a single late goal, headed in at the far post by Tony Adams.

A fortnight later the FA Cup finalists met first in the final of the League Cup. Level at half-time after an opening goal by John Harkes for Sheffield Wednesday and an equaliser from the day's most influential player Paul Merson, the young Arsenal midfielder Steve Morrow stabbed home his first goal for the club and what proved to be the winner. Many will best remember the occasion for the badly broken arm Morrow sustained during celebrations on the pitch after the match which saw him dispatched to hospital as his team-mates climbed to the Royal Box to collect their medals.

Morrow had to wait until Cup Final day, 15 May, to collect his before Arsenal and Wednesday kicked off. Within minutes it became clear that the two managers, George Graham and Trevor Francis, had thought long and hard about their sides' second Wembley appointment: defensive cover was so well-marshalled that it all but extinguished opportunities for creative play. Ian Wright put Arsenal ahead, David Hirst equalised just after the hour. Long before the end of extra-time both teams had settled into stalemate.

The replay, five days later on a drizzly Thursday night, attracted the lowest crowd ever for a Wembley Cup Final, 62,267, suggesting that for Wednesday fans in particular, because of their 350-mile round trip, the season had been too expensive already. The game was little better than the Saturday's but at least produced the kind of dramatic finish for which Arsenal had developed something of a reputation.

Ian Wright scored his fourth Cup Final goal to give Arsenal the lead, running on to Alan Smith's pass before flicking his shot deftly over Chris Woods. Chris Waddle's deflected drive brought Wednesday level and during an uncompromising period of extra-time both sets of fans steeled themselves for Wembley's first Cup Final penalty shoot-out. With seconds remaining, however, a Merson corner was met flush by the head of an unmarked Andy Linighan. Woods' parry only took the ball into the roof of the net. George Graham, thanks to goals from two of his squad's lesser lights, became the first man to win all three of English football's major domestic honours as a player and manager. The following May Arsenal would go on to Copenhagen to beat Parma by a single Alan Smith goal and become the second English side to win the European Cup Winners' Cup in the 1990s. The success was further reward for their efforts of the previous season, during which it had seemed, in the words of Tony Adams, as if 'Arsenal were at Wembley every other week'.

Arsenal's fifth visit to the stadium in 1993 was for the Charity Shield game against Manchester United in August. The match ended 1–1 and the players were making their way off the pitch when officials informed them that a penalty shoot-out would decide the result. The Arsenal goalkeeper David

Seaman took one, missed and handed victory to United. If the season started in confusing circumstances, by its end no one would be in any doubt that an Old Trafford dynasty was in place that could hope at last to emulate the achievements of the Busby era.

'Ince at his peak, Hughes at his peak, Kanchelskis flying ...' As Alex Ferguson would later recall, his team going into the 1993/94 season was full of stars, a splendid balance of pace, power and ingenuity. The previous campaign had seen United win the League for the first time in nearly thirty years and one player stood out as a catalyst, turning a good side into a great one.

Eric Cantona had helped Leeds United to the Championship in 1992. He then dazzled Wembley with a hat-trick against Liverpool in that year's Charity Shield before a surprising and controversial transfer took him to Old Trafford a few weeks later. The difference Cantona made to Manchester United was profound and dramatic; his vision, confidence and goals – at crucial times in crucial games – gave the team an extra dimension, lifting them clear of the best efforts of their peers.

The following season, 1992/93, was an auspicious one for the English game. Football's popularity, buoyed by England's good run in the 1990 World Cup, brought new fans into remodelled stadia made safer by the all-seater guidelines implemented in accordance with the Taylor Report. In response commercial interests began to invest in football through sponsorship, the use of executive facilities and even acquisition of the clubs themselves.

Sky TV were among the first into the new marketplace. The creation of the Premier League in 1992 and the signing over of live rights for television coverage to Rupert Murdoch's satellite stations brought £214 million into football over the course of a four-year deal. Manchester United's winning of the inaugural Premier League title put them on top of a very profitable pile. With the game apparently awash with money, success like United's could prove thereafter to be a licence to print one's own.

In 1994 Cantona and his team-mates completed the League and Cup double for the first time in United's history; only a 3–1 defeat by Aston Villa in the League Cup Final prevented them achieving an unprecedented clean sweep of the game's domestic honours. The club had hit the jackpot at exactly the right time.

Again the FA Cup semi-finals were played at Wembley. Chelsea reached the final with a routine 2–0 victory over Luton. United, on the other hand, struggled against Oldham Athletic. Alex Ferguson later described that game's closing stages: 'You always feel for your opponent when he loses a big game, especially at Wembley with practically the last kick. We were in the last minute when Hughes scored that incredible goal, completely out of the blue.' In fact, Mark Hughes' trademark volley was a last-gasp equaliser rather than a winning goal but, to all intents and purposes, it was enough to take United through, according to Ferguson: 'Oldham realised that that had been their chance and the replay was a formality.'

So, eventually, was the Final itself, although for nearly an hour Chelsea, their star rising under their new player-manager Glenn Hoddle, seemed well enough equipped to make a contest of it. The referee David Elleray awarded two controversial penalties which Cantona converted and, with further goals from Hughes and Brian McClair, United completed a second-half rout. Tony Banks, Sports Minister from 1997, speaks for all Chelsea fans when he says: 'I was very angry after the game; I still haven't got over those penalty decisions.'

Proof of how important Cantona's contribution had been came the following year, in notorious circumstances. The United star spent much of the season out of the game, banned after an extraordinary assault on a spectator during a League game at Selhurst Park against Crystal Palace; it explained, in part, why Ferguson's side fell short in May. Having lost out to Blackburn Rovers on the last day of the League season, United lost the Cup Final to a single goal by Everton's Paul Rideout.

The contest was far from memorable but the result provided a certain symmetry not lost on the managers involved. Joe Royle had been in charge of Oldham for the previous season's semi-final, as Ferguson recalls: 'He must have been gutted but that's life and you have to get up from your disappointments and bounce back. Wembley, though, isn't a place where you want to be a loser. I found that out in 1995 when we lost to Everton who, ironically, were managed by Joe Royle.'

By the time Cantona returned to the team, several of the senior players who had done so much to secure United's first Double had moved on: Paul Ince to Inter Milan, Mark Hughes to Chelsea and Andrei Kanchelskis to Everton. The side at Wembley to face Liverpool on 11 May 1996 was captained by the charismatic Frenchman and built around young talent which had been brought through United's youth development programme. At the start of the season the former Liverpool star Alan Hansen had reminded the world that 'you win nothing with kids'. Gary and Philip Neville, Ryan Giggs, Nicky Butt, David Beckham and Paul Scholes arrived at Wembley to explode the received wisdom.

With the League title already won, a single goal, driven in from the edge of the penalty area by Cantona – inevitably the hero of the day – was enough to secure a second Double and a place in history for United. As Alex Ferguson later observed: 'I think a lot of people would see the 1996 Double as our greatest achievement. The young lads handled it so well and lasted the distance despite what some people predicted. We had a bigger pool of players in 1994. The young players two years later were unbelievable.'

The chapter in the FA's official history of the England team which covers the period of Graham Taylor's management is entitled 'Best We Forget'. Watching the national side's decline from the heights scaled at Italia '90 was certainly an experience few will care to remember. Qualification for the 1992 European Championships was narrowly achieved after an uninspired campaign which included a scrambled draw against Ireland and an unconvincing 1–0 win over Turkey at Wembley.

The tournament in Sweden was to prove even more painful for the former Watford and Aston Villa manager. Taylor returned to England after the defeat by the host nation which eliminated them from the competition to find his head superimposed on a root vegetable beneath the score in banner headlines: 'Swedes 2 Turnips 1'. Worse followed during the national team's attempts to qualify for the 1994 World Cup.

In October 1992 a 1–1 draw in front of just over 50,000 enervated spectators at Wembley against Norway ensured that the coming months would become an endless struggle to make up lost ground. Although qualification was still theoretically possible until the last round of group matches, most England fans had abandoned realistic ambitions during the second half of a vital game against Holland at Wembley in April 1993.

England were 2–0 up within twenty-five minutes through goals from John Barnes and the prolific captain David Platt but hope drained away after Dennis Bergkamp put the Dutch back in contention with a marvellous solo effort against the run of play. Paul Gascoigne's cheekbone was then fractured in a crude challenge by Jan Wouters. The foul went unpunished; not so England's lack of staying power. Four minutes from time Des Walker, undone by the pace of Marc Overmars, conceded a penalty which gifted Holland a barely deserved equaliser.

England, having played so central and enterprising a part in 1990's World Cup, failed to qualify for USA '94. Taylor, a more than capable club manager but out of his depth – and pilloried for it – at international level, fell on his sword. Terry Venables, a popular if controversial figure, was appointed in his place, charged with the task of restoring a dispirited national team in time for England's hosting of the 1996 European Championships.

Venables' appointment brought an optimism which reflected, on one hand, the cheerful public image presented by the new manager and, on the other, perhaps a belief that England, having touched bottom, could only improve. Over 70,000 turned out at Wembley for Venables' first game in charge, a 1–0 win over Denmark, the start of a programme of friendlies, most of them at home, which the manager used to establish the personnel and pattern of play he intended to use in Euro '96.

The tournament, the first European Championships to be staged in England, kicked off on 8 June at Wembley, the host nation playing Switzerland. Behind the fanfare of the opening ceremony – forty-five minutes of high-tech meets Merrie Olde Englande – lay familiar doubts. Was Gascoigne, after his central role in a 'men behaving badly' episode on the other side of the world a fortnight previously, worth a place in the team? What had happened to Alan Shearer, last an England goalscorer nearly two years previously? Might hooliganism yet spoil the prospect of the biggest summer of football in England since 1966?

As Terry Venables later recalled: 'It wasn't just our first competitive game for nearly three years but the first game of the tournament. And when did you ever see a good opening match? There are peculiar tensions and pressures at work and the crowd was a bit subdued ... Perhaps they were nervous, too.' An early goal by Shearer, who as usual wrote his own script, settled players and spectators for a while. As England tired, however, the Swiss pressed forward and, late on, won a penalty when a Marco Grassi shot hit Stuart Pearce's arm. Kubilay Turkyilmaz equalised and at the final whistle Swiss fans, cowbells clanging, celebrated the draw as they might have the win some observers thought their team had deserved. Many England fans, meanwhile, having arrived at Wembley hoping for the best, drifted homewards fearing the worst.

The host nation's stumbling start brought Scots fans to Wembley, for the first time in nearly a decade, in good heart for the second group fixture the following Saturday. Scotland had the better of a goalless first half, the apparent balance of power celebrated by a raucous rendition of *Rocking All Over The World* from the tartan contingent during the break. England, however, outsung in the partisan and largely good-natured contest in the stands, regrouped to take control of matters on the pitch. Jamie Redknapp's arrival as substitute, although he lasted less than half an hour before sustaining an injury which put him out of the tournament, nonetheless turned the game England's way.

Busy in central midfield to release Gascoigne from defensive duties, Redknapp instigated the move from which Shearer put England ahead with a header from Gary Neville's cross. Fifteen minutes from the end, however, another penalty – this one after Adams' sliding tackle on Gordon Durie – gave Scotland the chance to equalise. As Gary McAllister ran up to take the kick, the ball rolled gently, strangely, a few inches off the penalty spot. The Scotland captain's shot lifted to a height which allowed David Seaman to divert it over the bar.

Within minutes the game was won in spectacular fashion. Darren Anderton sent a through-pass into the left of the Scotland penalty area. Gascoigne ran in, lifted the ball over the advancing defender, Colin Hendry, with his left foot and then volleyed past Andy Goram with his right. Venables' loyalty had been rewarded in some style, as the England manager would later recall: 'It was not only the best goal of the tournament but the best in the last two or three major tournaments. If Romario or Marco Van Basten had scored it, everyone would be raving about it still; but, being English, we tend to give only grudging respect to wonderful demonstrations of individual skill like that.'

The 2–0 win left England needing to beat Holland the following Tuesday to ensure that they would win their group and play their quarter-final at Wembley. The bare statistics – and 76,400 spectators' senses – were swept away for the night as the country died and went to football heaven. During an hour in which England's team played better than it had in living memory, four goals – two from Shearer, one a penalty, and two from Teddy Sheringham, his attacking partner – were deserved reward for something close to the 'total football' that was once the hallmark of the greatest Dutch sides. Delighted supporters were unsure whether they should be cheering or simply sitting in rapt admiration. As Richard Williams wrote in the *Guardian* the following day: 'When Teddy Sheringham slid the fourth goal past Van der Sar, the sound of pure joy was heard all around Wembley. England's fans had found eleven players whose deeds matched their dreams.'

Those fans, it transpired, had their part to play the following Saturday when Spain were England's quarter-final opponents. The game blew a cool breath of reality through a warm Wembley afternoon. Spain had much the better of a tense first half before England slowly began to turn the tide thanks, in the words of the *Independent*'s Ken Jones, to 'the spirit for which British football is famous. As only a few thousand Spaniards were present in the crowd, England had overwhelming support and they made the most of it'.

The game was goalless after ninety minutes and remained so during an increasingly nervous extra period, both sides apparently inhibited by the Golden Goal rule: one mistake might mean the end of the tournament for the team which made it. Instead an expectant Wembley prepared for its first international penalty shoot-out. Again the crowd played its part. According to Ken Jones: 'When Hierro strode up for the first penalty the whistling was enough to have drowned out the noise made by Concorde at take-off.' The Spaniard hit his shot against the crossbar.

After Shearer and Platt had scored, Stuart Pearce had the opportunity to make up for the disappointment of his penalty miss at Italia '90. As the ball flew in, Pearce charged towards the crowd, wide-eyed, open-mouthed, roaring, to provide one of Euro '96's enduring images. The fans bellowed with him, as did Venables: 'I've never seen a reaction like that from a penalty-taker before. I've seen celebration but that was sheer, bloody relief. It was really marvellous to watch.'

All that remained was a successful penalty from Gascoigne and a remarkable, athletic save from Miguel Angel Nadal by David Seaman. The game won, the chorus of *Football's Coming Home* – the crowd never did quite get the hang of the verses – rang out around Wembley. Matt Tench, writing in the *Independent* the following week, recalled: 'The joyous rendition of the song at the end of the Spain game was the best moment of a tense and slightly deflating afternoon. As we finished it for the second time the middle-aged woman in the row behind me could hold herself back no longer and began crying uncontrollably.'

She was one fan who would have been well-advised to save her tears for the following Wednesday when the semi-final against Germany ended in disappointment for England after a game as dramatic, in its way, as the World Cup Final thirty years previously. The evening of 26 June 1996 will last long in memory. Wembley that night, both despite and because of its heartbreaking climax, was a marvellous place to be.

The stadium was heaving, a mass of colour, echoing to the hope and expectation of the now familiar anthem long before kick-off. Less than three minutes into the game the old place exploded as Shearer, the tournament's leading scorer, stabbed England in front. The lead, though, did not last and Stefan Kuntz soon equalised. Thereafter a classic contest unfolded, England's spirit of adventure foundering on their opponents' indomitable resolve. England, Terry Venables would remember, 'were outstanding in the second half and perhaps even better in extra-time'. Anderton hit the woodwork, Gascoigne was inches away from a tap-in at the far post but, the more they monopolised possession, the more obstinate and dangerous on the break the Germans became.

For the first time in the tournament both sides had gone in search of the sudden-death winner, making for a breathless, enthralling extra half-hour. It was all in vain. The winners would be decided by another penalty shoot-out. Five were taken successfully by each side – every time a German ran up, thousands of whispers, 'Dave Seaman will stop one sooner or later', rustled through the stands – before Gareth Southgate volunteered to take England's sixth. Nearly 76,000 held their breath inside Wembley, as did millions more watching on TV. Up stepped Southgate, only to place his kick too close to the keeper. Andreas Kopke dived to his right to save and Andy Moller converted his side's sixth penalty to take Germany into the final.

Southgate, understandably inconsolable, was surrounded by team-mates. Jurgen Klinsmann, who missed the game through injury, came on too to commiserate. Venables declared: 'Football can be a cruel game but it can also be glorious. We have experienced both emotions in the last week. I am feeling for Gareth but he must not hurt too much . . . he comes out of this tournament with a lot of credit and should remember that.'

The German manager Bertie Vogts did not try to hide his relief. He described the England side as the best he had ever seen: 'I would also suggest that it was one of the best performances of all time by a German team and we were lucky to win, which says a lot of the England team.' The Wembley crowd offered a chorus of 'There's only one Gareth Southgate' before slipping quietly away, leaving the block of German fans to celebrate with their own rendition of 'Football's Coming Home'.

The match would have been as stirring a climax as Euro '96 might have hoped for but, as Matthew Engel pointed out in the *Guardian* the following day, 'the result was especially disastrous for anyone with a ticket for the final and thoughts of selling it; they will be difficult to give away now'. Germany v the Czech Republic attracted the smallest Wembley crowd of the tournament, 73,611, for a final that never shook off its sense of happening after the Lord Mayor's show.

The majority of partisans in the crowd, understandably, were German. Neutrals invested what emotion remained in the efforts of the underdogs. The Czechs, after losing their first game of Euro '96 to Germany, had improved steadily and took the lead at Wembley on the hour, Patrick Berger scoring from the spot after Karel Poborsky was judged to have been fouled inside the area.

Before the game Bertie Vogts had pointed out that 'for a player to play at Wembley is a very special moment in his career'. It was doubly so for Oliver Bierhoff, who came off the substitutes' bench after seventy-three minutes to equalise with his first touch of the ball. Five minutes into sudden-death extra-time he struck again, his shot bobbling past Petr Kouba and in off the far post to win the game and the tournament. A strange hiatus followed – the German celebrations briefly interrupted after a linesman appeared to indicate that Bierhoff had been offside – but the goal stood and Euro '96, in the words of Ken Jones, 'brought Germany their seventh major championship and left England and their supporters wondering what might have been'.

Apart from the delights and disappointments afforded by England's progress in the tournament, part of the spell cast on the country's football fans by Euro '96 was the novelty of watching international players from all over Europe who were already – or soon would be – playing their league football in the Premiership. Some of world football's biggest names – Ruud Gullit, Dennis Bergkamp, Jurgen Klinsmann – had already been attracted to the competition, the passion and, above all, the huge salaries which were becoming part and parcel of a domestic game in rude economic health.

Wembley's showpiece games during 1997 proved as exotic, in terms of personnel, as the previous summer's international tournament. Newly promoted Middlesbrough, managed by Bryan Robson, started life in the top division with a playing staff augmented by the Brazilian midfielders Junhino and Emerson and the Italian striker Fabrizio Ravanelli. During a confusing season, made more so by constant speculation that their foreign stars were on the point of packing their bags, Middlesbrough's relegation from the Premiership at the first time of asking was felt all the more intensely by players and fans for their having lost both League and FA Cup finals.

In April, after leading 1–0 through a Ravanelli goal in extra-time, Robson's team were held to a draw by Leicester City at Wembley and lost the Hillsborough replay to a single Steve Claridge goal. In a period during which most Boro fans hardly knew whether they and their team were coming or going, Robson likewise found himself at something of a loss: 'People have said that, if we'd won that game, it would have lifted our season but you don't know what would have happened. After we lost the replay against

Leicester we went on a very good run in the league. It's hard to know what effect games like the League Cup Final have on players.'

By 17 May and the FA Cup Final Middlesbrough had already been relegated. Their opponents, Chelsea, now managed by Ruud Gullit, had a cosmopolitan line-up of their own, including a Norwegian, a Romanian, a Frenchman and two experienced Italian internationals in Gianfranco Zola and Roberto Di Matteo, with a third, Gianluca Vialli, on the substitutes' bench. Di Matteo all but won the game in the first minute, scoring Wembley's quickest Cup Final goal with a shot from distance after only forty-three seconds.

Bryan Robson later said he felt even worse some twenty minutes later: 'By then not only were we 1–0 down but our most consistent player, Robbie Mustoe, had done his cartilage and Ravanelli's hamstring had gone. I thought the gods were against us.' A second goal, by the merely mortal Eddie Newton, was sufficient to put Boro out of their misery and secure Chelsea's first major trophy in more than twenty-five years. Ruud Gullit was able to look on and enjoy his team's display along with Chelsea's army of fans. As Tony Banks remembers: 'Our players stayed out on the pitch for half an hour after the game to celebrate. That's when you appreciate why Wembley is so special.'

Robson, meanwhile, who had competed so hard and successfully for Manchester United and England at Wembley, was left with memories of a frustrating afternoon: 'It was a great honour to lead the team out as a manager but I'd swap it all for being out there as a player again. Wembley is all about players and, as a manager, I found it really nerve-racking sitting on the bench, not being able to do anything about the situation. You just sit there wishing you could get out there and have some effect on a game at Wembley again.'

1991: JOHN ALDRIDGE

It's not as fierce as the England v Scotland game but there's still a rivalry. I played for Ireland four times against England: at the 1988 European Championships, the 1990 World Cup and home and away in qualifiers for the tournament in Sweden in 1992. We won one and drew three and my best memory of the one game at Wembley was our fans singing: *You'll never beat the Irish*. We had about 15,000 fans there that night but they sounded like 40,000. I suppose it helped that there's such a big Irish community in North London. Anyway they kept that song going the whole ninety minutes.

   It was a great game. We played really well the first half – better than we had for a long time. We dominated England completely for a lot of the time but just about the only shot they had they scored. But big Niall Quinn equalised and it finished up one-all. Ray Houghton had a great chance to score just before the end. We should have won that game and, if we had, we'd have qualified for those European Championships. Instead we lost out and England got through on goal difference or a point or something. But that was a good Wembley night and we had great support.

INTERVIEW, 1998

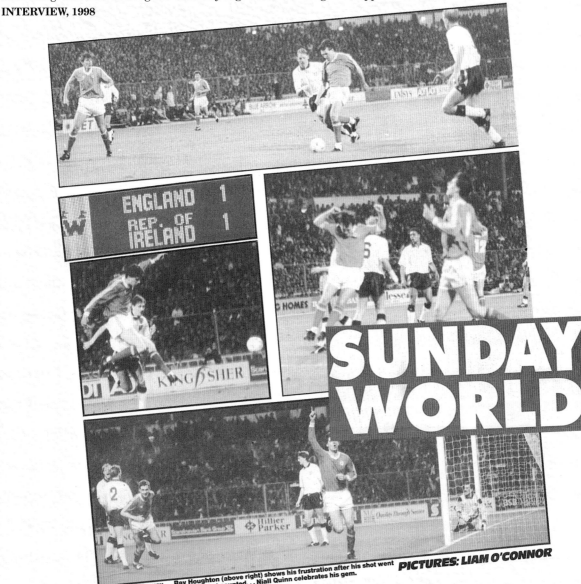

·The one that got away. . . Ray Houghton (above right) shows his frustration after his shot went narrowly wide. The one that counted. . . Niall Quinn celebrates his gem.

PICTURES: LIAM O'CONNOR

1991: GARY MABBUTT

In 1991, in the mind of our fans, we had already won a lot that season. To them, beating Arsenal in the semi-final at Wembley was as good as any Cup Final but, as professionals, we wanted to win the Cup. It had been an incredible season. The club was lurching from one problem to the next off the field with takeovers and financial problems, which made our achievement of getting to Wembley all the more remarkable.

The Cup Final against Nottingham Forest could not have started worse for us. Gazza lunged into a tackle on Gary Charles and picked up an injury and, from the free-kick, Stuart Pearce put Forest ahead. I was actually pushed out of the way on the end of the wall and he hit his shot through the gap created by that.

We did not realise how bad it was for Gazza until the game re-started after their goal. He went down again and was stretchered off. You got the feeling that it wasn't going to be our day, that nothing else could go wrong. But it got worse. We won a penalty and, with Gary Lineker around, you expect to score nine times out of ten but he missed and we went in at half-time wondering what had hit us.

It would have been easy for the younger players in our side to get overawed but Terry [Venables] told us to draw strength from that first half. We had been the better side in many ways and he told us that, if we kept going, it would happen for us. There was also a feeling that we should do it for Gazza. After all, he had got us to Wembley in the first place.

It was an excellent performance in the second half, with Paul Stewart equalising for us. After my experience of scoring an own goal in 1987, it was ironic that Des Walker's own goal won it for us this time. I was running in ready to head in but Des got his head there just before me and the ball looped in. When something like that happens, I think you know that fate has played a part in repaying you for what happened before. The emotion as the final whistle goes and you win the FA Cup is impossible to describe. As I waited to go up and collect the Cup, so many things flashed through my mind. I was now the person all the kids around the world, watching on TV, would want to emulate and it was a wonderful feeling. You could see from the smile on my face just what it meant.

INTERVIEW, 1997

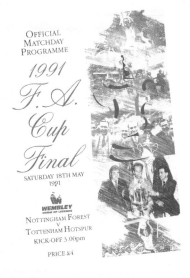

OFFICIAL MATCHDAY PROGRAMME

1991 F. A. Cup Final

SATURDAY 18TH MAY 1991

WEMBLEY
HOME OF LEGENDS

NOTTINGHAM FOREST
V
TOTTENHAM HOTSPUR
KICK-OFF 3.00pm

PRICE £4

smiles from the Spurs players as they pose with the trophy after their Wembley victory   Picture: TONY WARD

GAZZA'S £8m KO

1992: ALAN SHEARER

For my England debut Graham Taylor told me on the Tuesday morning that I was going to be playing up front with David Hirst and that he was leaving Gary Lineker on the bench. For me to be playing as a scrawny little twenty-year-old ahead of Lineker really was something. I don't imagine he was very happy about it, mind. He came on at half-time for Hirst, so I got a chance to play with him which was very exciting.

The whole day is a great experience. Sitting on the coach with all these great players, getting near the ground and seeing people walking to the game with their England shirts on, you realise that it really is happening. Once you are there you just want the game to happen. A lot of kids grew up dreaming of that moment, walking out of the tunnel. I was one of them and when it happened I did appreciate what it meant.

Once the whistle goes, you don't hear anything from the crowd, until you score, of course. My goal came from a corner from Nigel Clough in the last minute of the first half. Mark Wright got up and headed it down. I was about three or four yards away from the goal with my back to it. I just turned and hit it on the half-volley. I had a horrible feeling that, as I was standing on my own, I must be off-side but, as I turned around and saw it in the back of the net, I spotted someone standing on the goal-line and I knew what I'd done.

Walking down that tunnel again at half-time was great. You just want to go out and get a bit more of it in the second half and after Gary came on I was fortunate enough to set him up for a second on the night. The game just flew by. I couldn't believe it when the final whistle went. Everyone said enjoy it, people still say that to me now. Enjoy your career because it does fly by. I still get a great lift out of playing at Wembley. I've done it with Southampton, Blackburn, Newcastle and England and, when it is full, there are not many stadiums around the world that can match it.

INTERVIEW, 1997

WED 17 FEB 1993

1993: DAVID PLATT

My first game as England captain was against San Marino at Wembley. Graham Taylor called me into his office a couple of days beforehand and started talking about me playing up front rather than in midfield. I said I had no problem with that. Then, as I was leaving, he said he wanted me to lead the side out as Stuart Pearce was injured. It was such a lift: the adrenalin had me floating for the couple of days before the match.

The experience actually exceeded anything I'd imagined beforehand: putting on the armband; standing in the tunnel holding the pennant; coming out at the head of the team, knowing your family's there watching. It was the pinnacle as far as I was concerned. When you retire, looking back, what could be better than to have captained your country?

I've got the kit I wore that night at my house. It's filthy, probably stinks behind the glass: it's got the armband on and everything, as if I've just stepped out of it and put it into the frame. I wanted it unspoilt. It was the most fantastic feeling and I wanted the memory of it intact. Leading out the England team, it felt like Wembley was my ground; the night, everything, felt like it belonged to me
INTERVIEW, 1997

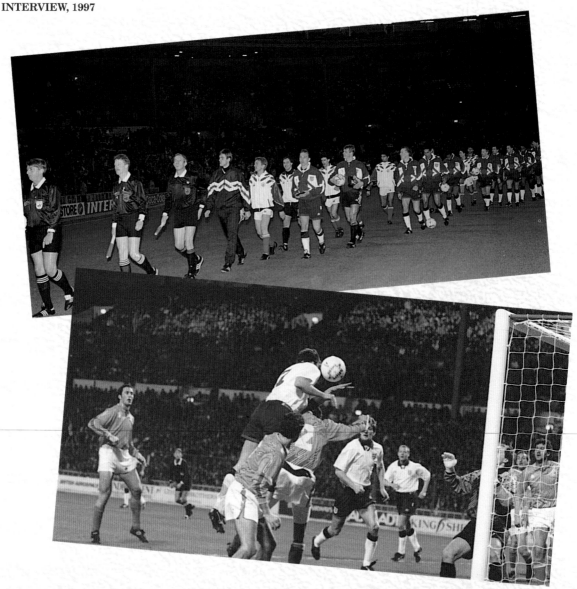

1993: GEORGE GRAHAM

In football you do have what you could call 'big-game players'. That's why, at a big club like Arsenal, when you buy players you've got to ask yourself not just *can he play?* but *can he put up with the pressure and play on the biggest stage?* Before a game at Wembley you can tell who's going to freeze and who might play well, who has the character to go with the ability, the personality to say: *Hey, this is my arena. I'm going to perform here.* Wembley definitely brings out the best in certain players while, for others, it's too big a stage. That's why you'll sometimes see weird team selections at Wembley and, of course, the manager can't really explain them truthfully.

Successful Arsenal teams have always had great players, but great players who'd integrate into the team. Even back in the thirties they had their stars – Male, Hapgood, Hulme, Bastin, Drake, James – but the success of the team unit was paramount. That's always been my philosophy and, when it came to Wembley, although we had a Wright or a Merson who could do something with an individual flash of brilliance, the team was the most important thing.

I decided very early in my managerial career that I wanted to win things. Football is conflict: two sides, a winner and a loser. You have to make up your mind which you want to be. You know what they say: a good loser is still a loser. It's a question of priorities. I remember before the finals against Sheffield Wednesday sitting down and going over the opposition, working out how to nullify their strengths, Chris Waddle's ability and John Sheridan's passing. I remember being criticised, being accused of 'spoiling' the Cup Finals. Well, if that was in the interests of making sure Arsenal won, then I'd say: *Yes. 100 per cent.* Who remembers losers in ten years' time? They were two very close games – and we knew they would be – but I was always confident we were going to win them both.

INTERVIEW, 1998

1994: SEGUN ODEGBAME

My generation of players, in the seventies, suffered from a psychological block. We didn't believe we could compete with the best. Wasn't that natural? We had never really played against any of the big teams in the world. We played against other African teams but when we went to Europe, for example, no national teams would play us. We would be given club sides to play against. The message we were given was that we were not good enough.

The breakthrough for Nigerian football came in 1985 when we won the world under-17 championships. Since then Nigerian footballers have believed they could play anywhere. After the '94 World Cup I was managing the national team, the Super Eagles. A company in England wanted to organise a game. I assured them that, if England would play Nigeria at Wembley, I could get the boys there. The fixture was confirmed by the English FA. I called the players, asked them to assemble in England. It wasn't difficult, they were very excited about playing at Wembley.

It was wonderful. I enjoyed myself so much. For the first time for a very long time I felt sad I had stopped playing. You know, you could play at Wembley and die. The pitch looked like a comfortable bed you could lie down and go to sleep on. We should have got a draw; we didn't deserve to lose. The boys made chances but missed them. England took their chance. It was tremendous. I still have a tape of the game.

You see, Nigeria now had respect. We'd gone to the World Cup and done well. Any country in the world would be ready to play against us now. We've earned and deserve that respect.

INTERVIEW, 1998

1995: SHAUN EDWARDS

Playing at Wembley so often was a definite advantage in games when we knew a lot of the opposition players hadn't played there before. They'd get carried away with the occasion, start waving to the crowd and looking out for their families. When we saw them trying to catch sight of their wives or girlfriends, we knew they'd lost it – that they'd bottled it – then and there. You know, rugby league is a very aggressive game. We knew those players were looking around for comfort. They didn't want to face the reality of having to take us on for eighty minutes. During the run of eight wins at Wembley we were very professional about it: get the job done and party afterwards. The best thing about a Wembley occasion is winning.

Two of the finals stick out for me personally. In 1990 against Warrington, quite early on, I kicked the ball through and someone caught me late with a shoulder charge. His head hit my face and I ended up with a multiple fracture of the eye socket and a depressed cheekbone. I thought I'd broken my jaw because it just wouldn't move and the double vision in my right eye was so bad I had to shut it to be able to pick up the ball with the other. I chose to carry on because it was just pain – I was in bloody agony – but it wasn't an injury that made me a hindrance to the team. Dean Bell did really well for me. In that situation, what you don't want is to feel sorry for yourself, have people asking you if you're all right. Dean just said: *Either you keep playing hard or get off. Keep going!*

In 1995 the Super League war had kicked off and, because I'd signed a long extension to my Wigan contract it looked like I might miss out on the loyalty bonuses when the League started. I felt I had a point to prove and, in that final against Leeds, I think I had one of my best games at Wembley. The whole team did well. It was a really strong Leeds side: Gary Schofield, Kevin Iro, Alan Tait, Ellery Hanley. But we destroyed them, really played some exceptional football. At the time I think Wigan were probably the best team in the world. And I got my loyalty bonus.

INTERVIEW, 1998

1996: GARY NEVILLE

The manager had been telling us for weeks what it would mean if we could win the biggest two trophies in the country so we didn't need time for it to sink in. And the fact that we beat Liverpool made it all the more sweet. They have been United's main rivals for the last 25 years and in that time they had been the ones winning trophies. I suppose we had aspired to be like them for a long time, so to clinch the Double by beating them at Wembley was something special. They must have wished they were like us for that day.

It was fitting that Eric Cantona won us the FA Cup. He had single-handedly won seven or eight games in the championship run-in which clinched the title and then he went and completed the Double with a moment of magic. There were only about five minutes to go and I was warming up behind the goal when Cantona hit this shot. I remember a mass of legs and bodies blocking the ball's path but it somehow got through. Seeing it on television afterwards made it seem even more amazing that it went in. When the final whistle went, we all ran into the centre circle and mobbed Eric. It was his season and his Cup Final. And for a lot of that team it was our first FA Cup winners' medal. The United team had changed a lot from the one that did the Double in 1994.

INTERVIEW, 1998

1996: GARETH SOUTHGATE

We thought Switzerland would be difficult but we expected to win. It was our first competitive game for two years and there was a huge difference from the friendlies we'd been playing: the speed of the play, the attitude of the opposition. You could even hear the away fans. The atmosphere was completely different.

We scored quite early on and I was really pleased Alan Shearer got the goal. Even the team had started to get worried that he hadn't been scoring. But in the second half we all seemed to run out of steam. The weather had suddenly changed from the week before and it was very warm, pushing up towards 100° on the pitch. In hindsight I think that during the week of preparation we'd perhaps trained too hard because we wanted everything just right.

The 1–1 draw turned out to be a huge anti-climax: whatever the score had been it couldn't have satisfied the expectation of the build-up, the opening ceremony and everything. I remember we were given the night off and I was going to drive home with my family. We came out of the stadium into the car park and it was empty. Nobody had hung around afterwards which was very unusual for an England game. Of course, listening to the radio phone-ins on the way home, it was already a national calamity: Euro '96 was already over.

INTERVIEW, 1997

WELCOME TO THE BIGGEST SPORTING EVENT to take place in ENGLAND FOR THIRTY YEARS

TEL'S BOYS WILL SEND US CUCKOO

1996: GARETH SOUTHGATE

I think the build-up to the Scotland game helped us and that the criticism from the Swiss game drew us together as a team. There was a lot made of the patriotism of the Scots, the whole Braveheart thing, and I remember thinking: *Don't you understand we're patriots, too? How much it means for me to play for my country?*

The first half was just a complete stalemate. At half-time, though, Terry changed it around a bit. I moved back, Jamie Redknapp came on in midfield and we started to get a grip. Gary Neville went flying down the right and whipped a great cross in for Alan to score but then, just like against Switzerland, we seemed to take our foot off the gas. And, of course, they got the penalty.

I'll never forget, as Gary McAllister ran up to take the kick, I saw the ball roll ever so slightly off the penalty spot. I thought he'd stop, but perhaps he was too far into his run-up to do anything. It must have crossed his mind: *That just moved.* For a split second it must distract you and Dave Seaman managed to get his elbow, I think it was, to the ball.

There was an incredible feeling of relief and then, just a few minutes later, Gazza's gone up the other end and scored the kind of goal which, if a Brazilian had scored it, we'd never have heard the end of it. His talent and personality making Paul the focus of so much of the criticism beforehand and scoring it against blokes he's playing with in Scotland every week made that goal all the more special.

INTERVIEW, 1997

EURO 96 England — KING GAZZA'S A CLASS APART!

1996: GARETH SOUTHGATE

It felt like the Wembley crowd began to feel optimistic after the
Scotland game. After the Holland game, of course, it was mayhem.
As an occasion and a result, to annihilate a team which, whatever
people said about them having problems off the field, was one of
the best in the world and one of the tournament favourites was
amazing. I'm sure it must have been one of the most intense nights ever at
the stadium.

From a defender's point of view it was a very difficult game: Bergkamp's performance was one of
the hardest I've ever had to defend against. We watched the goals go in and celebrated, of course, but
at the same time you couldn't quite believe it was happening. It was the same in the crowd, too, I
think. English players are supposed to be honest and hardworking but here we were, passing the ball
and beating the Dutch at their own game.

The setting was perfect. It was a balmy summer evening, the temperature was perfect for playing
football, and the colours in the stadium: Wembley seemed to be half-full of Dutch fans so there was
orange everywhere, reflecting the colour of the sun setting overhead. That game kicked the whole
tournament off, really. It was the first time I can remember the supporters all singing *Football's
Coming Home*, which became the anthem of the summer. It would be hard to better that night.

INTERVIEW, 1997

1996: GARETH SOUTHGATE

By now people were realising the route our coach took to Wembley and were coming out to cheer us on the way. There were Union Jacks flying from people's houses. When you walked out of the tunnel, every other person seemed to have their face painted with a Saint George's cross. The national anthem before each game was being sung with more and more passion.

Back at Wembley, three days after the Holland game, I think there was a feeling in the stadium – in the country – we were destined to win the tournament. The Spain game was one we just had to get through and people forgot how good they were, that they hadn't lost for two years. Like in any cup tie, every time the underdog attacked there was a kind of fear around the ground: *What's going on? The Spanish aren't supposed to be attacking!*

Extra-time was our first experience of the sudden-death situation. Scoring the winning goal and running straight off down the tunnel was quite an appealing idea but, of course, we hadn't had the chance to watch a game it happened in, so we didn't realise quite how tense it would be, that both teams would settle for not making a mistake. There's always that fear element in football and it's very difficult to overcome.

We all knew that, if it came to penalties, Stuart Pearce would take one, but the crowd possibly didn't. I think his reaction when he scored helped carry us through. He was so pumped up, the Spanish probably looked at him and thought: *Blimey, if he wants it that much we'd better let him have it!*

INTERVIEW, 1997

1996: GARETH SOUTHGATE

Everything in this country harks back to 1966. Even the video for
Football's Coming Home was about that World Cup Final. And here we
were, playing Germany at Wembley again. It brought all that history
and all those memories back for everybody, I think. To be honest, we
felt that if we beat the Germans we'd win Euro '96, especially after we
heard the Czechs had beaten France in the other semi-final.

We were very confident and scored early from a set-piece we'd
worked on in training. We really did think we were on our way –
destiny and all that – but we sat back for five minutes and they
equalised. It was an amazing game, two teams going at it hammer
and tongs, real end-to-end-stuff. And neither side held back in extra-
time: both teams were thinking, *if we win this, we'll win the
championship.* I thought we played very well on the night but that's
overshadowed, I suppose, by what happened in the end.

When it came to penalties, we knew who our first five guys were going to be. Before the game Terry
came up to me and said: *if it comes to a sixth one, would you take it?* The previous Saturday, I think
Gary Neville would have been in that situation but he didn't play against Germany.

I knew we were going to score our five and I thought they would too, so I was expecting to have to
take one. When it came to it, I remember it being the longest walk in the world from the centre circle
to the penalty spot. Then their keeper kicked the ball on his way to the goal-line. It hit the bar and
bounced away to the other side of the penalty area so I had to walk across to fetch it. I was very
conscious of the fact that it was just me out there and that there were a few people watching.

I knew exactly what I wanted to do. I put the penalty where I wanted but not far enough in the
corner. When he saved it, there was just an incredible sense of deflation, a sense of: this really wasn't
meant to happen. Stuart Pearce came straight up to me, I think, and said: *We're all in this together.*
But, you know, it doesn't really feel that way. I hardly even heard him.

There's nothing really to be said. For months afterwards it was all I could think about. Even though,
looking back, I was pleased with my performances, especially as I'd only won four caps before the
tournament started, I couldn't see that at the time. You get on with your life but, when you remember
that one moment, you're pretty much in it on your own.

What got me out of all that, I think, was the memory of the atmosphere at Wembley before the
opening game and remembering everything about the night we played Holland and the drama of that.
Not many players get the chance to play for England, fewer still in a major championship. I realised
how fortunate I was to play for my country in a tournament our generation will always remember.

INTERVIEW, 1998

Building On Tradition

1998

'And what of the Wembley Stadium 2,000 years hence? Who can foresee what changes will have occurred in British sport and building methods by then? He would indeed be a bold man who would dare to essay a prophecy. But one thing is certain. If the Roman amphitheatre at Nimes could outlast the centuries, so too will the Stadium at Wembley. For nothing more enduring than concrete has ever been used in building. In another 2,000 years the Stadium will still be able to house its 125,000 odd spectators drawn thereto possibly from motives of sentiment or archaeological study, perhaps – who knows? – from some desire to see the historic arena which was built in the quaint and archaic period when men were dabbling in the crude and long forgotten art and craft of wireless telephony.'

The volume published to describe 'The Building Of The Greatest Stadium In The World' by Sir Robert McAlpine Limited in 1923 closed with a look forward. Eyes lifted, briefly, from the detail of cost, measurement, design and engineering to gaze into a future imagined on a scale as grand as the project itself. Seventy-five years on this history, too, must finish with attention fixed not on what has passed but what, for Wembley, is to come.

In other circumstances the seventy-fifth anniversary of Wembley's first Cup Final, the only occasion on which the stadium housed '125,000 odd' spectators, would be an obvious time to celebrate the history and tradition of preceding decades. The pace of change, however, has seldom let up since opening day in 1923 and, as in the world outside its walls, has markedly increased in recent years. As a result 1998 has found Wembley, within its arena and behind the scenes, looking to the future rather than dwelling on the past. Never mind the next 2,000 years, it would take a 'bold man' to guess at what the next ten may hold.

Familiarity, they say, breeds contempt and attitudes to Wembley in the early nineties would seem to endorse the idea. As grounds around the country were modernised or rebuilt in line with the recommendations of the Taylor Report and with funds, private and public, available to a national game now profitable as never before, Wembley's shortcomings were thrown into sharp relief. Goodwill ebbed, the sense of Wembley's enduring and unique heritage counterbalanced by a degree of frustration with the outdated impracticalities of its setting.

Outside these shores, of course, Wembley's stature in no way was undermined. The stadium remains almost unique in world sport as a 'national' stadium in all but name. No other arena in the world can be seen as defining a country and its sporting history in the way Wembley does England and her national game. Wembley remains for international sports people, and musicians too, one of a handful of venues to appear at which satisfies the highest ambitions. Watch any visiting team train before an England game at Wembley: when the cones are put away, out come the cameras to capture a career highlight for posterity.

One of the most memorable aspects of Euro '96 was the opportunity it gave the Wembley crowd to rediscover the stadium, the chance to see it through the eyes of the unprecedented number of overseas supporters. Of course England's stirring progress to the semi-finals also made people happy to be there. Football came home, as the song said it would; and that meant to Wembley above all.

The timing was right. A year previously, as one of the five organisations in a position to award National Lottery grants, the Sports Council had canvassed the Football Association and the governing bodies of athletics and rugby league about the possibility of a new national sports stadium. All agreed that one was needed and committed themselves to staging their major events there should one be built. The Sports Council was prepared to release at least £100 million of Lottery money to the project. Applications were invited: Manchester, Birmingham, Sheffield and Bradford bid along with Wembley for the right to build an arena fit for the Millennium.

The latest financial storm to have broken over Wembley had recently been weathered. The PLC's attempts to diversify and expand in the teeth of early nineties' recession had backfired to the tune of a £140 million debt by 1994. Restructuring and refinancing at the behest of banks and new investors, however, had helped turn the business corner by the time, in the spring of 1996, the race for the national stadium had been narrowed to a straight contest between Wembley and Manchester. There was a certain inevitability in the outcome. Wembley offered expert staff, a track record, an established (and improvable) transport infrastructure, a London location and, irresistibly, more than 70 years of tradition and world-wide esteem. In October the FA, the Football League, the Rugby Football League and the British Athletic Federation all gave their public backing to Wembley's bid. The word was out long before 17 December when the Sports Council officially announced that a decision had been reached: the new national sports stadium would be built at Wembley.

Unsurprisingly, perhaps, the end of the process of choosing a venue was only the beginning of the more complicated practical undertaking which succeeded it. 1997 disappeared with little progress having been made. Who would take responsibility for the project? How much would it cost and, Lottery funding aside, who would pay for it? What would the new stadium look like and how would the different sports to be played there dovetail on a manageable basis?

By the middle of the year it had become clear that initial plans to complete Wembley's rebuilding – demolishing the present structure and starting again from scratch, retaining only the listed twin towers – by the year 2001, in time to stage the World Athletics Championships, would have to be revised. Only in November were architects, engineers and quantity surveyors first invited to tender for work on the new Wembley.

A further, unforeseen, ingredient was then dropped into Wembley's slowly boiling pot when Arsenal approached the stadium PLC with a view to buying what was clearly for sale. With capacity restricted to less than 40,000, the Highbury club faced problems of their own. Wembley seemed to offer a ready-made solution to Arsenal's dilemma, avoiding both the planning difficulties which came with redevelopment at their own site, hemmed in by residential property in Islington, and the prohibitive expense of relocation and building a new ground themselves elsewhere.

If nothing else, the approach by an alternative bidder concentrated the attentions of those involved in the national stadium project. In early April 1998 a deal was pronounced done, in principle at least: Wembley was to be sold to the English National Stadium Trust for something over £100 million and then redeveloped at a projected cost of £240 million, which would include a proportion of Lottery money. Where the cash for the purchase – and at least another £100 million for redevelopment – would come from remained unclear; indeed the Trust itself, in terms of structure and personnel, was as yet more idea than fact. In the coming months, however, the FA, always the most significant of a new stadium's potential end-users, emerged as the crucial player. Football, so decisive in making possible the construction of the Empire Stadium seventy-five years previously, has put its weight and new-found economic credibility behind the building of the old stadium's successor.

With dotted lines still lacking signatures in July, the FA's staff moved into offices at Wembley after a fire had destroyed much of its headquarters at Lancaster Gate and, although the arrangement was temporary, there seems every likelihood that when the new stadium opens – 2002 is the projected date – the FA, the Cup Final and the national team will be making themselves at home at Wembley on a permanent basis.

While Wembley's seventy-fifth year was full of uncertainty behind the scenes, the arena put on a succession of vintage shows to offer proof, if it were needed, that the future plans would be worth the trouble. 1998, a splendid Wembley year, was a birthday celebration in the best traditions of the stadium: marvellous games, capacity crowds, the brightest and most uplifting drama that contemporary sport has to offer, played out in a setting suffused by the spirit and warmth of times past. Appropriately, many of the year's events had about them, too, a freshness and optimism auguring well for the players and fans who wait to inherit Wembley's future.

In the autumn of 1996 Glenn Hoddle succeeded Terry Venables as England manager. His immediate task was to guide the national team through a qualifying campaign for the 1998 World Cup. During the next twelve months the Wembley crowd experienced both intense disappointment and heady optimism. A difficult group, which included Italy and England's old rivals Poland, appeared all the more challenging after the Italians won 1–0 at Wembley with a goal from Chelsea's Gianfranco Zola. Matthew Le Tissier, often touted previously as a world-class player, bore the brunt of the public and media blame for a frustratingly low-key team performance.

Encouraging displays, however, particularly away from home, kept England in with a chance of automatic qualification. The evening of 10

September 1997, only in part for football reasons, turned out to be as emotionally charged as any in recent Wembley history. That afternoon Italy had failed to win in Georgia, leaving England a victory and a draw away from a place in France. In normal circumstances the mood before the game against Moldova would have been high-spirited.

The fixture, though, took place ten days after the death of Diana, Princess of Wales. The Wembley occasion attracted considerable attention as the first 'national' event since the tragedy. The atmosphere on the night mixed the fervour of Euro '96 with the mourning of the previous few days, a definitively English blend of dignity and sentimentality. Candle-light and tears before kick-off gave way to the unfurling of a forest of flags of St George two hours later, after goals from Scholes and Gascoigne and two from an irrepressible Ian Wright had brought qualification a big step closer.

England's immediate future, a place at France '98, was sealed at the Olympic Stadium in Rome with a 0–0 draw a few weeks later. For a glimpse of the longer term fans had to wait until the following February. There can have been few international debuts as keenly awaited as that of the 17-year-old Michael Owen who, when he played in a friendly against Chile at Wembley, became the youngest man to represent England this century.

A self-possessed character and devastatingly quick footballer, the goodwill Owen attracted ensured the evening would belong to him. Although a patchwork England side stumbled to a 2–0 defeat, his enthusiasm, aggression and intelligence richly rewarded all expectation. Here clearly was a man on whom to hang hopes for England's future. Four months later Owen arrived in some style on the international stage with a goal against Argentina in the World Cup as exciting as any scored in the tournament. Having made his mark before football says goodbye to the old stadium, Owen seemed sure to be around, possibly approaching the height of his powers, when England step out for their first game at a new Wembley in 2002.

Where England would play during the building of the new national stadium and which venue would stage football's showpiece finals in the interim was still undecided by the summer of '98. Welsh rugby had faced the same problem in the previous twelve months while a new arena to replace Cardiff Arms Park was being built. Union, first played at Wembley during the Empire Exhibition, had been anything but a regular event there since. The English game, after all, has a home of its own across London at Twickenham, though a Test against Canada was played at Wembley in 1992, when rugby's headquarters were being refurbished. During 1997 and 1998, however, Wales contracted to play a Test against New Zealand and their home games in the Five Nations Championship at Wembley while construction on their own new ground got under way.

The Welsh took a hammering at the hands of the All Blacks in November 1997, losing 42–7. Their next Wembley appearance however, proved a happier experience for the thousands making their way up the M4 to north-west London. Both Wales and Scotland arrived at Wembley in March after heavy defeats, by England at Twickenham and France at Murrayfield, in their previous games in the 1998 Five Nations. The result, a barely deserved but hugely enjoyed 19–13 victory, was all-important for Wales as the *Observer*'s Eddie Butler pointed out the following day: 'Something stirred on the cold slab of the Five Nations yesterday. It wasn't exactly a resurrection of Welsh rugby but, after the shredding at Twickenham and the scarring of the subsequent post-mortem, any signs of life will do.'

Fortunately the partisan crowd made for an occasion considerably less gruesome than Butler's forensic analysis would suggest. Not since the 1927

WEMBLEY: THE GREATEST STAGE

Cup Final had so many Welshmen made the trip to Wembley – in 1994 Swansea had played Huddersfield in football's Autoglass Trophy, but at a half-full stadium – and the atmosphere, buoyed by the Scots contingent, was perhaps more inspiring than the rugby. The setting, at least, was a success.

Butler, though, was unimpressed with what the Welsh players had to offer: 'Wales did certain things well, only to mess them up with a nervousness once the phases became multiple and players were asked to perform skills in open play when they would prefer to be neatly obscured at the bottom of a pile of forwards.' A month later the entire Welsh XV were looking for somewhere to hide after their second Wembley 'home' Five Nations fixture saw them crumble 51–0 to the French.

That French victory was one for a team going into the game as firm favourites. The year's greatest Wembley upset arrived a few weeks later, on 3 May, in the other code's blue-riband final, the Challenge Cup. Wigan have enjoyed success at the stadium like no other club in the history of rugby league and, after two years away and a thorough overhaul on and off the pitch at Central Park, were odds-on to add to their record number of Wembley victories against Sheffield.

The obvious parallel is with Wimbledon's toppling of Liverpool in the FA Cup a decade previously. Certainly the result was as unexpected. The Sheffield Eagles had been in existence only thirteen years before reaching this, their first Wembley Final. That brief pedigree was betrayed by the empty seats at their end of the ground; the club had been unable to sell out their allocation. No matter: the team turned up and soon had 40,000 neutral fans roaring them on. Their coach John Kear remarked afterwards: 'Nobody thought we could win except the people in our dressing-room and they are the people that matter the most.' Even Kear, though, must have been pinching himself as the afternoon unfolded. His opposite number John Monie, after all, had never lost a Challenge Cup tie as Wigan coach.

Sheffield's defence stood firm each time Wigan wound themselves up and seemed set to bring matters back to earth while further forward Sheffield put points on the board at just the right times.

The moment when the crowd realised the unthinkable was about to happen came ten minutes into the second half. With Sheffield leading 11–2 at the break and Wigan having come out looking set to restore order after it, the substitute Darren Turner stretched out through a crowd of bodies to take the game beyond the favourites' best late efforts with the Eagle's third try. Beyond a dramatic upset the game put a new city on the rugby league map. Among his players, Kear declared, 'there was a unity of belief that 1998 was going to be Sheffield's year'.

Football's cup finals during the spring and summer failed to turn up a comparable shock, though there were games and stories enough to ensure that Wembley's seventy-fifth year would prove a memorable one for the national game, the future jostling with the past during the penultimate sequence of showpiece fixtures at the old stadium. The Coca-Cola Cup Final on 29 March rematched Chelsea and Middlesbrough, who had met at Wembley in 1997's FA Cup. Beforehand Wilf Mannion, a former Boro player and England star at the stadium in times past, was applauded up the steps outside by fans who had cheered him on after the Second World War. Once inside, however, Mannion suffered with his fellow Teessiders as their team lost a third final in 12 months, despite an appearance as substitute by the newly signed but barely fit Paul Gascoigne. Goals by Frank Sinclair and Roberto Di Matteo in extra-time sealed a 2–0 Chelsea win.

The victory was a personal triumph for Chelsea's new player-manager Gianluca Vialli, who had succeeded Ruud Gullit in controversial circumstances little more than a month previously. Vialli's decision not to include himself even among the substitutes impressed the Chelsea players sufficiently for them to insist he climbed the thirty-nine steps to the Royal Box afterwards to collect the cup. Less than two months later, in Gothenberg, Vialli had his hands on a second trophy after Chelsea beat Stuttgart to win the European Cup Winners' Cup.

The final of the Auto Windscreen Shield on 19 April saw Wembley welcome rather less starry company as Grimsby beat Bournemouth 2–1 with an extra-time 'golden goal' by Wayne Burnett. The occasion, though, was a perfect example of how Wembley can thrust parochial heroes blinking into the national spotlight. Bournemouth, recently in receivership before being bought and reconstituted as the only club in the country owned and run by its local community, could be forgiven for seeing the day out at Wembley as reward enough in itself. Mel Machin, the manager, put his team's defeat into some kind of perspective the evening after the game: 'This club was half an hour from going out of business not long ago and to see Bournemouth run out at Wembley was a wonderful moment for everyone.' For his opposite number, Grimsby's manager Alan Buckley, the victory itself seemed less important than where it had been won: 'I don't know what it is about Wembley but to win here means more than at any other ground in the world. It is history when you win here, whatever the trophy may be. I recall walking up Wembley Way with my father almost forty years ago for the 1959 FA Cup Final between Nottingham Forest and Luton. It was the start of my football dreams and they became reality today.'

As it turned out, 1998 was to be quite a year for Buckley and his team. In May Grimsby returned to beat Northampton Town 1–0 in the Second Division play-off final (after Colchester had beaten Torquay by the same score the previous evening in the Third Division game). While the trips to Wembley were doubtless enjoyed by the partisans present, neither match offered the excitement or quality truly to grace the setting, fuelling the arguments of those who claim that such fixtures – and the plethora of minor cup finals – have devalued the singular prestige of the stadium and a reputation established, in the early days, by virtue of one uniquely glamorous club game each year and an international every two.

Happily for the play-offs, which have done much to rekindle interest in the latter stages of recent Football League seasons, the First Division final was played in front of a near-capacity crowd. Even better, the game between Charlton Athletic and Sunderland, with the winner's reward a place aboard the Premiership gravy train, was arguably as thrilling and adventurous a contest as any in Wembley's long history. Two teams whose success thus far over a long season had depended on defensive stability and reliable organisation apparently threw caution to the wind. A splendid game of football ensued, aggressive, athletic and dramatic: a definitively English affair.

Charlton took the lead with the first of three goals by Clive Mendonca during what turned out to be a long afternoon. Niall Quinn, a goalscorer for Ireland at Wembley in previous years, headed Sunderland level. Thereafter they led three times, only for Charlton to equalise on each occasion, before the end of extra-time. With the score 4–4 after 120 minutes, the game – and the glittering prize of one season, at least, at football's top table – was decided by a penalty shoot-out. Six players from each team successfully converted. The crucial miss, after Charlton had scored a seventh, came from Sunderland's young defender Michael Gray whose under-hit shot, saved by Sasa Ilic, handed the Londoners victory.

Mendonca, the Charlton hero, grew up in Sunderland and is a lifelong fan of the club, which lent a bittersweet personal edge to his moment of professional triumph: 'I went to the same school as Michael Gray, so to see him miss that vital penalty hit me hard. It might sound strange for me to say that I am disappointed but that is the way I feel. I have scored a hat-trick at Wembley, my team have just won a place in the Premiership and I feel bad about it. What a strange day.'

It was an unforgettable one, though, for Charlton fans who, over the previous decade, had watched their homeless and near-destitute club return to its Valley ground in south-east London and prosper thanks to a groundswell of local support. What better place than Wembley to celebrate an achievement as laudable and satisfying, in its way, as FA Cup Final victory against Burnley had been more than 50 years before?

Each Wembley occasion carries within it the spirit of games, players and adventures past. That is the stadium's heritage and well worth the celebrating in its seventy-fifth year. Countless ghosts – heroes and villains beneath the towers since 1923 – haunt, enrich and inspire the Wembley of today. It is to be hoped they will do so still when the current building is replaced in the next century by a new stadium as ambitious and impressive, perhaps, as the Empire Stadium seemed to the 200,000 fans who found their way in on its opening day.

Since Bolton beat West Ham on 28 April 1923, each pair of competing teams have trodden in increasingly familiar footsteps on the way to glory or defeat (or both) within the stadium's walls, before leaving impressions of their own on Wembley's slowly evolving tradition. And down the years, too, each man appearing in the final of the game's oldest competition has taken away not only a winner's or a loser's medal but the proud memory of having played a part in football's great day on football's greatest stage.

During such a momentous year in Wembley's history it was appropriate that 1998's FA Cup Final was contested by clubs whose names and deeds have echoed around Wembley since the stadium's earliest days. Arsenal and Newcastle United are clubs with traditions as sustaining as Wembley's own. The former played in a Cup Final for the first time in 1927, the latter appeared at Wembley for the first time three days after King George V had opened the Empire Exhibition in 1924. They had met in Cup Finals in 1932 and 1952, Newcastle winning both. Names like James, Drake, George and Brady, Seymour, Milburn and Harvey are as important to the Wembley story as they are to the stories of those clubs where the reputations which have kept the names alive were made.

16 May dawned a traditionally perfect Cup Final day: warm, sunny and a gentle breeze. The two sets of fans – Newcastle's at the tunnel end – ensured the spectacle was colourful and raucous, all that participants and onlookers could wish for: a swath of black and white confronted a sea of red and white; the *Blaydon Races* rang out, *Good Old Arsenal* echoed back. The Londoners lacked the injured Dennis Bergkamp, Footballer of the Year and the inspiration during a memorable season which had already seen them win the Premiership at a late but irresistible canter. Newcastle, under-achieving miserably all season in the league, had been rescued by the return from injury of Alan Shearer in time to inspire the team to an unlikely run to Wembley in the Cup.

With the stage set, sadly only half the cast turned up. A cautious and dispirited Newcastle side proved no match for buoyant Arsenal who, without having to extend themselves, completed the second Double in the club's history with goals from an experienced winger, Marc Overmars, and a raw young centre-forward, Nicolas Anelka. These were modern times at Wembley indeed: a Dutchman and a Frenchman the match-winners, while players from Greece, Italy, Sweden, Georgia and Liberia also took the field in 1998's staging of this most English of sporting fixtures.

Shearer was a lonely figure all afternoon as his team-mates struggled with the pace of Overmars, Anelka and the man of the match Ray Parlour and the midfield drive of Vieira and Petit, World Cup winners later in the summer with France. The United number nine hit his only decent chance against the post. Although the game disappointed, however, Arsenal did not. Both ends of the stadium rose to applaud a team fit to stand comparison with any which has appeared in a Cup Final there.

Arsène Wenger, in his first full season in charge at Highbury, had brought fresh ideas, deployed with rare acumen, to bear on the business of breaking Manchester United's domination of the domestic game. Alex Ferguson, who had watched his own club complete Doubles in two of the four preceding seasons, was quick to recognise his rival's achievement: 'Wenger has done a brilliant job and blend is the secret.'

Arsenal's triumph had indeed been achieved by fastening the finesse of foreign newcomers to the reliability and spirit of the team's senior players and the club's traditional virtues. The mood was just right for such a significant year. The stadium, too, stood with one foot in a marvellous past, the other in an equally promising future. Oliver Holt, writing in *The Times*, was quite swept away by the timeless and uplifting spell cast over the grand old venue by this very modern football team: 'As they paraded the FA Cup around Wembley and supporters of both teams cheered them to the echo, the occasion seemed like a glorious harbinger ... players playing with verve, skill and assurance, fans applauding their teams and each other. It was like a glimpse of Arcadia.'

Wembley's seventy-fifth year was played out in a style befitting that which had gone before. Midway through its seventy-sixth, if things run according to plan, the curtain will come down on the greatest stage. The 1999 Cup Final will be the last before the stadium is demolished and building work starts on a successor to the 'great national sports ground' envisaged by the Prince of Wales in 1921. Before then another season will be checked off with relish on the calendar of British sport, its biggest occasions celebrated for the last time in the most familiar of arenas. England footballers will put the disappointment of last summer's penalty shoot-out in St Etienne behind them and kick off their qualifying campaign for the 2000 European Championships at the home of the national team. And, a twist in the tale,

Arsenal will compete in the 1998/99 Champions League at Wembley while their own ground remains too restricted to meet Uefa specifications for the competition and too small to welcome all those who want to follow them.

Wembley will be handed over to the architects, engineers, electricians and builders in the summer of 1999. A brand new structure, according to the best laid plans, will be handed back in 2002 to the players, the fans, the nation, to whom, in spirit if not in fact, Wembley and all it represents belongs. The bricks and mortar will probably be the Football Association's responsibility. Those who watch and play there will look after the tradition. The twin towers are likely to remain, as must a sense of Wembley's past. The history recorded in these pages, like that of any vibrant institution, should not be thought of as something merely to be preserved. Rather the memory of the past seventy-five years of life on the greatest stage deserves to be cherished, echoed and celebrated in the planning and substance of Wembley's future. That assured, it is high time to move forward. In 1999 this Wembley chapter will end and the next one can begin.

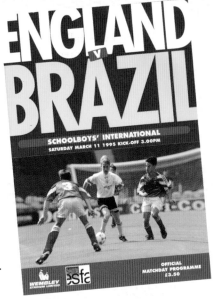

1998: MICHAEL OWEN

I was fifteen when I first played at Wembley. It was a schoolboy international and, although the crowd was about 40,000, there was a great atmosphere and it was even more of an occasion because we were playing Brazil. To score the winner against them seemed like a great achievement to me. The game at Wembley, the build-up seemed that bit more serious; there was an air of something special about to happen. I think the coaching staff, if anything, tried to play the occasion down because all of us were so made up about playing there. No one needed to tell us how big a day it was.

All I remember about the game was my goal. A young lad, James Bird, had run down the wing and the centre-half went out to cover him. That left me free and Jamie knocked it in. The keeper ran out to me. I took my first touch and took the ball round him. I saw a covering defender on the line. In hindsight I should have taken it to him, drawn him and put it in one of the corners but, on the spur of the moment, I just whacked it and it hit the bar and went in. I can't remember anything after the goal, not even my celebration.

Playing for England Schoolboys does give you an insight into the way different countries play. Brazil were so well organised even at that age, I hardly got a kick. The goal was the only opening I had all afternoon. They were like the full international teams I play against now. I thought at the time: *If this is what it's going to be like, it's going to be tough.*

Before I was called up for the full squad for the Chile game, I'd already been invited down to train a couple of times which I think is a really good idea; you get to know the players, the training and the routine. Glenn Hoddle told me I was going to play against Chile at the first session after we joined up. It was great. I didn't know whether I should laugh in his face or try to stay serious. What do you say? *Oh right?* I managed to keep my feelings to myself and got on with training.

The morning of the game we did some set-pieces and then rested all afternoon. It seemed like a very long ride on the coach to Wembley. I suppose I got nervous about ten or fifteen minutes before we got there but once we arrived and got in the dressing-room I was fine. All the other players were very encouraging, just telling me to play my natural game. I think they maybe thought I was going to be more nervous than I was. I was just looking forward to it. I like the big stage and there's no bigger stage than Wembley. I just wanted to be playing.

It seemed like a very long time since I'd been there as a schoolboy. Even though I'd played at Wembley before, it felt like the first time. Playing through the levels with England meant I wasn't surprised by how Chile played or anything but for the first ten or fifteen minutes I was a bit energetic. I was running all over the pitch. People kept having to tell me to get back into my position.

It was a great feeling, knowing people wanted me to do well, the crowd cheering when they announced my name during the warm-up. All my family was there: there's seven of us and, with aunties and uncles, there were fifteen or twenty in all. At the time I wasn't too happy with the way things went, because of the result I suppose. It didn't matter about my debut; we had to win. I was disappointed. But when you reflect on the game – the fact that we were an experimental side – and think about your own performance. I suppose I was reasonably pleased. *Reasonably* pleased!

INTERVIEW, 1998

75 Years of Wembley Memories

1923: Bolton beat West Ham 2–0 in Wembley's first FA Cup Final.

1924: The Empire Exhibition opens and England draw with Scotland in Wembley's first international.

1925: The Empire Exhibition closes after its second season.

1926: Ex-serviceman Arthur Elvin makes plans to buy Wembley stadium.

1927: The FA Cup leaves England for the first and only time, Cardiff City beating Arsenal 1–0 in the Final.

1928: Scotland's 'Wembley Wizards' beat England 5–1.

1929: In Wembley's first Rugby League Cup Final, Wigan beat Dewsbury 13–2.

1930: Herbert Chapman's Arsenal beat his former club Huddersfield 2–0 to win the FA Cup.

1931: Mick the Miller wins his last Greyhound St. Leger.

1932: After a dispute with the English FA, Scotland send a 'tartan' team of 11 Scottish-based players to Wembley. They lose 3–0.

1933: After a year's enforced absence the Rugby League Challenge Cup Final returns to Wembley for good.

1934: The Wembley complex grows: the Empire Pool opens next door.

1935: Having also scored in every previous round, Ellis Rimmer scores twice for Sheffield Wednesday to beat West Bromwich in the Cup Final.

1936: The first World Speedway Championships are held at Wembley.

1937: Sunderland v Preston is the first Final filmed by television cameras before the fixture is broadcast live the following year.

1938: In Wembley's first extra-time Cup Final, Preston beat Huddersfield with a 120th-minute penalty.

1939: The last Cup Final before World War Two is won by Portsmouth 4–1 against Wolves.

1940: Wales become the first side other than Scotland to play England at Wembley; they win 1–0.

1941: Prime Minister Churchill is introduced to the players before England beat Scotland 2–0.

1942: Hundreds of servicemen and women descend on Wembley for a series of Christmas parties.

1943: Arsenal beat Charlton 7–1 in the final of the League South Cup.

1944: Dwight D. Eisenhower is the guest of honour as Charlton beat Chelsea in the League South Final.

1945: France are England's first foreign opposition at Wembley, drawing 2–2 in a Victory International.

1946: In the first post-war Cup Final, Derby beat Charlton 4–1 in extra-time.

1947: State-of-the-art greyhound photo-finish equipment is installed.

1948: Wembley hosts the major events of the XIV Olympiad .

1949: The first Amateur Cup Final at Wembley Bromley v Romford, is watched by a 94,000 crowd.

1950: In Wembley's first Schoolboy International, England beat Scotland 8–2.

1951: England meet South American opposition at Wembley, beating Argentina 2–1 in a match celebrating the Festival of Britain.

1952: In the first of a series of Cup Finals marred by serious injuries, 10-man Arsenal lose 1–0 to Newcastle.

1953: Hungary become the first foreign team to win at Wembley, Puskas inspiring a 6-3 victory.

1954: After the excitement of Blackpool's victory in the previous year's 'Matthews' Final, Preston disappoint, losing the 'Finney' Final 3–2 to West Bromwich Albion.

1955: Newcastle, inspired by Jackie Milburn, win the Cup for the third time in five years.

1956: Manchester City goalkeeper Bert Trautmann plays the closing stages of the Cup Final despite sustaining a broken neck.

1957: Chairman Sir Arthur Elvin dies after 30 years spent directing Wembley's fortunes.

1958: Manchester United, in the wake of the Munich Air Disaster, lose to Bolton in the Cup Final.

1959: Roy Dwight, uncle of Sir Elton John, scores and breaks his leg in a Nottingham Forest Cup Final victory.

1960: England are named as hosts for the 1966 World Cup with the final to be staged at Wembley.

1961: Spurs complete the century's first League and Cup double with a 2–0 victory over Leicester.

1962: Spurs retain the Cup, Jimmy Greaves scoring in a 3–1 defeat of Burnley.

1963: In Wembley's first European Cup Final, AC Milan beat Benfica 2–1.

1964: Bobby Moore leads West Ham to a 3-2 victory over Preston in the Cup Final.

1965: West Ham beat Munich 1860 2–0 in Wembley's first European Cup Winners' Cup Final.

1966: England beat West Germany 4–2 after extra-time in the final and win the World Cup.

1967: Underdogs QPR beat West Bromwich Albion 3–2 in Wembley's first League Cup Final.

1968: Manchester United win the European Cup with a 4-1 victory in extra-time over Benfica.

1969: The Wembley pitch is ruined by a wet summer and the Royal International Horse Show.

1970: A Wembley FA Cup Final is drawn for the first time, Leeds and Chelsea sharing four goals.

1971: Arsenal beat Liverpool 2–1 in extra-time to complete the League and Cup double.

1972: Wembley's first pop music event features Bill Hayley, Little Richard and Billy Fury.

1973: England draw 1–1 with Poland at Wembley and fail to qualify for the 1974 World Cup.

1974: Kevin Keegan and Billy Bremner are sent off as Liverpool and Leeds meet in Wembley's first Charity Shield game.

1975: Bobby Moore's last Wembley appearance ends in defeat, Fulham losing to his former club, West Ham, 2–0 in the Cup Final.

1976: In their first-ever Wembley appearance, underdogs Southampton beat Manchester United 1–0 in the Cup Final.

1977: Manchester United return to Wembley to win the Cup by beating Liverpool 2–1.

1978: Liverpool retain the European Cup with a 1–0 Wembley victory over F.C. Brugge.

1979: Despite a late fight-back by Manchester United, Arsenal seal a 3–2 victory in the Cup Final with a last-minute goal.

1980: Paul Allen becomes Wembley's youngest Cup finalist as West Ham beat Arsenal 1–0.

1981: A Ricky Villa goal against Manchester City seals Spurs' victory in Wembley's first Cup Final replay.

1982: Bobby Robson's first home game as England manager ends in a 2–1 defeat by West Germany.

1983: American NFL teams play at Wembley for the first time, Minnesota defeating St Louis 28–10.

1984: Having lost the League Cup to Liverpool in Wembley's first all-Merseyside final, Everton win the FA Cup with a 2–0 victory over Watford.

1985: Bob Geldof organises the Live Aid concert to raise millions of pounds for African famine victims.

1986: Liverpool complete the Double with victory over Everton in the Cup Final.

1987: In Glenn Hoddle's last game for the club, Spurs are beaten 3–2 by Coventry in the Cup Final.

1988: Wimbledon beat Liverpool 1–0, John Aldridge becoming the first player to miss a Cup Final penalty.

1989: Liverpool beat Everton 3-2 in the 'Hillsborough' Cup Final.

1990: Graham Taylor's first game as England manager is marked by a 1–0 win over Hungary.

1991: Spurs beat Arsenal 3–1 in the first FA Cup semi-final to be staged at Wembley.

1992: A sell-out crowd attends a Freddie Mercury Tribute concert at the stadium.

1993: Arsenal win the League Cup and FA Cup in the same season, beating Sheffield Wednesday in both Wembley finals.

1994: Manchester United beat Chelsea 4–0 to complete the first of two Doubles in three years.

1995: Frank Bruno stops Oliver McCall at Wembley to become WBC Heavyweight World Champion.

1996: England lose to eventual winners Germany, on penalties in the semi-final of Euro '96.

1997: Roberto Di Matteo scores the quickest-ever FA Cup Final goal in Chelsea's 2-0 defeat of Middlesbrough.

1998: Arsenal complete the second Double in their history with a 2–0 Cup Final victory over Newcastle at Wembley.

1998: DENNIS BERGKAMP

I remember staying in and watching the FA Cup Final on television back home in Holland when I was growing up and then, after the game, you would go out with a football and pretend you were one of the players at Wembley. You do not appreciate what an impact this game has on so many people. It is as much Wembley that makes the Cup Final something different as anything else. It is not the biggest stadium in the world, but the way it is built, with it being so enclosed, means it creates a great atmosphere.

INTERVIEW, 1998

1998: TONY ADAMS

The thing I think of on Cup Final day is the colour on both sides. There is always something different about FA Cup Final day. It is the last game of the season, the curtain falls on the domestic season after this and people like to see a good game. When I was growing up, and still to this day, I think of Cup Final day as being very hot and sunny. That is how Wembley should be. Throughout the year you play in wind, rain, hail and snow but, when you get to this game, it always seems to be perfect conditions.

INTERVIEW, 1998

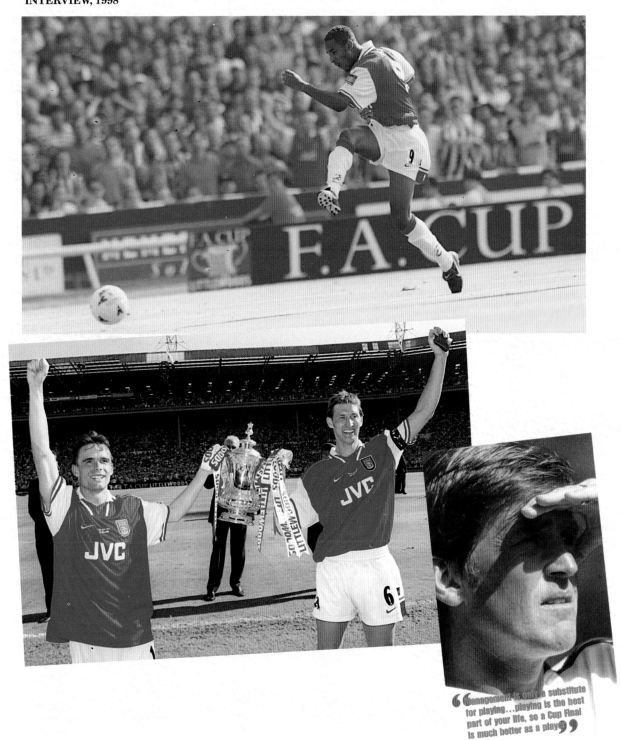

Management is only a substitute for playing...playing is the best part of your life, so a Cup Final is much better as a player

Wembley Bibliography

Allen, Ronnie: *It's Goals That Count*; Stanley Paul, 1955

Allison, George: *Allison Calling*; Staples Press, 1948

Ball, Alan: *It's All About A Ball*; WH Allen, 1978

Barnes, Walley: *Captain Of Wales*; Stanley Paul, 1953

Bartram, Sam: *Sam Bartram*; Burke, 1956

Birley, Derek: *Playing The Game*; Manchester University Press, 1995

British Olympic Association: 'Official Report Of The London Olympic Games'; World Sports, 1948

Buchan, Charles: *A Lifetime In Football*; Phoenix House, 1955

Busby, Matt: *My Story*; Souvenir Press, 1957

Cantwell, Noel: *United We Stand*; Stanley Pual, 1965

Carter, Raich: *Footballer's Progress*; Sporting Handbooks, 1950

Clayton, Ronnie: *A Slave To Soccer*; Stanley Paul, 1960

Clough, Brian: *The Autobiography*; Partridge, 1994

Cullis, Stan: *All For The Wolves*; Sportsmans Book Club, 1960

Daniels, Phil: *Moore Than A Legend*; Goal! Publications, 1997

Docherty, Tommy: *Soccer From The Shoulder*; Stanley Paul, 1960

Edworthy, Niall: *England The Official F.A. History*; Virgin, 1997

Eusebio: *My Name Is Eusebio*; Routledge & Kegan Paul, 1967

Finn, Ralph L.: *My Greatest Game*; Saturn Press, 1951

Finney, Tom: *Football Round The World*; Museum Press, 1953

Finney, Tom: *Finney On Football*; Nicholas Kaye, 1958

Flowers, Ron: *For Wolves And England*; Stanley Paul, 1962

Football Association: *Official F.A. and England Yearbook 1997/98*; Pan Books, 1997

Forsyth, Roddy: *The Only Game*; Mainstream Publishing, 1990

Foulkes, Bill: *Back At The Top*; Pelham Books, 1965

Franklin, Neil: *Soccer At Home And Abroad*; Stanley Paul, 1956

Fynn, Alex: *Out Of Time*; Simon & Schuster, 1994

Glanville, Brian: *The History Of The World Cup*; Faber & Faber, 1980

Greaves, Jimmy & Gutteridge, Reg: *Let's Be Honest*; Pelham Books, 1972.

Gregg, Harry: *Wild About Football*; Souvenir Press, 1961

Griffiths, Mervyn: *The Man In The Middle*; Stanley Paul, 1958

Guiney, David: *The Dunlop Book Of The World Cup*; Eastland Press, 1973

Hapgood, Eddie: *Football Ambassador*; Sporting Handbooks, 1945

Harris, Ron: *Soccer The Hard Way*; Pelham Books, 1970

Hewlett, Geoffrey ed.: *A History Of Wembley*; Brent Library Service, 1979

Hill, Dave: *Out Of His Skin*; Faber, 1989

Hunt, Roger: *Hunt For Goals*; Pelham Books, 1969

Huxley, John: *The Rugby League Challenge Cup*; Guinness, 1992

Inglis, Simon: *Football Grounds Of Great Britain*; Willow, 1983

James, Brian: *England v Scotland*; Pelham Books, 1969

Johnston, Harry: *The Rocky Road To Wembley*; Museum Press, 1954

Kelly, Stephen (ed.): *A Game Of Two Halves*; Mandarin, 1992

Kelly, Stephen (ed.): *The Pick Of The Season*; Mainstream Publishing, 1996

Kelsey, Jack: *Over The Bar*; Stanley Paul, 1958

Labone, Brian: *Defence At The Top*; Pelham Books, 1968

Lawton, Tommy: *Football is My Business*; Sporting Handbooks, 1946

Liddell, Billy: *My Soccer Story*; Stanley Paul, 1960

Lofthouse, Nat: *Goals Galore*; Stanley Paul, 1954

Mackay, Dave: *Soccer My Spur*; Stanley Paul, 1961

Matthews, Stanley: *Feet First*; Ewan & Dale, 1948

McParland, Peter: *Going For Goal*; Souvenir Press, 1960

McNeill, Billy: *For Celtic And Scotland*; Pelham Books, 1966

Merrick, Gil: *I See It All*; Museum Press, 1954

Milburn, Jackie: *Golden Goals*; Stanley Paul, 1957

Milburn, Jackie & Gibson, John: *Jackie Milburn's Newcastle United Scrapbook*; Souvenir Press, 1981

Miller, David: *Father Of Football*; Pavilion, 1994

Moore, Bobby: *My Soccer Story*; Stanley Paul, 1966

Mortensen, Stanley: *Football Is My Game*; Sampson, Low, 1949

Nawrat, Chris et al: *The Sunday Times Chronicle Of Twentieth Century Sport*; Reed International, 1992

Neill, Terry: *Revelations Of A Football Manager*; Guild Publishing, 1985

Platt, David: *Achieving The Goal*; Richard Cohen, 1995

Ponting, Ivan: *The F.A. Cup Final, A Post-War History*; Tony Williams Publishing, 1993

Puskas, Ferenc: *Captain Of Hungary*; Cassell & Co, 1955

Ramsey, Alf: *Talking Football*; Stanley Paul, 1952

Raynor, George: *Football Ambassador At Large*; Stanley Paul, 1960

Revie, Alistair: *All Roads Lead To Wembley*; Pelham Books, 1971

Revie, Don: *Soccer's Happy Wanderer*; Museum Press, 1955

Rollin, Jack: *Soccer At War 1939–45*; Collins, 1985

Russell, Ian F.: *Sir Robert McAlpine & Sons – The Early Years*; Parthenon, 1988

Seed, Jimmy: *The Jimmy Seed Story*; Phoenix Books, 1957

Sephton, George: *This Is Anfield Calling*; Red Rag, 1998

Shepherd, Richard: *Cardiff City FC 1899–1947*; Chalford, 1996

Shepherdson, Harold: *The Magic Sponge*; Pelham Books, 1968

Soar, Phil & Tyler, Martin: *Arsenal Official History*; Hamlyn, 1986

St. John, Ian: *Room At The Kop*; Pelham Books, 1966

Swift, Frank: *Football From The Goalmouth*; Sporting Handbooks, 1948

Taylor, Rogan & Ward, Andrew: *Three Sides Of The Mersey*; Robson Books, 1993

Thomas, Clive: *By The Book*; Willow, 1984

Thompson, Phil: *Shankly*; Bluecoat Press, 1993

Thomson, David: *4–2*; Bloomsbury, 1996

Trautmann, Bert: *Steppes To Wembley*; Robert Hale, 1956

Tyler, Martin: *Cup Final Extra!*; Hamlyn, 1981

Unknown: *The Building Of The Greatest Stadium In The World*; St. James, 1923

Various: *Wembley 1923–1973*; Kelly & Kelly Ltd, 1973

Venables, Terry: *Venables*; Michael Joseph, 1994

Venables, Terry: *The Best Game In The World*; Century, 1996

Walker, Billy: *Soccer In The Blood*; Stanley Paul, 1960

Walvin, James: *The People's Game*; Mainstream Publishing, 1994

Whittaker, Tom: *Tom Whittaker's Arsenal Story*; Sportsmans Book Club, 1958

Wilson, Ray: *My Life In Soccer*; Pelham Books, 1969

Wright, Billy: *Football Is My Passport*; Stanley Paul, 1957

Wright, Billy: *One Hundred Caps And All That*; Robert Hale, 1962

Young, Alex: *Goals At Goodison*; Pelham Books, 1968

Young, George: *Captain Of Scotland*; Stanley Paul, 1958

Young, George: *George Young Talks Football*; Stanley Paul, 1958

The majority of illustrative material used in this book is the property of Wembley Stadium. Permission has been obtained from Action Images and Graham Smith for the material they have supplied and the *Daily Mirror* for reproducing material from their newspaper.

With thanks to Souvenir Press for permission to quote from *My Story* by Matt Busby; St James Advertising for *The Story Of The Building Of The Greatest Stadium In The World*; Robson Books for *Three Sides Of The Mersey* by Andrew Ward & Rogan Taylor.

Additional permission has been given for use of the following; 1927 Cup Final © Hulton Getty; Photo of the pitch divided into squares and advert © Radio Times; 1933 Rugby Cup Final (Warrington v Huddersfield) © Hulton Getty; 1941 War Cup Final (Arsenal v Preston) © Hulton Getty; 1953 Hungary v England. The two teams walking on to the pitch © Hulton Getty; 1959 Cup Final. Dwight carried off © Hulton Getty; 1960 Cup Final. Whelan carried off © Hulton Getty; Picture of Murphy & Busby © Coloursport; World Cup cover for stamp book © Royal Mail; 1973 England v Poland. Two pictures of Peter Shilton © Hulton Getty; 1975 Picture of Bobby Moore © Hulton Getty

Where we have been unable to ascertain copyright, we will be pleased to correct the copyright details in any future editions of this book.